FinTech

FinTech

FinTech
The Technology Driving Disruption in the Financial Services Industry

Parag Y. Arjunwadkar

CRC Press
Taylor & Francis Group
Boca Raton London New York

CRC Press is an imprint of the
Taylor & Francis Group, an **informa** business
AN AUERBACH BOOK

CRC Press
Taylor & Francis Group
6000 Broken Sound Parkway NW, Suite 300
Boca Raton, FL 33487-2742

First issued in paperback 2020

© 2018 by Taylor & Francis Group, LLC
CRC Press is an imprint of Taylor & Francis Group, an Informa business

No claim to original U.S. Government works

ISBN 13: 978-0-367-65728-4 (pbk)
ISBN 13: 978-1-138-29479-0 (hbk)

**Visit the Taylor & Francis Web site at
http://www.taylorandfrancis.com**

**and the CRC Press Web site at
http://www.crcpress.com**

Contents

Introduction

The financial services industry from the beginning of human civilization has been built on trust and the confidence of people to honor the liability they undertake, being the guardian of finances. The financial industry over centuries developed into banking, wealth management and the insurance industry. The basic principle behind the banking and insurance industry was pooling money amongst its members, with an underlying assumption that only a small percentage of them will claim from the pool. The pool of money was therefore required to be invested further in order to get enough returns for the banking and insurance companies to make profit, and thus emerged the wealth management industry. The very nature of the industry demands that there should be high trust between members and the companies managing the pool of money. Unfortunately, time and again the trust was broken. The most recent one being the 2008 financial crisis, wherein not only people lost their invested money and jobs, but also countries lost taxpayers' money to keep the crisis ridden firms capitalized.

An after-effect of all this was the emergence of technology start-ups in the financial domain that started with the premise of operating with complete trust and transparency. These companies that started disrupting the financial services business domains were primarily technology companies and were therefore being collectively referred to as FinTechs. FinTechs by the very nature of their formation were agile, asset-light and disruptive in nature. Unlike their established peers, they were starting from scratch. They had to bring about offerings that were superior in customer experience and were cost-effective at the same time. They were also starting at a time when investment capital was difficult to come by. Even though there were these and many other challenges in front of FinTechs, they also had advantages in the form of less regulatory pressure and they were free to offer unconventional ways of doing traditional business. All of these factors resulted in multiple FinTechs emerging in the payments, lending, wealth management and insurance space.

The interesting thing about most of these FinTechs is that they were not only making the customer interface better, but they were also offering products that could plug gaps in the current offerings of established financial firms. An example would be the insurance FinTech firm that offers an individual to change his/her life insurance commitment based on life-changing events, instead of being tied down to a single premium for rest of his/her life. FinTechs also started offering services that were transparent in nature and they would even declare the commission they would charge for transactions. Peer-to-peer (P2P) lending and P2P insurance is an example of the same, where companies started acting as a marketplace to connect borrowers and lenders transparently. The P2P theme was new to the market, and people could see how and where their money was getting used. Some of the FinTechs went a step further by connecting business with charity. Through these FinTechs an individual was able to donate money for a cause while insuring himself/herself. All of these FinTechs, besides providing a transparent way of conducting business, were also providing ways to bring superior customer experience at an affordable cost.

Wealth management FinTechs have started bringing affordable wealth advising to everybody by using robo-advisors. Additionally, these companies have dashboards that reflect the investments transparently, including the fees charged by them. Payment and wallet companies introduced P2P money transfers, thus bringing an entirely new level of transparency and customer experience using social networks. Some of the other FinTechs redefined financial planning for customers by aggregating all the banks accounts in real-time, thus offering an entirely superior customer experience compared to an in-person financial planning-led session. FinTech platforms help investors to invest in only those companies that meet the investor's values. Though there are established wealth management firms, FinTechs have been able to differentiate themselves by providing a superior experience at an affordable cost and at the same time delivering services in areas that established firms were not able to address.

Technology has also played a decisive role in enabling FinTechs to deliver differentiated services. FinTechs being agile, nimble and starting from scratch as compared to their established peers were able to use the new age technologies to deliver superior customer experience. The first and foremost technology disruption that influenced the financial services industry and tilted the balance in favor of the FinTech industry was the introduction of mobile devices. Mobile devices with high processing capabilities using high data transmission speed, made possible through 4G networks took the FinTech revolution to the next level. Using mobile devices, FinTechs made banking anywhere, anytime a possibility. Additionally, using embedded sensors and cameras within mobile devices, FinTechs were able to offer location-specific promotional coupon offers. Using a NFC chip and biometrics, FinTechs have completely transformed the payment experience, reducing it to just tapping or swiping the phone. Internet of things, which is a network of smart sensors, have further simplified the process by helping monitor driver behavior, thus reducing claims for the insurance industry. FinTechs have gone a step further to provide pay-per-use insurance using IOT devices. These FinTechs lets an individual pay for insurance only while the individual is driving his/her vehicle.

FinTechs have also been key catalysts in transforming the traditional ways of doing business using artificial intelligence and blockchain technologies. Artificial intelligence has been actively used by FinTechs to define alternate ways of determining credit score as well as detecting the chances of loan default by individual borrowers. Similarly, finetchs have been able to leverage blockchain to build an exchange for cryptocurrencies. They have also put blockchain to use in offering cross-border and other multiparty transactions where trust and consensus is important.

Initially, FinTechs were being looked upon by the investor community with skepticism, but with some of the successful investments, a large number of investors started rushing to invest with a hope of finding the next Apple or Microsoft. With more than $100+ billion invested across thousands of start-ups and a sizeable number having valuations more than a billion dollars (referred to as unicorns), and more investments flowing in every year, the optimism for the success of FinTechs is at its prime. Increasing investments have also encouraged a large number of first-time entrepreneurs to take the plunge. To help these entrepreneurs launch themselves in a low-cost setup and at the same time validate their business models, incubators and accelerator platforms emerged. A large number of existing unicorns have been facilitated by some of the renowned accelerator platforms. These platforms have been one of the crucial elements in the success of some of today's unicorns. The success of FinTechs have also made the established firms take notice. Established firms have also been quick to realize that they have to be a part of this FinTech revolution or else they may be left out. This has led them to co-innovate with FinTech firms by setting up their own accelerators and innovation hubs.

The FinTech revolution started in the United States and soon spread to the UK and other European countries. The reason for the emergence and success of these FinTechs have been the same across these countries. Some of the common reasons for the rise of FinTechs in these countries have been the financial crisis of 2008, better customer experience from FinTechs and an alternative, yet affordable, business model from them. Soon other countries like India and China started their own FinTech revolution, though the reasons were more centered around financial inclusion and a better customer experience. FinTechs also soon started emerging into African nations to solve some of the financial inclusion problems by introducing alternate currencies like mobile money and Bitcoins. Finetchs in African countries have also been pioneers in using blockchain for cross-border transactions. Summarily, it can be said that the FinTech revolution is spreading like wild fire globally and the established firms stand challenged.

The future of FinTechs is filled with excitement and a journey that is changing direction very frequently. It is very possible that FinTechs become big enough to overtake the existing financial firms and subsequently marginalize them. There is also a possibility that they will coexist in a synergetic relationship. Millenials can be a big factor in the direction that FinTech firms take in future. It is highly probable that millenials and digital natives start adopting the sharing economy. The sharing economy would also mean that there is service consolidation and outsourcing. Furthering this cause would be regulations like the second payment services directive (PSD2) and government support. This could make the existence of business functions available as a single qualified offerings obsolete and thereby forcing the established firms to go the FinTech way, i.e., fragment the service offerings into microservices. Irrespective of what the future is for FinTechs, they are causing anxiety in the industry today and helping build a better and more trustworthy business environment for the future.

We see more than a million start-ups and FinTech organizations emerging across the globe, with multiple overlaps of customer journeys. It is evident that only the ones that address the customer needs and remain profitable will succeed in the future. Nonetheless, the learning and transformation that these start-ups are driving will present an entirely new way of managing finances in the next decade, including probably dismantling the categorization of the industry as a financial services industry.

Author

Parag Y. Arjunwadkar is a certified technical architect from The Open Group Architecture Framework and a certified project management professional from Project Management Institute. He MBA in international business and BE in electronics and telecommunication from Pune University, Pune, India. Parag has won the MahaIntraprenuer 2014 Award—an award jointly established by Praj Industries, Pune, India, a global process solution company, and Symbiosis International University, Pune, India, an international university excelling in management sciences. The award is an acknowledgment of individuals acting as entrepreneurs within their existing organizations. Parag is a transformation solution strategist with a right combination of techno-functional skills with more than 20 years of experience in business and technology consulting. Parag has been instrumental in incubating multiple COEs and building industrialized yet disruptive offerings for organizations such as enterprise gamification, innovation as a service, customer journey transformation, and accelerated delivery platforms. He has been involved in strategizing and implementing the digital transformation road map for large financial and insurance companies including marketplace transformations, re-platforming core banking and cards systems, and redefining customer journeys. Parag has built an ecosystem of leading multichannel solutions and leading FinTech organizations in the space of omni-channel solutions, artificial intelligence, block chain, Internet of things (IOT), security, and customer experience transformation. He has also conceptualized and built multiple shared service development and testing platforms for mobile, IOT, cloud, and omni-channel solutions. Leveraging the ecosystems and laboratories, Parag has conceptualized and implemented multiple products and product platforms including financial planners, on-boarding solutions, mobile application development, and management platforms. He has been a mentor for one of the finalist teams in a popular techno-functional television show, elaborating rural inclusion for a large fast moving consumer goods global organization. Parag has been recognized as an expert in digital customer experience within his current organization and has written multiple blogs and delivered multiple presentations on enterprise gamification, payments, and digital customer experience in various conferences and in social media, including the "Enabling Superior Digital Engagement" conference hosted by Dun & Bradstreet.

Chapter 1

Evolution of the Financial Services Industry

The financial services industry has existed since the beginning of human civilization. At the very beginning of human civilization, societies were formed. Societies were based on the principles of mutual trust, transparency, and helping each other. Helping another individual or groups was either out of good gesture or was remunerative. In the initial days of civilization barter mechanism was prevalent, which meant exchanging goods for remuneration of services delivered. The services delivered were in the form of help, a favor or assistance. The help would include helping another individual in his/her times of distress, provide expertise in a certain field of work, assisting in an activity, looking after each other's children and many more such activities. The barter trade subsequently developed into giving out loans, credits and insurance. The loans and credits were in the form of providing aid (monetary) to an individual in his/her times of distress. The insurance was typically an agreed obligation that the insurer would payback in case there was damage to the property/person in question.

The financial services industry from the beginning of civilization was based on the concept of honoring the commitment to pay in presentment of a mutually binding financial instrument. The payout mechanism in each of these cases was therefore honored by paying in coins, gold ornaments or by giving away large pieces of land. It was not until 300 BC that the first form of "money"/"currency" in the form of a wooden piece came into existence. In the initial days of currency, it was only the royal family who was entitled to distribute these currencies to their patrons, workforce, helpers and generals, as remuneration of excellent services delivered to them. Therefore, an individual was able to claim extraordinary returns for the currencies coming from royal families. It was only during the 19th and 20th century,

1

long after the industrial revolution started, that the term financial services became more prevalent in the United States. The term was commonly used to represent the banking, capital markets and insurance industries. The popularity of the term also could be attributed to the Gramm–Leach–Bliley Act, enacted in 1999, that allowed different financial services companies from the banking, insurance and capital markets industry to merge.

Financial services in the initial days were meant to provide all the services associated with monetary transactions, and most often these transactions would be between individuals or between a corporation and individual entity. Subsequently, the arrangement became complex with the involvement of multiple intermediaries. Adding to the complexity was creation/development of financial instruments that were a complex mix of other basic financial instruments. Soon people started making profits using these instruments and such an arrangement was categorized as derivatives trading or mutual fund investing. Consequently, all such trading was together termed as wealth management or investment banking.

There emerged investors who could invest wisely in these complex instruments and make profits from them. A large number of people in order to make similar profits started investing in these complex instruments in the hope of multiplying their savings. The complex instruments soon sprang up in all the different areas of financial services including lending, taxation, equities, savings, credits and insurance. Each of these instruments had multiple stakeholders putting their bets in for the very same asset. Soon it was a challenge to identify the actual entity to own the underlying asset.

During the 18th and 19th century, central banks were created by countries who would act as lender of the last resort, i.e., they would be the go-to banks to help in case there is run on any of the other banks. These banks who acted as a lender of last resort and were sponsored by the central governments of a country were later on referred as a central bank of that specific country. During the 1930 financial crisis in the United States, even the central bank of the United States could not support honoring a large number of claims, owing to the complexity and size of the claims. This led to erosion of faith in the system and therefore regulatory authorities were introduced who would act as watchdogs to monitor the transactions that were happening throughout. Despite all of this, the system was not able to stop the failure of big banks less than a century later in the United States, leading to a worldwide recession.

In 2008, about 80 years later from the last financial crisis, the financial industry was again on the verge of collapse, followed by the worst recession till date. In 2008, large financial institutions (FIs) defaulted on honoring the claims of their funds due to inadequate capital and high leverage. Soon a chain of defaults from multiple entities who were a part of the investment chain followed. It triggered a wave of huge defaults resulting in the bankruptcy of a large number of banks, central banks and the financial services industry overall. It was around this time that a large number of financial start-ups emerged who would change the ways of conducting financial business. These start-ups were primarily financial services business firms and were causing the disruption using technology. Therefore, the term "FinTech came into existence to represent all of these companies as a group. These FinTechs started by transforming a niche segment of the financial services business and they soon spread into multiple areas of financial business, thus disrupting the entire industry.

FinTech emergence can also be partially attributed to the interest of venture capitalists (VCs) in investing into the financial services industry. The VCs invest in a start-up on the basis of an idea or the proposed future product, and continue investing during the different stages of the formation and buildup of the start-up. The investment is usually done in exchange of equity from the start-up. The investors exit the start-up when it gets acquired or merged or it goes public or decides to acquire another entity. Irrespective of the mode of investing and exits, VCs have ushered in a culture of technology start-ups. A large part of VC investment was focused only on creating technology start-ups until the late 20th century, and helped bring up companies like Google and Apple. In the 21st century, the VCs started focusing on business domains like transportation, retail and the hotel industry. Consequently, unicorns like Uber, Amazon and Airbnb were born. The trend of the post financial crisis in 2008 veered toward investing in start-ups from the financial services domain. With more than $50 billion invested in 2,500+ companies by 2010, and 23+ unicorns, it can be clearly said that the age of FinTech has arrived.

A large part of the book will discuss the disruptions caused by these FinTechs, and how the entire phenomenon has been catalyzed by simultaneous disruptions in the technology. In the end, we talk about the overall ecosystem for FinTechs and some of the success and failures of FinTechs. The book concludes with the author's viewpoint on the future of FinTechs.

The Evolution of Banks: Temples to Challenger Banks

Banks were the first constituents of the financial industry and have been around since the time the concept of currency originated. The currency itself graduated from a wooden plank to coins and then subsequently in the form of paper bills. Records from ancient times indicate that temples were used to keep the coins in safe custody of priests. The temples were also involved in loaning out the money, and therefore could be regarded as the earliest form of banks. Besides, there were wealthy merchants, who were able to accumulate these coins and were able to lend them to a borrower, albeit with interest. Some of the earlier civilizations started conducting banking through a separate institution housed in buildings. All the government spending and individual financial transactions were handled by these institutions. In some of the other civilizations the kings and royal families became the default banks for the kingdom. It was these royal families who would collect taxes from the people to fill up the kingdom's coffers. The kingdom would then pay its soldiers, artisans, etc. from the coffers as remuneration of the services rendered. These people in turn would pay farmers and downstream service providers using the coins received by the kingdom. Therefore, the economy usually circled around the kingdom, with the treasury acting as the default bank. The latter form of banking continued for long time, and history has evidence where one kingdom was taken over by another king because the kingdom was in huge debt and not able to pay salary to its people.

In the 17th century most of the European nations have had a more formal banking system with initial banks being formed by wealthy families. The first bank to issue banknotes was the Bank of England in 1695. The bank was originally a private institution, but by 1870 it accepted the role of a lender of last resort or as the central bank of England. The banking system was making great strides the world over and the services offered by banks increased to include operations like check deposits, clearing and investments. In most of the other European countries, central banks were established during the 19th century. The postal saving system was introduced in Great Britain in 1861 to promote saving among the poor and rural communities. Similar institutions were created in a number of different countries in Europe and the United States.

During the same time frame, small banks emerged around the world in the form of society banks, community banks and cooperative banks. These were mutual savings banks created to address the banking requirements of a specific community or group of people. It was around the same time private banks were created by wealthy merchants' the world over. The trend further continued in the United States, and a large number of small banks emerged. The life span of most of these banks was limited and often marred with robbery and corruption. J.P. Morgan emerged as head of the merchants' bank in the 1800s and created U.S. Steel, AT&T and multiple other conglomerates through the use of trusts. It was not until 1907 when there was a large-scale run on the bank money, caused because of the collapse of copper trust shares. J.P. Morgan being the largest bank, tried to manage the situation through multiple initiatives, but the incident highlighted the importance of the central bank in managing the situation. The central bank therefore became the primary stakeholder of the banking system in most of the countries and the private/merchant banks were relegated to be operating within the norms set by the central bank. In the beginning of the 20th century, private banks in the United States and the world over were providing savings, lending and investment services to individuals and corporations alike.

In 1929, large numbers of banks in the United States were providing money to traders and investors at 10% margin money. It was all good until the shares of some companies collapsed and there was a run on the banks' money. The Federal Reserve could not do much to contain the situation and the country plunged into a depression. During the first few months in 1930, 700+ U.S. banks failed. In all, close to 10,000 banks failed. The depression had global impact and many countries significantly increased financial regulation. As an after effect of the crisis, the United States established the Securities and Exchange Commission in 1933 and

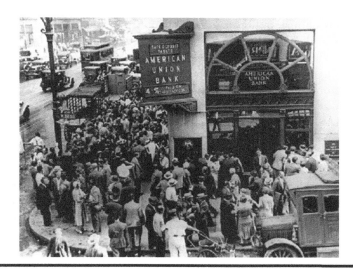

Figure 1.1   A run on one of the banks in New York.

Source: https://commons.wikimedia.org/wiki/File:American_union_bank.gif# filelinks.

passed the Glass–Steagall Act, that separated investment banking and commercial banking (Figure 1.1).

The charge card industry has a similar interesting evolution history. In the early 20th century, department stores in the United States started providing charge cards made of metals or card boards to their customers as prepaid cards that can be used only in their stores. In mid-20th century, A New York businessman started Diners Club with a vision that the Diners Club cardboard credit card would be accepted at all the restaurants in New York. It charged merchants a fee on each transaction, but assured the merchants that customers with cards would spend more than the customers who did not have one. Soon it started becoming a status symbol for card-holders and they would get a monthly dining bill. These cards required payment in full each month and therefore were more of a charge card, than a credit card. Within a year of its operations, Diners Club had attracted thousands of members, and a couple of years later it became the first internationally accepted charge card. By end of the decade, major companies joined the competition including American Express, Bank of America, Wells Fargo and multiple other banks. Thus, banks and nonbanks joined in this new form of lending, wherein there was a preapproved credit limit for individuals to spend on their charge/credit cards.

As banking systems evolved in multiple countries, international finance started evolving to become an industry in itself. Some of the wealthy families with global business pioneered international finance in the early 19th century, and these families were also pivotal in providing loans to large banks. Subsequently in the late 20th century, a large number of private and merchant banks started becoming global in order to expand their balance sheets and customer base. Some of the large banks were also providing cross-border transactions and investment services. While banks were expanding their operations beyond countries, the international monetary system evolved from the gold standard in 1865, followed by the Bretton Woods system after World War II. One of the primary agreements of Bretton Woods system was to identify the U.S. dollar as a reserve currency, and the only currency in the world to be backed by gold. In 1971, the U.S. government stopped exchanging U.S. dollars for gold because there was very little gold in the U.S Treasury, leading to the collapse of the Bretton Woods system. Following the collapse of the Bretton Woods system, the countries worldwide adopted floating foreign exchange rates. Under the floating exchange rates, countries adopted one of following three methods – (1) using a foreign currency as its national currency – El Salvador uses the U.S. dollar as its currency; (2) a country fixes its exchange rate to a foreign currency – China pegged the yuan to the U.S. dollar between 1997 and 2005; and (3) determining exchange rates based on demand and supply, usually managed by central banks. Owing to the complexity of cross-border transactions and country-specific regulatory requirements, banks now have a separate department/division looking into matters of international finance and cross-border transactions.

For a significant time period, bookkeeping in banks was done using voluminous registers. Therefore, even simple banking operations like depositing and withdrawing money took a lot of time and was prone to manual errors and fraud. It was not until the 1960s when IBM mainframe computers were introduced in the banking world, and this transformed the banking industry completely. Leveraging mainframe and similar systems, core banking solutions and credit card processing and management solutions were developed. The systems automated a large portion of banking and card transactions. In less than a decade most of these systems were built and were deployed across all the banks. It now became much simpler for the banks to maintain their transaction records, and simplified reporting. Therefore, the introduction of IBM mainframe computers brought in automation, speed, transparency and "trust" in the system. These solutions, when developed, required trained professionals to operate, and their usage was restricted to the employees within the bank. The bank branches, which usually had stacks of registers with bank account details, now had information stored in computers. Though the banks were completely computerized and a majority of banking processes were automated leading to faster transactions, but from a customer's perspective, besides getting the work done faster, there was very little change in the overall experience.

Computerization of banking operations made automated teller machines (ATMs) a reality. ATMs were introduced between the 1960s and 1970s to cater to off-working hours' cash withdrawal requirement. ATMs in subsequent years started providing additional services like account balance inquiries, password change and altering profile details. Individuals could perform these operations using their own debit or credit cards over an ATM. The major difference between credit and debit cards is that credit cards are debt instruments allowing an individual to withdraw until the pre-approved credit limit set by the bank is met, whereas with debit cards, an individual can withdraw only up to the amount of cash available in the persons' savings account. The introduction of the ATM was a step toward branchless banking and has become very popular in the decades that followed. Some estimates put the total number of ATMs globally to be over 3 million.

The emergence of the Internet in the 1990s coupled with the invention of desktop computers, altered the way users accessed information. The information exchange using the Internet soon evolved into interactions between business to consumer (B2C) and business to business (B2B). Banks leveraged the Internet to create applications that would enable a customer to do transactions through a website while sitting at his/her home or office. Customer interaction with bank branches was minimized and the user experience was dramatically transformed. The banking functions were directly available to customers online through a website that was previously restricted to bank employees only. Online systems and solutions coupled with ATMs created an ecosystem for branchless banking. Soon multiple "online-only" banks and credit card companies emerged worldwide. Online-only banks and credit card companies would have websites, a network of ATMs and very few branches, thus creating low-cost financial services catering to online-only customers. Consequently "banking anytime" was now possible.

The Internet changed the way customers interacted with banks and banking started moving toward branchless banking. Mobile banking transformed the customer experience entirely by bringing the bank to the fingertips of the customer. SMS banking was the earliest form of mobile banking available on feature phones launched in late 1990s. The success of the iPhone, followed by exponential growth of smart phones led to the inevitability of mobile apps. Most of the banks made their banking applications available through these apps. With the advent of client-side technologies like HTML5 and CSS3, a large number of banks transitioned their online applications to be available across all the mobile devices. Now the customer was able to operate his/her account while travelling, while at home or even outdoors; therefore it can be said that mobile banking made "banking anywhere" a reality. Thus, all three together, ATM, online banking applications and mobile banking applications led to the popular concept of "banking anytime and anywhere."

Mobile devices are personalized devices and therefore they have been used extensively to store and carry individual's preferences. The preferences could be – the type of food one likes to eat, the mode of travel an individual prefers and multiple other things. Additionally, modern-day mobile devices have multiple security features like fingerprint authentication and application "sandboxing." Business intelligence and analytics in combination with user information and enhanced security on mobile devices have enabled banks to launch personalized offering to their customers. All of these technologies have also transformed the loyalty business entirely. Earlier, a large part of loyalty and offers information was routed either directly by a bank or by co-branding the same with a retail store. With mobile devices, it was possible to take the entire loyalty use case out of the bank and run it as a separate application which would connect to the respective bank only for payment-related transactions.

The Internet and e-commerce revolution led to disruption in the online payment space as well, which was further fueled by mobile devices. Though Electronic Data Interchange (EDI) is believed to have started e-commerce, it was the Internet that catalyzed the adoption of e-commerce in a big way. In 1995, Amazon was launched as a bookstore initially. Amazon is now an e-commerce site with a wide range of products available. PayPal is an Internet payment service that was introduced in 1998. Customers using PayPal did not have had to take out their debit or credit cards to make a purchase; instead they would do it online using a PayPal account. PayPal would internally charge the credit and debit cards provided by the customer in his/her preference. This mechanism of quickly making a payment through a single service which in turn stores the actual payment details and shipping details started being referred to as wallets. Therefore, PayPal could be considered as a pioneer in providing wallet services. In subsequent decades, wallet services were enhanced to store multiple other secured information like User ID, passwords and multiple card information. Because mobile devices were secure, personal and handy, the wallet on mobile devices became hugely popular and is aiming to replace the physical wallet. Therefore, Internet, e-commerce, mobile devices and wallets brought in an entirely new payment interface for the customers which was secure and intuitive to use.

Mobile devices brought a significant change in the way people interacted with banks. Mobile banking, wallet services, loyalty applications and personal financial planning are now available as separate applications on mobile devices. Mobile devices also completely changed the way lending and payments were done by banks. Alternative finance in the form of peer-to-peer lending, small- and medium-sized enterprise (SME) lending and microfinancing were all made possible because of peer-to-peer communication capability between individuals with their mobile devices. Similarly, in the payment space, multiple card-service providers and payment providers brought in their own application and wallet services to enable mobile payments. In some countries like India, dedicated payment banks have also become a reality.

Artificial intelligence (AI) marked the transformation from human-led interaction to machine-driven interaction and automation. Chatbots or software robots have been employed by banks extensively to interact with customers. Bots are driven by machine-learning algorithms, with their response getting enriched based on the experience and learning they have from the past interactions. Banks are using AI to improve response-time and accuracy for functions like credit scoring and fraud management.

Mobile devices also changed the way communication was done between individuals. It was through feature phones that individuals were able to communicate via text messages. Smartphones brought in multiple applications that would redefine the way communication was done. Internet ushered in an era of communicating over social media and has become hugely popular in last decade. The banking industry has also embraced social media to provide banking functionalities like sales, customer management and payment through social media. Analytics-based financial applications have used social media to provide disruptive solutions by gathering information about a customer in the social media for business functions like credit scoring, know your customer (KYC) and fraud detection.

Blockchain is an algorithm that helps generate cryptocurrencies and helps maintain distributed ledgers between multiple entities. It has a consensus mechanism, an auto executing smart contract and an unmatched security provision. All of these have made blockchain the most sought-after algorithm in the highly secure banking ecosystem. Banks have started testing and using blockchain for functions like KYC and cross-border transactions. These transactions require multiple entities in different countries to update the records based on a consensus between authorized entities. Though a large part of blockchain projects are being run as proof-of-concept (POC) or as experimental projects, but it is being acknowledged to have the maximum disruption potential among all other innovations in the recent past.

Innovations in technology and business is also leading to the emergence of alternate currencies worldwide. These currencies are being viewed as having a similar impact as the collapse of the gold standard system on currencies worldwide. Bitcoin and other cryptocurrencies generated through blockchain is one such currency which is truly global and not country specific. In some parts of the world telecom operators and mobile application developers are creating a different kind of currency called mobile money. Mobile money is a digital currency typically managed and maintained by the telecom operator and can be used in place of cash, especially in countries where the unbanked population is large. Though there has been a debate among countries about acceptability of such currencies, there exists apps and wallets that help generate and exchange these currencies. Owing to controversies around the sanctity of such currencies, a formal banking system has not yet ventured into these alternate currencies.

Financial regulations are a form of guidelines for financial authorities to comply. These regulations are very country-specific, though some regulations could be applicable to multiple countries depending on the agreements the participating countries might have adopted. There have been multiple financial regulations worldwide which has impacted the way banking is done including the Glass–Steagall Act. One of the recent regulations adopted in the European Union and the U.K. has been to implement a PSD2 (revised payment services directive). Under the directive, customers (individuals and corporates) of a bank can use third-party providers to manage their finances. Banks in turn are obligated to provide these third-party providers access to their customers' accounts through open application program interfaces (APIs). The regulation/directive has been disruptive for FinTechs and banks alike as this would enforce a greater collaboration between the two, instead of competition.

In the aftermath of the 2008 financial crisis, the Bank of England lowered the capital requirements to set up a bank. Challenger banks that were online-only banks with less initial capital emerged in next couple of years. Banks like Atom Bank, Monzo Bank, Starling and Tandem are a new breed of mobile and online only challenger banks. Challenger banks are therefore the new face of banking which is agile and have adopted nonconventional ways of carrying out banking transactions. Banks therefore have evolved from being run in temples to today's challenger banks that customers can access through their mobile devices.

Technologies like mobile, AI, social medial and blockchain coupled with regulations like PSD2 have ushered in an era of open banking in the new millennium. A large number of financial services start-ups, driven by the new-age technologies and regulations, have forayed into providing banking services either in part or full. Globally, 2,000 FinTechs, $23+ billion of investment and 23+ unicorns (start-ups with valuation greater than a billion dollars) in last 5 years is evident of the disruption that is changing the banking industry like never before.

The Evolution of the Wealth Management Industry: Merchant Banking to Robo-Advising

Merchant banks emerged in the Middle Ages from the Italian grain and cloth merchants' community. Merchants and bankers from these high yielding plains became wealthy and popular owing to the high crop yields. They were soon displaced by Florentine merchants. These merchants on one hand were traders of grain and cloths themselves and they also financed long trading journeys for others. These traders in the Lombardy plains started lending money to farmers in return for grain-sale rights against the eventual harvest. They also offered advance payment against the future delivery of grain shipped to distant ports. Thus emerged a concept similar to "futures" in the present trading world. Soon there arose a class of merchants who were trading grain debt instead of grain themselves. Therefore, this can be considered as the beginning of financial traders and trading, albeit in commodities.

Merchant banking further evolved into settling trades for traders and holding deposits to honor claims from traders who were dealing with the actual grain. Subsequently, most families who were goldsmiths also moved into banking. In the late 18th century, multiple Protestant families began to move into banking as well. In the late 19th century, private merchant banks emerged in the United States. In the 20th century, corporations started owning large merchant banks also known as commercial banks or investment banks in the United States. The primary aim of these banks besides financing was to deal in securities of businesses directly or through derivative products with a retail or corporate investor.

The Glass–Steagall Act in 1933 was a trigger for transformation in the banking and wealth-management industry. The Act emphasized that commercial banking and investment banking needed to be separated. This is when investment banks emerged globally and wealth management became a different function from banking. In the initial days, investing was restricted primarily to debts and equities together called as securities by retail or corporate investors. Subsequently, as the products matured, investing spread over various areas like forex and commodities as well. In the last couple of decades, a new trend of investing such as a contrarian or as a hedge fund is picking up as well.

Investors trade financial securities, commodities, foreign exchange and other financial instruments in the financial markets. The financial markets can be further categorized as below:

1. Capital markets deal in equity and bonds
2. Commodity markets enable trading in commodities
3. Money markets provide short-term debt financing and investment
4. Derivatives markets help manage financial risk
5. Futures markets manage the future trading value of a financial instrument or commodity
6. There are other markets like forex market dealing in foreign currencies, spot market, etc.

Capital markets are the markets wherein the wealth of investors is used to buy, sell and trade equity-backed securities and corporate and government debts. There are two types of capital markets – primary and secondary markets. Primary markets are involved in trading new equity or bond issues. Investment banks, fund houses and high networth individuals (HNIs) are the buyers and sellers in the primary market. Investment banks also act as underwriters for securities in primary markets and ask brokers and agents to further sell the securities to their customers. In secondary markets, already existing securities (equities and bonds) are traded through an exchange. A security can be traded in secondary markets multiple times. In case of high-frequency trading, which is usually performed through high-performance computers, a security can be traded multiple times in an hour. Individual customers operate through a broker, who then buys and sells securities in a secondary market on behalf of the customer. Investment banks have capital market specialists who keep track of both primary and secondary markets and advise major clients on potential opportunities. An investor can invest using any of the following instruments:

1. Bonds – these are debt instruments issued by an organization or government
2. Equity – these are shares of a company issued to make investors own a piece of the company
3. Different type of funds – funds are an aggregation of multiple stock, bonds and other financial instruments of multiple corporations and governments. There are multiple constructs of fund types that define different types of financial instruments for the fund managers, i.e., hedge fund, wealth fund, pension fund, etc.

In the common man's terminology, most of the financial markets together are called stock markets. A stock market in modern times is an aggregation of buyers and sellers of stocks or securities at a physical location or at a virtual place. As of 2015, there were 60 stock exchanges with a total market capitalization of $50+ trillion. Stock markets enable the trading of stocks through stock exchanges. The stock exchange could be a physical place or a virtual gathering of traders to trade for a particular stock. Trading on a stock exchange is handled by designated traders also known as brokers.

The courretiers de change in 12th-century France traded debts of the agriculture community and banks. Therefore, they can be considered as first brokers. Informal gathering of traders started around late 13th and 14th centuries, and Belgium is known to have had one of the first gathering of traders in a building, similar to a stock exchange. In the 17th century, multiple European nations gave a charter to a country-specific "East India Company" to carry out voyage expeditions to India and other Asian countries. The voyages were funded by insurers with a percentage of return on a successful voyage. Subsequently, the companies started issuing dividend-paying stocks wherein the dividend was paid based on proceeds from all the successful voyages. It was contrary to being paid only after every successful voyage as the dividends were being paid despite some failed voyages by a voyage company. They were the first joint stock companies, and allowed companies to demand more for their shares and build a larger fleet. The trading at this point would happen in coffee shops around London. Multiple other companies soon came up with their shares and a promise of high returns. Some of them had no previous success stories, yet because of the speculative valuations people bought into them. This resulted in the crash of these stocks a few years down the line. Soon stock trading was banned until 1825 in London.

The first stock exchange in London was formed in 1773, although it was not allowed to trade in stocks until 1825. The Philadelphia Stock Exchange was the first stock exchange in the United States. The New York Stock Exchange was formed on Wall Street 19 years after the London Stock Exchange and traded in stocks since its inception. The Nasdaq, a brainchild of the Financial Industry Regulatory Authority (FINRA), was founded in 1971 and is a virtual exchange. It is the second largest exchange in the world by market capitalization and has its share listed on the same exchange. Therefore, stock exchanges and trading of securities have evolved from benches in Italy to virtual stock exchanges.

In the 16th and 17th centuries, share prices were published twice a week on a 10×4-in. sheet of paper and distributed from Jonathan's Coffee-House in London. Trading in a stock market/exchange was typically done through buyers and sellers trading face-to-face on trading floors. The quotations were shouted, and buyers or sellers would subscribe to the number of shares either by shouting or by showing hand gestures. It was not until 1986 when stock exchanges automated their quotation system and replaced the trading floor. This screen-based quotation system was used by brokers to buy and sell stocks. Consequently, a year later, most of the stock exchanges multiplied their businesses exponential. In 1987 there was a big crash which was further accelerated because of technology, as there were no controls on the execution of the trade. Soon enough, circuit breakers were introduced that slowed down the sudden fall or rise of securities, and trading would stop after falling beyond a certain point.

Transactions on trading floors were traditionally handled manually between brokers or counterparties. In fact, until the 1970s, the trading on most of the exchanges were known as floor trading and was done using open cry and telephones (Figure 1.2).

However, by 1970 a large proportion of trading was done using electronic trading platforms. An electronic trading platform, or online trading platform, is a computer-driven software that is used to place buy–sell and other forms of trading orders online through a financial intermediary. The Electronic Communications Network (ECN) was used by brokerages to display bids and ask prices in the 1970s. In 1982, the first full-service consumer equity trading system was introduced. The system was capable of trading in stocks, mutual funds and commodities. There were other companies that offered some of the first retail trading platforms on AOL (America Online) and CompuServe. In 1995, TD Ameritrade acquired a company that had an online stock trading platform and with multiple other acquisitions became one of the largest online brokerages. Charles Schwab became another leader in offering online trading in the late 1990s and providing Web presence in 1995.

Online trading enabled end customers and brokers to place orders from anywhere, even sitting at their home. Most of the exchanges have now adopted online trading as an evolution to the floor trading that used open outcry and

Figure 1.2   Image showing the NYSE trade floor in the 1960s.

Source: https://commons.wikimedia.org/wiki/File:NY_stock_exchange_traders_floor_LC-U9-10548-6.jpg.

telephone-based trading. The first electronic trading platforms were terminals that would enable a broker to execute a trade remotely using an application that was hosted with the exchange itself. The earlier systems had quite a lag in terms of placing an order and executing an order. Therefore, the prices would be approximately managed and intraday trading was more of an individual's skill to estimate price movements. With online Internet-based electronic trading platforms and real-time stock feeds, instant order execution has been possible in recent days. In the last decade, most of these trading platforms have been opened to a large section of the customers, connected through their trading and/or investing accounts. These platforms have been enhanced to provide charts, real-time feeds, information from analysts and the brokerage house recommendations. Today's retail investor can therefore make his/her decisions directly without taking any service from brokerage houses. Automation in these platforms have made algorithmic trading and robo-advising a reality.

Electronic trading platforms enables scheduling an order online and usually during the opening and closing hours of the exchange. This type of trading is known as program trading. Program trading is a trade comprising of buying or selling of a sizeable number of stocks valued for over a million dollars. In the 1980s, program trading became very popular, especially for trading in futures. Traders used this to take advantage of lower openings and higher endings of the stock market prices during a bull run and vice versa during a bear phase. There were multiple such strategies that were being adopted by traders to take advantage of arbitrage opportunities that were possible only due to the high speed of execution by a computer program. Some of the widely used techniques which have had their share of popularity and criticism are index arbitrage and portfolio insurance. In the 1980s, most of the markets were capable of executing orders electronically using different forms of ECN. This led to program trading becoming enormously popular. The program trading algorithm started by considering only a certain set of parameters like time, price and volume and became quite complex with multiple input parameters and a lot of automation built into the algorithm. Since a large part of trading was now being handled by algorithms (program logic), therefore over time, program trading started being known as algorithmic trading.

Many more strategies got introduced for algorithmic trading with the increased computational capability of computers and more markets becoming electronic. These techniques are largely used by investment banks, fund houses and institutional traders to execute large orders. In 2001, a team of IBM researchers proved that, in a laboratory research setup, algorithmic trading was more successful than human traders.

Some of the techniques involved in algorithmic trading fall into the category of high frequency trading (HFT). Though there is no specific definition for HFT, it can be described as large number of trade orders being executed at high speeds resulting in high turnover. These trades leverage electronic tools and financial data feeds at high speeds to make faster trading decisions. HFTs are characterized by complex algorithms that run trading deals with a very short-term investment strategy. It uses the fast speed of computers to move in and out of trading positions in seconds or fraction of seconds. Some estimates have put that HFT comprises about half of equity trading volumes.

The start of HFT can be traced back to 1983 when the NASDAQ introduced an electronic form of trading. Initially the trading times of HFT were in seconds and by 2011 the same have been reduced to milliseconds and microseconds. The high frequency strategy was made first popular by Renaissance Technologies. In 2010, HFTs was estimated to be half of the equity trades in the United States and a third in Europe. With more HFT strategies being deployed in the market, it will become difficult to deploy them profitably.

As different banking applications were interconnected, people started earning interest through arbitrage opportunities across multiple banks. Soon people started investing in securities of different companies. Individuals started maintaining an investment account, and investment banks started advising on where the money should be invested to get better returns. Soon after, advising on wealth management became a profession with certified wealth management advisors from investment banks advising their customers on ways and means to manage their wealth. Wealth management advice subsequently started covering aspects of customer financial management as well. The wealth advisors started being referred to as financial planners or advisors.

A financial planner prepares financial plans for his/her customers and includes cash flow management, retirement planning, investment planning, financial risk management and in some cases, insurance-related planning as well. In the initial days, it was a broker who would do the financial planning for a customer. It was done quite ad hoc and continues until the date for informal financial planning. The focus of these advisors/planners was to drive customers into buying funds and securities that the brokerage firms or large banks or their employers wanted to push. In this process, everybody made a certain percentage of the commission. The focus subsequently shifted toward making more commission than thinking about the welfare of the customer in the long term. It was not until the 1970s that a financial planning discipline was established. The financial planning started with Loren Dunton setting up a financial planning profession in 1969. The first graduates passed out from the financial planning college that was set up in 1973. Financial planners are certified by respective financial planning colleges worldwide. There are thousands of certified financial planners worldwide. Financial planning changed the way people looked at investing, estate planning, retirement planning and tax planning.

The purpose of planning was not to push for any specific product or investment type. The focus instead was on planning for an individual based on his/her goals. The amount that should be invested for a particular goal, and the monitoring and tracking of the progress and achievement of that goal. In the initial days, the planning exercise was a time-consuming exercise with planning spread over months. The planners would gather data about sources of income and financial commitments of the customers. The information, once collected, would then be analyzed by the planner based on the experience, knowledge and how frequently the planner updated himself/herself on different investment instruments. After the analysis, the planner would come back with suggested investment avenues and instruments for the customer to meet his/her goals. A large part of this planning was done through tools like Excel sheets, residing in the personal computer of the financial planners. One of the drawbacks of these tools was that they were merely data-collecting tools and the advisor/planner would then go back to his/her office and analyze the information and then propose the best possible alternatives. There was no possibility in the tools to apply multiple what-if scenarios right there in front of the customers to check different possible alternatives. In recent years, there have been multiple softwares that have the capability to do financial planning interactively.

The introduction of mobile devices radically transformed financial planning. Advisors carrying mobile devices could now have face-to-face discussions with their customers almost anywhere – in a café, at a customer's house or even at a customer's office. The financial planning applications on mobile devices enabled advisors to apply multiple what-if scenarios instantly and present different proposals immediately. The availability of investment product-related information at their fingertips simplified communication between the advisors and their customers. Recently, social media is also being used extensively by financial planners to engage and communicate with their customers. Texting has also been a popular communication medium between the planners and customers. It is usually used to make quick decisions on certain investment opportunities available. The planning industry has therefore come a long way from using Excel sheets to using mobile devices and communications using social media.

Services like financial planning, investment portfolio management and managing other wealth instruments is collectively called wealth management. The term was used more generally in the late 1990s within the private wealth management divisions of large investment firms. The private wealth management divisions would typically manage the wealth of high net worth investors and wealthy retail clients. Wealth managers today are using mobile devices and social media to give the right information to their customers and make timely decisions on investments.

The 2008 financial crisis has left a sense of mistrust toward big FIs, and the ire continued toward anybody who was propagating the investment theories popularized by these institutions. During the same time, middle-class income globally started rising, partially due to inflationary pressure and partially due to increasing productivity led by automation. Unfortunately, these people did not have the time to do research related to securities on their own and did not find it worthwhile to hire a financial advisor with hefty commissions. It was also a well-accepted fact that anybody giving free advice was trying to push products with bigger commissions than those instruments that were benefiting the investors. Consequently, a large number of investors (retail and corporate) were now looking for a solution that did not involve a human interface. They were looking for a self-help platform capable of carrying out investments with predefined parameters. In and around 2008 such platforms commonly known as robo-advisors emerged in the United States, and until 2011 they were being used in all the major countries and stock markets around the world.

Robo-advisor is a name given to a collection of software/solution that provides financial advice through online channels with moderate to minimal human intervention. The financial advice by a robo-advisor is generated using complex mathematical calculations and algorithms. Users specify their criterion for investment and accordingly appropriate investment products are suggested to the user. The user then selects the right investment product as part of his/her portfolio. Mobile and email notifications are used to provide periodic updates to the customer regarding his/her investments, goals and trading decisions. In some of the solutions the investment products matching the criterion are selected by the platforms on their own. The platform further provides a regular update on the overall portfolio through alerts and notifications. The platform is similar to that used by financial advisors, but with automation and rules built into it for operating with the least manual intervention.

Robo-advisors have driven down the customer acquisition cost significantly and the portfolio management expenses are also minimal. This has made robo-advisors affordable to the middle class, leading to a significant increase in total assets under management (AUM) by robo-advisors. There are now hundreds of robo-advisory services actively managing over billions of dollars worth of assets under management. Charles Schwab, Wealthfront and Betterment and Vanguard were some of the early robo-advisory services in the United States.

In the last decade, ventures raising funds from the common man (referred as crowd) in return for a share or reward has become quite popular. This form of alternative financing is known as crowdfunding. Crowdfunding has been present for a long time and was extensively used by artisans and authors to fund their work. The same has been used during war through war bonds. In the 20th century, crowdfunding had also been used by scientists worldwide to fund their expensive experiments. It was not until the 21st century when crowdfunding became popular among investors and became mainstream. The Internet has been used for crowdfunding the ventures in a more formal manner. In this type of funding, the projects, assignments or an idea is listed on the crowdfunding website. Members of the website can then invest in the idea/project/assignment for a share of equity or for some rewards or purely on goodwill/patronage. Some of the popular platforms in crowdfunding space include Kiva, IndieGoGo and Kickstarter. It is estimated that there are currently about 2,000+ crowdfunding sites.

The Evolution of the Insurance Industry: Lloyd's of London to Pay per Mile Insurance

The insurance industry insures an individual, a corporation or any such entity to compensate against an eventuality happening due to a certain risk. The compensation would be monetary in nature and in exceptional cases could involve other grants like land, livestock, etc. The insurance industry generates its own capital corpus by pooling in money from all the members insured for a specific risk. Compensation claims are restricted to a certain percentage of the capital corpus. Thus, the insurance industry helps to spread the risk from an individual to a larger community who believes they share the same risks.

The origins of the insurance industry, similar to the banking industry, can be dated back to the beginning of human civilization. There are folk tales which narrate how a businessman or a peasant would keep one of their kin, ornaments or farmland as insurance until a certain objective set by the king or moneylender is not met. In some civilizations, the community of traders would pool their money to help anyone being impacted/effected by a natural calamity or sudden demise of the breadwinner. Insurance in some economies existed as an agreement of mutual aid. Granaries and financial reserves kept aside by kings to cater in difficult times like famine and war can be considered as a certain form of insurance. The first formal form of insurance can be traced to Babylonian traders who insured their loan for a voyage by paying an additional sum to compensate for their inability to pay back the loan in case something happened to their ship. Their loan was also waived off by the lender in case something happened to the ship.

About 3,000 years ago, the merchants from Rhodes would pay an additional amount of money in groups to insure their shipment. The collected amount was then used to compensate a merchant incurring a loss of merchandise due to a storm or the sinking of the ship. During the same time, the Romans and Greeks created societies that would take care of the families of deceased members, which can be called the earliest form of health and life insurance. In the 14th century, insurance contracts were invented that were pure insurance pools backed by estates. In the 15th century, maritime insurance developed into a full-fledged insurance. A more-formal set of insurance policies emerged in Europe for maritime businesses. Traders would pool in money to insure against voyage risk and if something happened to the crew, ship or cargo in transit, the compensation would be handed over to the next of kin.

A major fire in London in the 16th century, known as the "Great Fire of London," devoured thousands of houses. Soon thereafter, insurance to protect the property from fire came into existence in London with the formation of the first fire insurance company "Insurance Office for Houses." The insurance insured all brick and frame homes with an initial count of few thousand homes being insured. The Sun Fire Office is one of the oldest existing property insurance companies in the UK. Benjamin Franklin founded one of the first property insurance companies in the United States in the 18th century that insured property from fire. Taking a cue from the success of initial insurance companies, multiple other insurance companies emerged in the UK and the United States.

Business and maritime insurance started from a coffeehouse opened by Edward Lloyd in London in the 17th century. Initially the merchants would meet informally to insure cargoes and ships (Figure 1.3).

The same was later established as Lloyd's of London insurance market. In the 18th century, the first company to offer life insurance started in London as a society of participating members. It was a society of few thousand members at the start, wherein each member paid a fixed share depending on the age of the members. At the end of the year, a portion of the contribution would be divided among the wives and children of the deceased in proportion to the amount of shares the heirs owned. The first life table was written by Edmund Halley in 1693, but it was not until 1750 that necessary mathematical and statistical tools were in place for the development of modern life insurance. A life table is a table in actuarial science that shows the probability of a mortality across different ages and genders. It was in 1762 that Edward Rowe Mores established the "Society for Equitable Assurances on Lives and Survivorship," one of the first mutual insurers to pioneer age-based premiums on mortality rates, thus providing a framework for scientific insurance practices that also serves as the basis for most of the modern life insurance policies.

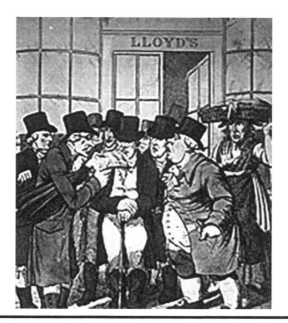

Figure 1.3   Coffeehouse by Lloyds.

Source: https://commons.wikimedia.org/wiki/File:Lloyd%27s_coffee_house_drawing.jpg.

Premiums were regulated per age and anybody could be admitted despite their state of health and circumstances.

The first accident insurance was offered by Railway Passenger Assurance Company to cover claims related to railway. The insurance was sold as a package deal along with tickets. The premiums were based on the class of the ticket. Soon thereafter, multiple countries introduced insurance programs to cover claims arising out of sickness and old age. In the 1880s, Germany introduced age-old pensions, accident insurance and medical care. The 1911 National Insurance Act gave the British working classes insurance against illness and unemployment. The Social Security Act was passed in the United States in 1935 that sought to provide insurance for individual financial security.

Seven years after establishing fire insurance, Benjamin Franklin started a life insurance company in the United States. Thereafter, multiple insurance companies sprung up – some of them were successful, but a large number of them ended up in bankruptcy as well. The primary reason for these companies going bankrupt was they did not have enough capital to back the claims. Soon the government introduced laws to ensure insurance companies maintained a certain minimum balance always. In 1864, the Travelers Insurance Company sold its first accident policy and in 1889 saw the first auto insurance policy being rolled out. In 2010, Congress passed the Dodd–Frank Wall Street Reform and Consumer Protection Act that is a mandate to provide oversight to all FIs and has established a Federal Insurance Office in the Department of the Treasury. The insurance industry in the United States is divided into two main categories, life and health insurance as one category and property and casualty as the other. U.S. insurers wrote about a third of all premiums collected worldwide.

One of the key functions of the insurance industry is to process data and information about their customers and provide them with the relevant quotes and premiums, and then issue a policy. The data processing is required again for annuity/claim payouts. Therefore, data processing capability and performance-intensive computational capability is central to the technology systems in the insurance industry. Until a large part of 19th and 20th centuries, most of the data processing functions for insurance companies were done manually. In the late 19th century, insurance firms adopted tabulating technology to speed up manual processes of sorting, counting and adding numerical data. In 1895, an actuary for the Prudential Life Insurance Company invented the Gore sorter algorithm which improved the sorting technology, and was used for multicompany mortality studies. Most insurance functions involved the generation of reports for internal use and policies to be issued to external parties. Therefore, insurance companies were the earliest adopters of Powers printing tabulators in 1915, capable of printing reports and policies data. During the same time, the Metropolitan Life Insurance Company was planning to build its own printing tabulator. These printers were only capable of printing numbers and were not capable of printing alphabets. Therefore, these printers were of limited use. By the end of the 1920s, IBM, through its acquisitions and partnerships, brought in the capability of alphabet printing along with number printing. From 1928 to 1950, the printers evolved to alphanumeric printing with a wide array of continuous forms. By the early 1950s, a large number of insurance firms were able to print most of the documents related to policy.

The high usage of tabulating equipment, increasing information volume and rising labor costs were pushing the insurance industry toward inventing and adopting machines with better computing capability. In 1950, The Univac division of Remington Rand introduced its first Univac computer. In 1951, Metropolitan Life took the delivery of Univac. The next Univac was delivered to the Franklin Life Insurance Company in the latter part of the same year. It is interesting to note that Franklin Life Insurance, which was a much smaller firm than Metropolitan Life, used the Univac for more functions and was able to generate greater savings. In the following year two more insurance firms bought Univac. In 1954, IBM introduced a smaller yet more efficient computer known as 650s at a much lesser price than Univac. John Hancock was one of the first buyers of the 650s and soon the sales of 650s picked up surpassing Univac by large numbers. It was much more economical and convenient, contractually and technically, for companies to replace one IBM machine (tabulating machine) with another (650s), compared to replacing IBM machines with Univac.

The introduction of the 650s and multiple versions until 1970 mandated that the software be built specifically for the machine. Therefore, a large number of insurance companies started developing their own insurance applications. This led to an increased expense for programming the computers for an insurance company. In 1970, IBM provided machines that enabled the unbundling of software and hardware. This led to the proliferation of multiple software packages specific to insurance. In 1980, IBM introduced its personal computer and from 1980 to 1990, multiple insurance applications were built on the personal computer. During the same time, the introduction of the laptop computer by IBM changed the way insurance agents/advisors interacted with the customers. The agent equipped with a laptop could meet with a customer face-to-face at a café, at a customer's residence or even at his office and come up with multiple different proposals. Since the laptop could not connect to the office network at most of the outdoor locations, the proposal and information to some extent would be based on stored information and not real time.

The Internet transformed the internal and external applications deployed by insurance companies. There were now online applications available for customer acquisition, customer management and entire policy life cycle management. The agents were now able to get connected to the insurance providers remotely and exchange information and data relating to prospects, new products and were able to communicating their monthly progress as well. The Internet helped agents to instantly provide benefit illustration and stay connected with their customers after the initial sale. The customer experience also dramatically transformed for the insured. Internet also marked the emergence of insurance aggregators that helped a customer to identify the best insurance alternatives. The customers were now able to search for insurance policies from a personal computer (PC) or a laptop. The communication between the insurance company and the customer was also simplified through email communication and online chat applications. Insurance claims became quite simplified as well, since the customer could now scan all of the relevant documents and upload them through an online portal.

Mobile devices further transformed the customer experience by providing all of the abovementioned online capabilities at their fingertips anytime. The telecom revolution with Wi-Fi and mobile connectivity at most of the outdoor locations enabled the advisors to be equipped with the latest information at their fingertips. Therefore, it was possible for a customer to compare quotes, pay premiums and chat with an insurance agent while traveling. The agent could now sit face-to-face with a prospect and provide different what-if scenarios to customers, by choosing different options on an iPad application. The built-in camera capability also helped customers file claims faster as they could take a photo of the accident and upload for faster and easier claim processing. The geolocation capability of phones also helped provide real-time access to emergency and other related services.

One of the key aspects of insurance is to prevent an eventuality from happening by taking necessary precautions. Mobile devices coupled with wearable devices are helping an individual to avoid health-related risks through regular health monitoring. These devices additionally suggest a workout plan and ensure customers to follow their routines through alerts and notifications. The wearable devices monitor pulse rates and will indicate if there is a chance of a heart attack. The usage of mobile devices to remotely communicate with doctors are also helping patients with chronic illnesses, thus, bringing down the overall healthcare bills and lesser accidents.

In recent years, sensors embedded in everyday devices alert customers for any damage to property because of fire, water and snow. Collectively these devices, when operating in a network to communicate meaningful information, are called the Internet of things (IOT). IOT has also been extensively used by corporations to prevent damages to industrial assets and processes. IOT is also being used in the automotive industry to track and alert driver behaviors to prevent accidents. Drones are being used by surveyors to assess the damage to property where it is not possible for humans to reach. IOT devices are also enabling insurers to provide pay per mile insurance, wherein the customer pays for insurance based on the miles the vehicle is being driven.

Disruptive technologies like blockchain, business intelligence and analytics are being used by insurance agencies to build new business models. Blockchain is being used to maintain a unique distributed ledger of assets and maintain a transaction history of assets to prevent fraud and theft. Business intelligence and analytics are being used to understand patterns that emerge after analyzing inputs received from multiple sources. These patterns are then being used by insurance agencies to charge differential premiums specific to an identified pattern of risks.

It is believed that insurance companies have been the key enablers of data processing technologies and enhancing the computational capability of computers. Cloud computing and AI-related technologies have been therefore adopted by the insurance industry to multiple solutions like customer management, policy administration and claims management. API-fication has also helped insurance companies to share information and prevent frauds.

FinTechs have been a key catalyst in adopting disruptive technologies and are transforming the way insurance business is done. The era can be compared to how the insurance industry transformed from the days when the first formal insurance was being conceptualized in the coffeehouse in London to the adoption of Univac computers. In subsequent chapters, examples of different insurance companies reveal how they are revolutionizing the business model by adopting disruptive technologies.

Emerging FinTechs

In 1980s, central banks globally started adopting inflationary policies boosting the investment in multiple assets like gold, real estate and stocks. In 2001, the crash of the dot-com companies resulted in people moving away from equities and started investing more in traditional assets like real estate. In 2008, due to the real estate crash, one of the worst financial crises happened leading to collapse of large banks globally. The financial crisis of 2007–2008 is known to be worst financial crisis after the Great Depression of the 1930s. It began in 2007 with a crisis in subprime mortgages in the United States and developed into a full-blown international banking crisis with the collapse of the investment bank Lehman Brothers in 2008. There was a combination of multiple causes that led to the crisis, though there is no evidence of any particular cause being responsible for the same in isolation. Some of the causes that led to the crisis are

1. Low interest rates prevailing in the United States before the crisis, led to multiple people investing in real estate with very low equated monthly installments (EMIs), and the collateral for these mortgages was the property that was being purchased.
2. High-risk loans issued to help low- and moderate-income Americans.
3. The high-risk mortgages were further bundled and sold as securities to quasi-government bodies and investment banks.

Simplistically, it could be said that there were multiple claims to a high-risk overvalued real estate asset.

The US Central Bank lowered the interest rates significantly to offset the downturn in the economy resulting from the September 2001 terrorist attack and the dot-com bubble bust. Owing to low interest rates, a new kind of asset bubble was in the making. Low interest rates and high mortgage approval rates were driving housing prices higher every day. More people were purchasing houses with the hope that they would get a much better deal right away than in the near future. A large number of houses (about 40%) were being bought for investment purposes or as weekend homes and were not intended to be a primary residence. The household debt to disposable personal income rose from two thirds of the income in 1990 to about 25% more than the existing income by the end of 2007.

The U.S. current account deficit increased to half a trillion and about four times as percentage of GDP between 1996 and 2004. The United States attracted huge foreign investment inflows mainly from the emerging economies in Asia and oil-exporting nations. Inflow of huge funds primarily due to the housing bubble combined with low interest rates created an easy credit situation. There were multiple adjustable interest rate schemes announced that enabled people to initially pay less interest rate/EMI on the borrowed amount and the interest rate/EMI would increase two to three times after a couple of years. This coerced people into borrowing with riskier loans, with a belief that let us borrow now and we would hopefully be able to meet the increased EMI demand in the next couple of years owing to their salary rise, etc.

To capitalize on the housing boom scenario, multiple investment banks introduced mortgage-backed securities (MBSs). Investors in these securities would indirectly provide the capital for banks to be mortgaged to the end-consumer. All the interest rate incomes would be shared back in the form of dividends or as appreciation of the security value. All the timely loan repayments by borrowers would make these securities more tradeable as opposed to securities with a high-loan default rate. Therefore, the security valuations were dependent on the mortgage repayment by home borrowers. Soon, multiple investment banks and financial entities within the United States and across the globe bought into the MBSs, presuming it to give better returns than other forms of investment. The investment banks and hedge funds were also issuing mortgages albeit with much less regulatory compliance as compared to the depository banks. Their share in the mortgage market had also become significant by 2007 and they were able to mask it by complex off-balance sheet arrangements and securitization.

As interest rates started rising in 2004 to 2006, borrowers started defaulting on their mortgages. The housing market also peaked in 2006 and started declining thereafter. The investment in MBSs, including global investors, started declining along with the fall in housing prices. One of the largest global banks wrote $10+ billion in subprime related mortgage securities during the same year. During 2007, as investor capital dried up, more than 100 mortgage companies who were reliant on the pool of capital generated through the origination and sale of mortgages closed down. Mortgage defaults, reduction in additional loans and falling home prices fueled the collapse in value of MBSs resulting in a further reduction in investments in MBSs and increase in redemption pressure. There was a spiraling effect on all the dependent funds and securities. Soon, Bear Stearns announced two of its hedge funds had imploded and the French bank BNP Paribas announced it was halting redemptions on three of investment funds due to subprime issues.

Investment banks under redemption pressure started borrowing from Asia and the Middle East during 2007. This lead to a high debt to equity ratio for most of the investment banks, thus leading them further to insolvency. Unable to withstand its operation, Bear Stearns was rescued from collapse by J.P. Morgan Chase with a multibillion dollar guarantee from the Federal Reserve in early 2008. Soon thereafter, by September 2008 Lehman Brothers collapsed, Merrill Lynch was purchased by Bank of America, Goldman Sachs and Morgan Stanley received access to credit lines from the Federal Reserve. Fannie Mae and Freddie Mac were taken over by the government. AIG that sold protection similar to insurance for mortgage-backed securities, was bailed out by the government through a $100 billion+ bailout plan. A large number of fund houses closed down giving in to the redemption pressures. The United States introduced a $700 billion emergency bailout plan of the banking system. In the last quarter of 2008, multiple U.S. and European central banks injected trillions of dollars as capital into the financial system followed by near zero interest rates for many subsequent years. This had a cascading effect on the economies worldwide and soon the recession began, leading to huge job losses and many of them losing their investments. The trust of people in the banking system to protect their capital was shaken once again (Figure 1.4).

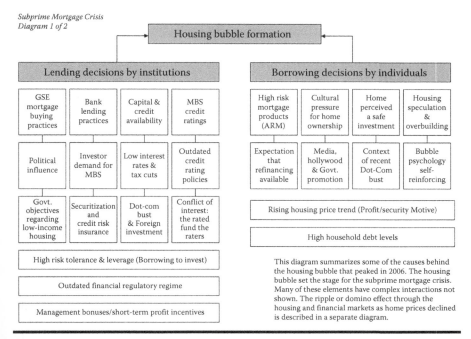

Figure 1.4   Causes for the financial crisis.

Source: https://commons.wikimedia.org/w/index.php?curid=11778063.

Subsequent to 2008, banks were mandated to follow a range of regulatory and statutory requirements with a strong oversight from multiple government agencies. The regulations helped build safeguards into the system, but at the same time it made the entire banking system rigid. The banks again became very stringent in issuing loans/mortgages. Additionally, the banking system had to follow stringent capital-related requirements. In order to comply with new regulatory requirements, the financial industry ended up incurring capital expenditures on account of building the desired checks and balances in their information technology (IT) systems.

The financial industry has been one of the biggest contributor and consumer of technology. They have been at the forefront of multiple technology innovations like the ATM machines in the 1960s and the introduction of Univacs and PCs in the 1980s. From 1980s onward, a greater focus of the financial industry was toward upgrading and fine tuning their backend processing system. The IT systems of these institutions were quite monolithic and homegrown with very little standardization. Thus, they were less agile in responding to the changing demands of the customer.

As FIs worldwide were either shutting down or were getting acquired/merged, a large number of people were being handed pink slips. Some of these were top notch technologies and business SMEs. They started grouping together to create start-ups, which were implementing financial business processes using technology as the disruptor. Thus, FinTechs, a name commonly given to technology-driven financial service start-ups were born. There were technology firms servicing the financial industry that existed before FinTechs but almost all of them were technology enablers rather than disruptors. In contrast, FinTechs were disrupting the financial business model. Therefore, they were in the truest sense, competing with most of the large FIs rather than enabling them. While FinTechs were disrupting the financial services landscape, the large financial firms were saddled with age-old technology and business processes. The digital native generations, therefore, were attracted toward the disruption caused by FinTechs as their offerings were intuitive, transparent and cost-effective.

The generation born at the beginning of the 21st century is referred to as millennials and generations just prior to that are called Gen X, Gen Y and Gen Z respectively. All of these generations were born in an era when technology innovations were at their peaks. Consequently, for a large part of this generation, technology terminology like Wi-Fi, 3G, mobile and Google are a part of their everyday vocabulary. These generations can collectively be said to be the digital native generation. Their use of devices has graduated from playing games to using business applications. Therefore, they consider a good customer experience more important than associating with a name or brand that has long existed. In one of the surveys it is said that millennials would switch banks if they do not get a satisfactory experience, albeit the bank may have a long-standing record of being a well-known brand otherwise.

A large number of legacy FIs, instead of spending on innovation and customer experience, were investing in fine tuning their backend processing and meeting compliance-related requirements. Additionally, the monolithic nature of most of the banking applications made it difficult to decouple customer experience from transaction processing. In the meantime, business and technology SMEs who lost jobs during the financial crisis from reputed FIs started building products and creating start-ups that would transform the customer experience radically. Additionally, they had the advantage of starting from scratch, and therefore they were able to create better customer experience supported by agile business processes. Customers quickly adopted these companies as they were using new-age technology like social media, mobile devices and wearables to provide a unique and personalized customer experience. Soon FinTechs started becoming a revolution in itself.

Another aftereffect of the 2008 crisis was that there were very less investment alternatives available for large investors. The real estate market showed no signs of recovery. The dot-com bubble had created a bad experience in the equity markets. The hedge fund collapse had taken the sheen out of alternative financing market. The angel investors and venture capitalist (VC) firms were sitting on huge money to be invested in potentially high-performing industries. The emergence of the FinTech industry was a potential investment opportunity for VCs and angel investors.

Additionally all the FinTechs are advantaged by using the shared services model and pay-per-use model instead of investing in infrastructure. The main focus of the FinTechs is to build a cost-optimized set-up and pass on the benefits to the customers. The cost-optimized offerings with a far superior customer experience resulted in a significant customer adoption. Since they were operating low-cost operations and they had a sizeable customer base, they were able to negotiate better rates with their vendors and partners. This created an ecosystem of providing low costs yet better or similar services compared to the large monolithic FIs. An example is affordable wealth management services provided by wealth FinTechs like Wealthfront and Betterment, proved that a customer could get similar returns as compared to their large monolithic peers. Therefore, FinTechs could bring in better earnings with an increased customer base while keeping the investments low. Consequently, the valuations of FinTech companies multiplied exponentially, thus bringing in an ever-increasing number of investors into investing in FinTechs.

The Rise of FinTechs

At the start of this century, financial technology start-ups had started disrupting the FI primarily in the payments, loyalty, lending, wealth management, financial planning and insurance domains.

The credit card industry had come a long way from the Diners Club card to ATM machines and using credit cards over the Internet for e-commerce transactions. The point of sale (POS) machines or card readers also had evolved over time. Even though the payment experience was changing, the traditional payment processing companies and card companies were not paying much attention to customer experience and innovation. A large part of their investments and efforts were being spent on compliance requirements, consequent to the 2008 financial crisis. In the meantime, start-ups like PayPal were already revolutionizing the payment space by providing a seamless payment experience through their wallet services. Using wallets, users would have to specify the credential for the wallet only while making an online purchase. The wallets in turn would manage details like personal information, card details and shipping details. Soon multiple companies started introducing wallet services, including retailers and telecom companies. FinTechs disrupted the payments domain further by enabling peer-to-peer (P2P) payments using social media.Wallets had an impact on loyalty as well. Since each superstore had its own loyalty program, wallets were a much better interface for the customer. Through wallets, customers could now tie up loyalty cards of different stores to a single wallet interface.

The financial crisis of 2008 resulted in low capital availability with most of the large banks. Additionally, new regulations regarding risk and compliance made it difficult for most of the lenders to develop any innovative lending products. FinTechs were smaller in size and agile; therefore, they were able to develop innovative lending business models like P2P lending, Payday lending and Crowdfunding. P2P lending has been the most popular form of lending in recent years. FinTechs have enabled P2P lending in multiple different models. In some cases, FinTechs merely act as aggregators or market places to get lenders and borrowers together. In some of the other models, FinTechs have provided additional security like protection from default. Lending Club, On Deck and Zopa are some of the FinTechs that are enabling P2P lending.

Payday lending and micro lending was clearly out of bounds for large lenders because it comprised of – large number of low-value transactions and borrowing by people with low credit scores. This type of lending also necessitated that the overall cost overheads are low and the underlying IT systems are cost-effective and agile. FinTechs built upon the vacuum left by the large lenders and very soon created robust organizations that would provide payday lending. Zest Finance and Wonga are some of the FinTechs that are offering payday lending.

Funding projects and experiments through patrons and crowdfunding was again something that was not possible for big investment banks. FinTechs like Kickstarter were able to build upon the model successfully. SME loans and microfinance were other lending offerings that FinTechs were able to offer. All of these offerings would have been difficult, if not impossible, for big established lenders to offer, owing to the complexity and the regulatory compliance issues involved.

FinTechs have also been able to tap into a large part of the middle-class population by providing affordable wealth management and advisory services. The middle-class population was largely ignored by large investment banks, as their cost structures would not justify investing below a certain minimum threshold value.

FinTechs have brought the next level of investing to middle-class investors by offering them robo-advising services. Since most of the middle-class population does not get enough time to spend on tracking investing trends, robo-advising has been a welcome offering and made some of these firms hugely popular. FinTechs have also been instrumental in enabling investing using state-of-the-art technologies like robo-investing for social causes. There are FinTechs that employ robo-investing techniques to invest in firms engaged in social causes matching the investor's preference. Additionally, some of the FinTechss have been able to aggregate bank accounts for a customer and provide personal financial management along with wealth advisory services.

Financial technology start-ups in insurance, also known as Insuretech, have also been instrumental in transforming the way insurance is done. Similar to the banking and wealth management industry, established players in the insurance industry have also been less agile and innovative owing to regulatory compliance and high-cost structures because of their size. FinTechs have been instrumental in offering on-demand insurance coverage using a mobile app by providing the user to toggle insurance coverage on a weekly, daily and hourly on a click of a button. These FinTechs, besides offering a good overall customer experience, are also helping save money for the user by charging the customer on a pay-per-use basis. The usage of sensors and devices like drones have helped insuretechs to collect information from inaccessible places, thus, providing a more accurate version of the accident conditions and suggesting preventive and corrective measure. Some of the FinTechs are helping insurance companies to decide insurance premium and claim settlements based on individual's behavior. FinTechs like lemonade are enabling P2P insurance, and there are other FinTechs that are transforming P2P insurance by pooling money from like-minded people.

In contrast to large monolithic core systems in large FIs, FinTechs have much simpler core systems to manage. Technology disruptions like high network speed, faster computing, mobile devices, Web 2.0, cloud computing and IOT have also been helping FinTechs to drive the transformation. Owing to these technology disruptions, it was possible for FinTechs to bring in innovative products and engage customers with intuitive business processes. The new-age technologies were also instrumental in lowering the cost of doing business for FinTechs, albeit providing a much better customer experience. The customer was now getting a better and personalized experience at lower cost. Soon a large number of FinTechs were popular with high customer adoption through word-of-mouth and social media publicity. A larger FinTech adoption brought in investors and ultimately started the chain of disruption in the industry.

FinTechs, therefore, not only started offering alternative business models, but they were disrupting the financial industry in a big way. Increasing network speeds from telecom operators and reduced data costs have been a critical factor in the success and rise of FinTechs. Right from the introduction of 1G networks to the existing 4G networks there has been a steady increase in the network speeds and a decrease in the cost of transmitting the data. 4G networks brought in a speed of 100 mbps to 1 gbps at very low cost, thereby driving the data revolution. Additionally, the telecom networks have enabled the transmission of voice, Internet access, video and multimedia messages through mobile devices. FinTechs have used the prowess of telecom networks coupled with the capability of mobile devices in the last decade to provide an unmatched customer experience anytime, anywhere, with high speed and at an affordable price.

The mobile phones themselves have been a major technology disruption fueling the rise of FinTechs. Mobile phones started off by being a device to talk remotely and wirelessly with another individual. The introduction of smartphones in late 1990s and early 2000s transformed the digital economy drastically. Prior to the iPhone, smartphones were primarily used by business professionals or by the affluent. Apple disrupted the mobile phone industry by bringing in the iPhone. The iPhone provided a customer interface that was extremely intuitive and soon was adopted by a large population. Around the same time, other phone companies launched their smartphones as well. The entire phone industry transformed from a simple telecalling industry to a smartphone industry with the emphasis on apps and data formats. Also at the same time, the concept of the cloud and software as a service started becoming prominent in the technology space. The FinTech industry harnessed this concept to its full potential and way ahead of time.

Smartphones have multiple sensors built inside them including the ability to capture biometrics information. The embedded camera in mobile devices is capable of capturing high-resolution images and videos. This capability when coupled with high-speed networks enabled these devices to transmit photos and videos between devices instantly. All these features in addition to the enormous computing capability of mobile devices enabled FinTechs to launch apps like instant onboarding. These apps were capable of capturing biometrics information, photos of the customer and onboarding details. Once collected, the information was sent to a centralized location in no time via high-speed 4G connections. The agile systems at the centralized location, coupled with AI was able to process and confirm the onboarding back to the mobile device in minutes. This process of onboarding a customer in the traditional set-up would take weeks, which FinTechs were able to complete in minutes. FinTechs, therefore, were able to disrupt the business by harnessing the technical abilities of mobile devices. Soon mobile phones reached all the places including the areas where the formal economy was not able to make inroads. It is forecasted that there would be around 5+ billion mobile phones worldwide in 2018. Essentially, there are now more mobile phones in the world than the number of people.

The smartphone industry also introduced App Stores wherein any developer (individual/corporate) could develop his/her app and upload it to the App Store wherefrom it could be consumed by any smartphone user. Therefore, developing and publishing apps became hugely popular, taking the count from about 500+ apps in 2008 to millions of apps now with billions of downloads. Initially there were utility- and media-related apps in the App Stores, but over time, the App Stores started getting first versions of mobile commerce applications. Soon e-commerce firms started conducting a large part of their business using the application in the App Store. This was the first sign of FinTechs becoming a major force in the financial services industry.

As the hardware and software capabilities on phones started becoming better, the first set of financial start-ups like Square and Groupon emerged. Some of these companies were using the geolocation capability on the device to provide best offers near the user. Subsequently, a host of financial start-ups emerged with innovative applications in the App Stores. Some of the innovative apps launched in the App Stores included, applications for banking, wealth management, lending, loyalty, insurance and payments. Some of the apps, that started as a personal financial management (PFM) tool, soon evolved into a full-fledged financial app with features like account aggregation, financial planning and setting financial goals.

The smartphones were also instrumental in transforming the payment industry by the introduction of near-field communication (NFC) chips and the capability to host wallets. Wallets, as explained earlier, are applications that try to emulate the capability of a physical wallet virtually. Therefore, a user can manage identity, card and cash information using wallets. Additionally, the wallets provide a single interface for all payments. Wallets dedicated to carrying out payment transactions are called payment wallets. The payment wallets are capable of conducting payment transactions using a wide variety of currencies. In Africa, the wallets have enabled financial transactions to a large unbanked population by using mobile money as an intermediate currency. Mobile money could be bought/exchanged from telecom operators similar to any other currency exchange and a mobile connection becomes the basis for identifying an individual. There are also wallets available that help buying, selling and exchanging cryptocurrencies.

Smartphones and mobile devices are also transforming the health insurance industry by enabling applications that help you get home delivery of medicines, applications that can schedule an appointment with doctor, applications that notify a patient with a medication schedule and multiple other applications. The camera and video streaming capability on phones is helping doctors diagnose and prescribe drugs to the patients remotely.

Cloud technology has helped start-ups by limiting their start-up costs on infrastructure, as they now have access to state-of-the-art infrastructure in a pay-per-use model. All the mobile and online applications need to interface remotely with a server at the back end. A start-up in the initial days after their formation are not sure of the usage capacity of their infrastructure, therefore a dedicated infrastructure would mean either building too much or too less. Cloud technology has come in as a savior, since it would charge on a pay-per-use model. Thus, start-ups would end up paying what is proportionate to their usage (success) instead of loading the infrastructure cost up front. This has lowered the initial investment for venture funds, consequently increasing the number of VCs and investors willing to invest in early-stage start-ups. Consequently, financial start-ups would not need to latch onto large IT infrastructure for managing the load of their subscribers, but instead they could partner with firms, and directly interface with their back end infrastructure through a public/private cloud. Summarily, the mobile/online apps and cloud revolution together has made software-as-a-service a reality. Infrastructure providers like Amazon is an example of such a cloud service provider. Challenger banks, a name given to an all online banks with less capital requirements, are using cloud technology to keep their costs down.

In the initial days, most of the websites were rendered from a centralized server onto the user's browser – there was very little content that was exchanged locally with a user's machine. Additionally, since these websites were only suitable to be accessed on desktops/laptops, therefore interaction using these websites was very limited. The Web 2.0 guidelines enabled the end user to own, change or append the existing website content. The responsive design ensured that the new websites could be rendered seamlessly on mobile devices. The responsive design could be achieved only if the websites were developed using client-side scripting technologies. Start-ups were building the system from scratch, and it was fast and easy for them to adopt to this new-age technology compared to the large FIs. Large FIs had to take a two-step approach to make their websites responsive. The first step was to fragment their applications to expose core functionalities as services, collectively known as microservices. Second step was to develop websites using client-side scripting. These websites would then use the services created in first step for rendering content and information. Consequently, adopting the new technologies, start-ups were able to launch their offerings faster in market, thus encashing the first mover advantage.

Technology disruptions mentioned above along with regulatory pressure, pushed businesses toward exposing their functionality and data using API-fication. API-fication has helped businesses in unbundling different components of the application like the customer experience, the core processing engine and intermediate workflows. An example would be a robo-advising FinTech who can offer only the core engine capability using APIs, instead of mandating the customer to buy the entire platform including the user interface. A large number of FinTechs have been able to use this as an additional revenue stream, besides running their own platform. An example could be payment FinTechs offering their APIs to businesses for integrating the same in their commercial apps and applications. Another shot in the arm for FinTechs have been the second payment services directive (PSD2) regulation in Europe and the UK. It mandates that all FIs should provide authorized access to their data and functionality. Consequently, FinTechs can now integrate data and core functionality from large FIs. The information from FIs coupled with unique customer journeys will enable FinTechs to disrupt the way business is done. Access to data and information from large FIs will also help FinTechs to cut down customer acquisition time and ultimately reduce their go-to-market time.

FinTechs have been very innovative in their approach toward using technology to find a business solution. Some of the most innovative FinTechs are using

IOT and gamification to imbibe saving habits into customers while doing financial planning for them. These FinTechs use health habits like the number of steps taken to transfer a predefined amount to a savings account. Direct payments from connected cars at tollbooths at the time of crossing the booth is already being prototyped by FinTechs. FinTechs are also providing a very personalized customer experience using technologies like business intelligence (BI), analytics and AI. A group of FinTechs are using BI, analytics and AI to provide high-impact market news for companies that exists in the portfolio of an investor. Some other FinTechs are providing intelligent search engines using Big Data and AI. Therefore, using IOT, AI, gamification, BI and analytics, FinTechs have been able to leverage the technology innovatively to bring about new ways of doing business. These technologies have helped start-ups redefine individual financial functions like lending, onboarding, etc. as separate personalized user-journeys.

FinTechs as mentioned earlier are building their platforms from scratch. Consequently, some of them have opted to build their platforms using blockchain. Blockchain at a very high level can be described to have the following components – (a) a distributed ledger that can store unique transactions, (b) a consensus mechanism that ensures there is authorization for a transaction from authorized entities, and (c) the transaction is secured through cryptography and chaining the transaction blocks. The financial world is also characterized by all of the above requirements in regard to financial transactions. Therefore, there is a clear overlap from a technology fitment perspective. There is a distributed ledger built by FinTech company that has more than 80 banks participating in its creation and usage. Blockchain is also used in the generation and exchange of cryptocurrencies like Bitcoin, Etherium, etc. There are FinTechs based out of Africa that are using Bitcoin as an intermediate currency in a cross-border currency exchange and instant payment. Blockchain is being touted as the biggest technology disruption after the Internet.

All of the abovementioned technologies have therefore given an edge to start-ups since they are providing one of the best customer experiences at affordable costs. It is no surprise that more than $50 billion has been invested across 2,500+ companies globally since 2010. The subsequent chapters detail disruptive business models adopted by FinTechs using new-age technology. There are also examples of how FinTechs are trying to help social causes and how innovations have been used to reach out to unbanked and informal economies. FinTechs are not only disrupting in developed nations but are coming up with innovative solutions in emerging and developing countries including Africa. Chapter 4 describes the emergence of FinTech in different parts of the world. The existence of an ecosystem is essential for entrepreneurs and Chapter 5 describes the enabling environments for FinTechs globally. Chapter 6 also talks about how established FIs are collaborating, encouraging and helping FinTechs grow. In the end the authors perspective on the future and what lies ahead for FinTechs as an industry is elaborated.

Chapter 2

Reshaping the Financial Services Industry

The fable of David and Goliath talks about how Goliath, a giant with all the protective Armor, challenged the opponents for a fight. Ultimately, one fine day a young boy carrying a pouch full of stones challenged Goliath. The boy's name was David, and he hits Goliath on his forehead with the stones in his pouch using a sling. This leads to Goliath falling and David cutting off his head.

Giant financial services institutions with multi billion dollars of global assets, clothed in 600 years of industry dominance, came out each day challenging entrepreneurs to disrupt the way they did the business. One day a young industry named FinTech started challenging the existing banking institutions, clothed in simplicity and convenience and armored with mobile technology. In contrast to the corollary, FinTechs have not been able to end the dominance of established financial services players. But they have been able to cause enough disruption for investors to bet on them as torch bearers of the future of the financial services industry.

A research report by analysts in early 2015 estimated that more than a quarter of the traditional financial services' revenue is at risk of being displaced by FinTechs. Another analysts report reveals that as much as half of revenues and profits are at risk of the established financial institutions (FIs). The reduction in revenues is from a combination of various factors such as dwindling margins and many others. One of the key reasons for drop in revenue is also competition from FinTech start-ups. A research report published in 2016 by a leading consulting and analyst firm concluded that top banking executives fear that more than a quarter of the traditional financial services businesses will be at risk of being taken away by FinTechs by 2020. All indicators are therefore indicating that FinTech is disrupting the financial industry in a big way. One of the main reasons they have been so successful is their ability to provide transformational products at affordable costs.

Wealth management has been one of the financial services that has been disrupted in a big way by FinTech firms. The wealth management industry for the last 30–40 years has primarily been driven by financial advisors and wealth advisors. Some of these advisors act independently, others are associated with a large investment bank or a fund house. The independent financial advisors suffer from a credibility standpoint and the latter are viewed by investors as pushing the products preferred by their banks or fund houses. A large part of the wealth management is done through face-to-face interactions in a traditional set-up, and seldom does the advisor explain multiple what-if scenarios. Lastly, most of these advisors charge a hefty fee, even though they might be conducting a commission-free trade themselves.

The biggest disruption by FinTechs has been caused by automating the financial advice part with the introduction of robo-advisors. Global assets under management (AUM) by robo-advisors are predicted to become a multitrillion dollar business by 2020. The year-end 2016 AUM of robo-advisor firms was estimated to be quarter of trillion dollars by leading analysts. The automation has helped FinTechs to charge very low commissions and some FinTechs are even offering commission-free trades.

Almost all the FinTech firms provide wealth management/financial advice through their digital platforms and can be accessed by customer through their mobile devices. There are now a large number of online advice firms, up from just a couple in 2000. A report by leading analyst indicates nearly half of the customers who changed their wealth management firm moved to a digitally led firm, and about three fourth of investors under the age of 40 said they would be comfortable working with a virtual financial advisor. Thus, FinTechs have been able to differentiate themselves, by offering a digital customer experience in contrast to an in person face-to-face interaction all the time by their established peers. Additionally, FinTechs have been able to provide transformational products like investment products for midmarket employers, which was traditionally not catered to by large investment banks.

A large number of investment firms, before the FinTechs came into picture, used to earn large sums of money by taking commissions out of the trades they made. FinTechs in fact are now reversing the trend by not charging any commission for the trade an individual makes, but instead charge an annual or monthly subscription fee. Therefore, FinTechs have brought the existing technology to the retail brokerage market, offering a commission-free stock brokerage.

Some of these FinTech firms have been able to conduct transactions in excess of a billion dollars through their portal and app. Though this might be a small percentage of the overall online trades, it definitely is an amount that has made large investment banks understand the potential of the FinTechs. Some of these FinTechs are also planning to release the application program interface (API) for their applications so that the same can be used by financial websites and investment advisors alike.

Some of the other FinTech companies introduced a business model wherein they would have a fee structure and a less entry amount as compared to the established FIs. Consumers always wanted a platform that could help them buy fractional shares so that their money does not sit idle in their accounts. Established investment banks were not able to offer such systems because of their rigid monolithic systems and processes. This prompted the FinTechs to introduce transformational products where a customer was able to buy fractional shares. These FinTech firms brought in all of these features coupled with a more customer-friendly financial advice and personalized the way of investing. This was in contrast to proposing a set of standard funds that a financial advisor from an established investment bank would propose. Additionally, some of these FinTech firms took to managing even the retirement funds using robo-advisors including 401(k) platforms aimed at midmarket employers. These platforms offered implementing the same investment strategies as traditional plans but at a much lesser cost. Again, this is an instance of bringing in a transformational product and cashing in on an opportunity ignored by established FIs. A large number of these FinTech companies are also encouraging collaboration by providing their application features as open source software or API and providing critical market information thus helping analyze financial data/ information for a specific financial instrument. It is an approach quite different from the closed approach followed by established FIs.

Robo-advising FinTechs, besides providing a compelling user experience and a proprietary platform at very low fees, have ushered in an era of alternative business processes. Some of the alternative business processes introduced by these FinTechs include:

1. Providing free service for a certain fixed amount of investment and then charging a nominal transaction fee thereafter.
2. Offering free financial advice for a certain amount based on referrals provided.
3. Facilitating trade and robo-advising across multiple businesses like real estate, natural resources and commodities besides trading in equities.
4. Investing the earnings in the form of dividends or through an exceptionally beneficial trade across other equities rather than investing it in the same equities and mutual funds time and again.

The introduction of alternate business models is also prevalent with mortgage FinTechs that are offering personal and payday loans. They are offering the same loans through a very simple and transparent application and approval process. These FinTech firms have adopted processes that do not have loan approvals dependent on credit scores, as is the case of large mortagage banking firms, but instead they provide loans through the assessment of the customer's financial situation and capability to repay the loans. Some of these FinTechs help customers to reduce the interest rates by taking classes for the timely repaying of loans. Clearly these mortgage and lending FinTech firms, along with the established lending platforms are disrupting the entire lending and mortgage business. All of these firms are challenging the Goliaths of industry through their automated- and artificial intelligence-driven (AI-driven) models to define a customized rate for each individual customer. They are also ensuring that the risk is vetted on actual data than just relying on credit scores, and thereby giving access to millions of unbanked or underbanked Americans. They have in no time become challengers to most of the large mortgage banks in capitalizing on an industry that was never considered worth investing in by the Goliaths.

FinTechs offering financial management services are delivering the same with a transformational user experience, by enabling the users to track their bank accounts, credit card details, investment details, loan balances and transactions through a single-user interface. Some of the other FinTech financial advising firms are targeting a specific segment like financial advising solutions for women only or for millennials only. Doing this is helping these firms to reach out to a customer base that was until now ignored by the large investment banks. Additionally, this new customer group is getting the advice in a transparent manner and in a manner that could help them understand how their decisions are impacting their returns. They are therefore greatly benefitted by the same as well. Some of these offerings are making this group, especially women, a key decision-maker in financial planning and ultimately leading to financial independence.

These FinTechs have built multiple tools to help individuals do their financial planning, manage their mortgages and ensure they have enough savings planned for a rainy day. Most of these FinTechs have a digital interface supported by an app that helps individual retail customers automatically track their cash flow, reinforce positive habits and provide insights about spending and saving behaviors. Therefore, FinTechs have occupied the opportunity space created by retail investors needing financial advice but do not have big bank balances. For a very small amount of money, FinTechs provide personalized financial advice to its customers, thus providing an alternate business model at an affordable cost.

These FinTechs are venturing into an area which either the Goliath's missed out on or did not think was lucrative enough. The FinTechs cashed in on these opportunities and are now challenging Goliaths at their own game. Another financial domain which was a forte for established FIs was the payment function. Until FinTechs arrived, it was perceived that a payment is an integrated function of banking and cannot be made available to the customers in isolation. The FIs were instrumental in propagating the belief for a long time that it is mandatory to have a bank account to carry out payments for purchases and at any point-of-sale. FinTechs besides enabling payments without a bank account also broke the myth that the only way of doing payments at a point-of-sale was through cash or cards. Therefore the payment FinTechs transformed the way payments have traditionally been done. According to the data accumulated by the leading analysts on FinTechs, payments and loyalty companies raised almost half of the total funds raised by FinTechs in 2016. Therefore, it can be said that the payment FinTechs are disrupting the financial industry in a big way, followed by lending and wealth management FinTechs.

FinTechs, as in other financial domains, are transforming the payment industry as well by introducing alternative business models. Some of the transformative models brought in by FinTechs are listed below:

1. Through payment wallets, they have been able to establish that payments could be done peer-to-peer (P2P) and does not necessarily need intermediaries like banks and credit card companies.
2. They have also transformed the usual way of dealing in cash by making the payment interfaces seamless.
3. Facilitating payments between friends and family using phone contacts and social media.

P2P FinTechs are facilitating money transfer services through social media. People can find friends or family through email, phones or mobile devices and transfer money between themselves. These applications function similar to a digital wallet and maintains a balance of its own. The wallets can also be linked to respective bank accounts, debit cards or credit cards to the account.

The popular social media companies like Snapchat and Facebook are also now providing P2P payments. These social media companies have launched their P2P payment platform where the user can send money to their contacts using debit/credit cards. There is another P2P service by these platforms that help small businesses and individuals transfer and process payments.

The impact of disruption caused by payment FinTechs in the industry has made the Goliaths take notice of them. The P2P FinTechs are therefore taking a huge chunk of more than a $3 trillion pie of the overall P2P payment industry. This is an indication that though individual FinTech players may be small in transaction volumes and revenue generation, they are all together taking away a significant revenue share of the entire industry. Thus, most of the large banks have started their own P2P services independently or jointly to compete with the FinTechs in this space. Some of the banks now let users send funds directly from their bank accounts to their recipient's bank account using only an email address or mobile phone number. This was launched initially only for corporates but is all set to be launched as a retail P2P payment service. Some other banks are partnering with FinTechs to adopt the disruption caused by them.

FinTechs in the Payments Industry

The payments industry is one of the most complex industries in the financial world. There are multiple players in this industry who work in tandem to make a payment transactions work. The payments were initially handled by banks in return of the presentment of a check, draft or a withdrawal note. In the initial days, a payment was only possible to the bearer of a check, draft or a withdrawal note if specified accordingly, or else, the payment was transferred to the account, specified on the check. Therefore, for a large part payments were handled in cash, until the first credit card was introduced. Thereafter, multiple banks introduced their own credit cards. Similar to the revolution brought about by the introduction of credit cards in the banking industry, the FinTechs are reshaping the payment industry by bringing in innovative customer journeys.

A brief understanding of the entire payment ecosystem and different entities involved is essential to understand the impact caused by FinTechs from a business and technology perspective. The moment an individual swipes his/her credit card at a point of sale (POS), the payment process begins and different entities of the ecosystem start interacting with each other. Let us begin by taking a hypothetical case of an individual purchasing coffee from a coffee shop and explore all the entities involved therein by the transaction.

Let us take the case of Susan, a hypothetical customer, swiping her card at a hypothetical coffee shop called StarCoffee. In the payment ecosystem, the coffee shop is called a "merchant" and Susan is described as a "card holder." StarCoffee would have a bank account, and the bank holding this account would be called an "acquirer" bank. Susan would also have a relationship with a specific bank who would have issued a credit card to Susan. This bank is called as "issuer" bank and in most cases the issuer bank will issue cards associated with different card schemes like Mastercard and Visa. The card scheme is an intermediary who is responsible for connecting all the entities in the ecosystem. The moment Susan swipes her card at the coffee shop, an authorization request is sent from the point-of-sale system to the merchant's acquirer bank. The point-of-sale system is typically a credit card swipe machine, a Europay, Mastercard and Visa (EMV) credit card or a tap card machine. The acquirer bank then forwards the request to the "card scheme." The card scheme works with the issuing bank to understand if the customer is eligible for the desired credit and if the customer has a relevant balance in his/her bank account. If all goes through well, Susan is allowed to conduct the purchase and she walks out of the store with her coffee. The merchant provides a bill to her and keeps a copy of it, as a proof of the transaction.

Once the transaction is completed at the POS, there are multiple transactions carried out at a later time to close settlements for the transactions initiated. The acquirer bank then creates batches of settlements and sends the details of these transactions to the respective card schemes. The card schemes then process this information and create batches of settlement requests to be sent to the respective issuing bank. Upon getting the payment request, the issuing bank pays the card scheme and which in turn pays the acquiring bank. In some cases, the card processing companies like American Express and Discover play a dual role of issuing a bank and card scheme as well.

This is a very simplified version of the complexities and variations involved in processing the transactions across multiple banks, merchants and credit card-issuing companies globally. Since the process is complex and usually the commission charged is correlated to the number of entities involved, the FinTechs have started disrupting this market by letting payments happen differently.

As mentioned above, investments in a payment FinTech has been the highest followed by FinTechs in the wealth management space. P2P payments, wallets and POS solutions are some of the areas that have been disrupted by FinTechs. Besides the FinTechs transforming the payment space directly, there are FinTechs that are disrupting the industry that enables the payment business. The business functions that these FinTechs are disrupting include on-boarding, know-your-customer (KYC) and loyalty-related solutions. Since the disruption caused by P2P payment FinTechs have been elaborated in the Chapter 1, this chapter elaborates on how wallet and POS solution FinTechs are disrupting the industry.

Multichannel Digital Wallets

With the introduction of wallet companies like PayPal in the late 1990s, the wallet revolution had already begun, but it was intensified with the advancement in mobile technology and the availability of client-side scripting technology. With the launch of the first generation iPhone the smartphone industry and later other mobile devices transformed the way business was being done. Mobile devices slowly started becoming the preferred channel for e-commerce transactions. A large number of apps were launched that were facilitating shopping using the mobile device directly. At the end of the purchase process, the customer would make the payments. After the purchase was done, the customer would initiate a payment using his/her card information. At this point the mobile application enabling shopping would make a request to the payment gateway to execute the transaction. In this process, a customer has to remember his/her credit card information and there could be multiple cards he/she would wish to use. Additionally, every time, the user would have to specify his/her shipping and invoicing details. In some cases, the user would have to provide the loyalty information as well to accumulate miles from the purchase made. All of this together made the payment interface quite complex for a customer.

A more simplified version of the same could be wherein a consumer stores all his/her credit card/debit card/banking information in a single application and all his/her purchases can then be routed through this application. Such an application that could enable payments using a single interface for purchases made using online or mobile channels is called a digital wallet. The digital wallet in turn could potentially store the credit card details, identity details, shipping and invoicing information and even could store loyalty-related information.

Mobile devices are personal devices and are secured with features like a one-time password, biometrics authentication and sandboxing of the application. The digital wallet applications can leverage these features to provide a secure interface to conduct payment transactions for a customer. Soon multiple start-ups began providing digital wallet solutions including established telecom providers and phone manufacturers. Apple Pay and Google Wallets are some of the popular wallets from the phone manufacturers Apple and Google respectively. The digital wallet reached a new level of popularity and adoption with the embedding of a near-field communication (NFC) chip in mobile devices and POS systems. Consequently, NFC-enabled devices in close proximity could transfer information with each other, including payment information, through a simple tap. This transformed the payment experience as the customer was now able to carry out payments by just tapping the device or bringing it near to POS. The customer experience was far better than handing over his/her card/cash at cash counters followed by entering the pin and authorization numbers and ending with a paper confirmation of the payment. Additionally, with tokenization solutions and security solutions being standardized, the frauds in digital wallets are going down, driving their adoption and popularity further.

The introduction of multiple different currencies other than government-issued denominations like mobile money and cryptocurrencies drove the success and popularity of digital wallets to a new high. Some of the wallets are also enabling payments using cryptocurrencies like Bitcoin. One of the reasons for the popularity of wallets have been the offers and coupons issued by different wallet companies for using their wallets.

The adoption of digital wallets and people moving to online shopping and digital payments has prompted a lot of telecom providers and retail stores like Walmart (walmartpay) and Reliance in India (Jio Wallet) to enable their own wallet solutions. The digital wallet industry can be further categorized into:

- Digital wallets
- Application supporting wallets
- Onboarding and KYC applications

Digital Wallets

Digital wallets as explained above are solutions that provide a common interface for conducting payments online or through a mobile device. The wallets in turn store the credit card details, identity details, shipping and invoicing information and even could store loyalty-related information. The wallets that store this information on a server are called server-side wallets. Then there are wallets that store the information on client devices and therefore do not store an individual-specific information on the server. The client side wallets are more popular than server side wallets. There are about 1,000+ FinTechs worldwide in this business. The wallet function, though, works the same across providers, but their popularity and adoption can be correlated to the type of providers. Wallet services from the below-mentioned categories of providers have been relatively popular and have been more widely accepted than the other types of providers:

a. Stand-alone digital wallet providers
b. Wallets introduced by banks/credit card companies
c. Wallets introduced by device manufacturers, software product firms and integrators
d. Wallets introduced by retailers
e. Wallets introduced by telecom providers
f. Wallets for cyptocurrency/Bitcoin

A detailed elaboration of different wallet providers in each of the above-mentioned categories is as follows:

a. Stand-alone digital wallet providers—The wallet concept was pioneered by some of the stand-alone start-ups not affiliated to any bank, device manufacturer, retailers, etc.
   • Some of the prominent wallets started with being an Internet banking solution that transformed themselves into a money-transfer service, and with the popularity of e-commerce, it became one of the key mechanisms of payment for most of the e-commerce transactions. Some of these wallets subsequently built in P2P money-transfer services as well as money transfer through debit and credit cards.
   • China enabling its telecom infrastructure has resulted in the introduction of wallets by some of the leading e-commerce companies in China that has become one of the mainstays for most of the e-commerce transactions.
   • In India, the government pushed to adopt digital transactions, and with one of the world's largest mobile penetrations in terms of volumes, have seen the introduction of multiple digital wallets enabling payments through mobile phones. One could also buy tickets for movies, hotels, flights, etc. using these wallets through mobile phones.
   • There are other mobile wallet services that enable customers to store their credit/debit cards and bank information into a digital wallet. Some of these wallets convert the mobile device into a wallet, enabling the direct purchase from the device.
b. Wallets introduced by banks/credit card companies—Taking a cue from the success of stand-alone wallet solutions and the increased share of digital business, has pushed most of the banks and credit card companies to provide

digital wallet solutions. The digital wallet solution from banks and credit card companies is usually an extension of their banking/card apps. Banks and credit card companies have issued wallets as a separate app in order to separate payment and banking functions. In some cases, the banks and credit card companies are even using different names for their wallets to promote it as a next generation brand image for themselves. Stand-alone wallet companies, taking away a major share of the overall digital payment pie has also been a reason for banks to push their wallet solutions. Some of the bank and card companies in order to launch a faster go-to-market payment offering have partnered with stand-alone wallet solutions to provide a cobranded wallet service. Some of the examples below illustrate how the established players are entering into the wallet business:

- A well-known card company has built solutions that would help banks embed wallets as part of their applications.
- A similar example is wherein one of the large global bank has partnered with leading payment wallet provider in India to provide the wallet solution in India.
- American Express, Bank of America in North America, and SBI, HDFC Bank and ICICI Bank in India are some of the banks that are providing home-grown wallet services.

The wallet services from banks globally also are accepted across major POS systems. Almost all of these wallets also have location-based offers (LBO) and also facilitate loyalty-point accumulation. One of the things that have driven these wallet services is the ease of transferring money between the wallet and bank or credit card account. Additionally, offers like cash-back schemes have made them popular.

c. Wallets introduced by device manufacturers, software product firms and integrators.

Apple Pay, Android Pay, Microsoft Pay, FIS, Finacle, etc. are some of the examples of these types of wallet services. These wallet service providers have an inherent advantage by providing wallet applications as part of their defacto hardware/software. This is also convenient for the consumers and merchants since they do not have to worry about infrastructure, security and performance. The key feature that will drive adoption for these wallet services is their capability to integrate across multiple devices, operating devices, ease of branding customization and merchants/customers commission arrangements. Some of these wallet service providers have restricted the usage of their wallets only to the devices manufactured by them.

d. Wallets introduced by retailers—A large number of the above-mentioned digital wallet solutions are being used for conducting payments for a purchase at an e-commerce site. The e-commerce site could be an online retailer like Amazon or a travel booking site like Cleartrip or for buying movies on Netflix, etc. The retailers with a large brick and mortar presence realized that they will have to introduce their own wallets in order to provide a one-stop shop experience from purchase to payment, ensuring customer stickiness and provide loyalty benefits directly. Additionally, the retailer would be able to negotiate a better pricing from different card companies based on the wallet usage. The retailers would also be able to drive better order processing, promotions and offers through their own wallets. A more indirect benefit was they could utilize the large float of money, subject to regulatory conditions, from the time a customer pays the money at a retail counter to the time the merchant actually pays its downstream providers. Some of the retailers have set up full-fledged IT departments to rollout wallet services across the board that are not restricted to only their stores. Also, reports by leading analysts suggest that the in-store payment volumes would rise about 8-fold in next 5 years. Some of the examples of wallets launched by successful retailers are Walmart Pay by Walmart and wallets introduced by Starbucks, Kohl's, Macy's, Dunkin' Donuts and CVS. Some of the differentiating features of these wallets are listed as below:

- Some of these digital wallets have a cool feature, wherein a consumer can directly pay for all the scanned items using a quick response (QR) code and a mobile device at POS terminals. The app from some of the retail chains enables a customer to do online purchasing and then announce his/her arrival at the store to pickup, so that his/her materials are already packaged and ready.
- They also enable a customer to pay by shaking the mobile device and have an option to pay a tip as well.
- The wallets integrated into pharmacy apps offer prescription pickup and their integration to the loyalty program.
- These wallets additionally offer special schemes and offers for purchases and payments at retail supermarkets.

There has been a mixed success for wallet services from these retailers. There has been a visible shift of wallet strategy by retailers to provide an in-app solution instead of collaborating with pure-play digital wallet providers. A majority of retailers are also enabling payments at POS using wallets provided by device manufacturers like Apple Pay, etc. or telecom vendors.

e. Wallets introduced by telecom vendors—Since most of the wallet transactions were being done using mobile devices and over a telecom network, telecom vendors similar to retailers realized that they could build brand loyalty, drive offers, promotions and capitalize on an available float (a pool of money that has not yet been claimed) by introducing their own wallets. In early 2011, different telecom vendors globally came up with a wallet that uses SIM cards as a technology to embed debit/credit card information. The event marked the beginning of telecom companies offering wallet services.

Soon the wallet applications and services were developed by telecom providers to harness the opportunity. As part of offering wallets, telecom providers are also providing prepaid cards and mobile money as alternative currencies for conducting transactions. This has catalyzed success and proliferation of such services in the overall ecosystem. Some of the examples below illustrate the ups and downs in the wallet services introduced by telecom providers:

- In and around 2010, multiple North American telecom companies were embarking on an initiative to have a common wallet and a mobile payment network.
- In 2011, multiple European telecom providers had come together to build a universal wallet.
- There are a large number of telecom companies in Canada that offer wallet services. In fact, there are so many players, that some of these companies had to shut down owing to increased competition.
- New Zealanders use digital wallets provided by telecom companies to make payments and use the same on a public transport.
- Telecom companies in Africa have introduced their own digital wallets, and some of these wallets use their own digital currency to conduct e-commerce and in-store transactions.
- Telecom providers in India have launched their own wallets that enables customers to credit or debit cash directly from and through the wallet service.

An additional outcome of telecom companies offering wallets is they can now mine huge amounts of data using different tools to understand the purchasing and behavior patterns of a customer. This in turn would help them to do targeted promotion and advertising, resulting in better conversion and better advertisement revenue receipts.

f. Wallets for cryptocurrencies/Bitcoin—Around 2009, blockchain, an algorithm to generate cryptocurrencies, started generating Bitcoin. Bitcoin soon became popular as an acceptable currency for payments in the online world. There are over 100,000 merchants and vendors accepting Bitcoin as payment. Since Bitcoin was becoming accepted as a mechanism for payment, there were wallets that enabled an individual to carry out purchases using it. There are around 30+ Bitcoin wallets. Some of the companies that offer Bitcoin wallets are Coinapult, Coinomi Wallets (they offer wallets for altcoins as well), Electrum and many more. There are wallets that allow an individual to store multiple digital or cryptocurrencies including Bitcoin, Etherium and Litecoin. These wallets also provide for using fiat currency, i.e., currency issued by the central governments.

Digital wallets can also be categorized based on the reach and membership type they encourage. The three types of a typical digital wallet are:

1. Closed wallets—These are wallets that can be used only by the issuing brand, with some of the wallets issued by retailers being a typical example. They are primarily used in a business to consumer (B2C) scenario and are restricted to the issuing merchant.
2. Semi-closed wallets—These are the wallets where the issuer (banks/businesses) have arrangements with select establishments and merchants for the use of their digital wallets. They have a wider reach and membership as multiple entities are involved. Wallets introduced by telecom vendors working only with certain merchants are examples of semi-closed wallets.
3. Open wallets—Issued only by banks, card companies or payment platforms that have universal recognition. These wallets can be used at any merchant establishment. The wallet introduced by credit card processing companies and credit card companies is an example of the same.

Applications Supporting Wallets

Besides the digital wallets discussed above, there are applications that work as an enabler for using wallets. There are FinTechs that have developed these enabler applications separately or as part of the standard wallet. Some of the enabler applications provided by a wallet service are:

a. A password manager utility along with a digital wallet. Usually most of the sensitive data stored in the wallet is related to bank/credit card accounts. Therefore it is an important utility that works with the digital wallet solution.
b. Wallet providers also enable their merchants end-to-end by equipping them with solutions for gifts, loyalty, POS, data analytics, etc. These solutions can be integrated into wallet services or are available as stand-alone solutions.
c. Utilities that help manage gift cards and their spending along with a standard digital wallet.
d. Some of the wallets help store loyalty cards and manage associated loyalty information coupled with offers and promotions.
e. Utilities that help find out the best deals and offers from businesses. They also provide a way to store these offers and other important data while working as a wallet as well.
f. Some of the mobile apps enable looking for a restaurant, menu and even ordering food at the same time while having their own digital wallets to facilitate payments immediately after ordering.
g. Some of the wallets offered by cab companies have a provision to store money with them by transferring from a credit/debit card and then using it to pay for the ride instantly from their app directly. This again is a similar example of a wallet as well as being a cab booking app.

h. Utility applications with associated hardware help simulate the physical card on a mobile app. The customer therefore ends up using a single card for all the loyalty/debit/credit cards and activate the one that is relevant for the transaction.

i. Some of the wallets have an associated electronic account that is similar to a bank account. The account can be used by customers to store and spend money in it besides providing a digital wallet.

j. There are other applications that are not necessarily a wallet but provide a data management platform to companies to make most of the information from their wallet platforms.

k. Applications that help digitize all kinds of cards besides the wallet like loyalty cards, bus travel cards, etc.

l. Applications that help sell, buy or send and receive money using social platforms like Twitter, Instagram, etc. You can post a buy/sell proposition on these portals and then use a standard wallet to make the transactions.

Onboarding and KYC Applications

Onboarding is the first touchpoint that a customer has with the financial institution, and if the same is appalling, there is a big chance that the customer may switch to another service provider. FinTechs, owing to their agility and ability to build innovative customer journeys, have been able to disrupt the onboarding function. Some of the differentiation features introduced in onboarding solutions by FinTech companies that have redefined on-boarding for customers are:

1. The introduction of an onboarding solution that has very limited text input and believes that an account for a customer can be opened in less than 4 minutes. It collects information/data through carrier information, from driver's licenses using optical character recognition (OCR) technology. ID Analytics uses a complex analytics algorithm to prefill the data required for onboarding.

2. Onboarding solutions that help customers to be onboarded into multiple banking products through a compelling user experience.

3. An application wherein the user is able to start his/her onboarding process right from watching an advertisement and then getting help through an AI bot to help gather and correct information from other sources.

One of the areas besides onboarding that is attracting a host of FinTech solution providers is KYC. According to leading analysts, banks spend about half a trillion dollars every year for KYC compliance and customer due diligence. There are a lot of FinTech players that are emerging in the entire KYC process. The regulatory and legislative changes, besides the lack of qualified people, are some of the reasons for the increase in total time for KYC and onboarding. Therefore, a host of FinTechs, also categorized now as regtechs, have come up that act as data aggregators and ensure how compliance-related information can be gathered in an effective manner. These start-ups are also employing OCR to extract related information from an individual's license, passport or similar documents. Some FinTechs are even doing KYC and onboarding using tax documents. In India, most of the establishments can tap into the government database (Aadhaar) for doing a preliminary KYC compliance. KYC in the current world of identity thefts and data breaches needs a qualitative evaluation of the individual and the intent of the transaction, besides the usual data validation. Below is a list of some of the innovative applications and platforms introduced by FinTechs for onboarding and KYC:

- Applications that allow opening a bank account using a selfie is one of the most innovative ways of onboarding and doing a KYC together.
- Applications that enhance KYC through digital identities. The digital identity of an individual is created by capturing his/her digital footprints in multiple digital domains including social media. The application then runs an AI algorithm to assess the credibility of the person for transactions like lending, investing, etc. There are a host of start-ups in this field.
- Some of the start-ups are using blockchain as a technology for simplifying and securing the KYC information. They use information voluntarily shared by the community to form the basis of an individual identity information and uses blockchain to maintain unique documentation and identities. Blockchain also helps prevent duplicating identities.
- Since KYC and onboarding requirements vary from country to country, it also needs to be compliant with regulatory requirements time and again. Therefore, there are FinTechs that collect real-time data about regulations and apply them directly to its clients.
- There are KYC validation tools that offer other services like anti-money laundering (AML) and fraud detection. Some of the platforms also ensure compliance like global anti-terrorism laws, etc. using workflow, visualization and machine learning.
- Applications and platforms that scan media information for negative news to provide a real-time KYC and AML view of individuals or corporates.
- Some of the platforms provide digital fingerprinting technology for real-time customer identification.

The KYC information that is now required by most of the organizations typically wants the following to be covered:

1. Is the physical and digital identity of the entity relevant and true?
2. Is the organization exchanging the information authorized to exchange the relevant identity-related information?
3. Is it trustworthy to do business with the entity in question?

4. What are the risks involved in conducting the transactions with the associated entities?
5. How to ensure that the transactions being conducted are unique and not fraudulent?
6. Is there an audit and traceability with all the entities participating in the transactions?

As the regulatory mechanisms become complex, more requirements will emerge for identity verification. Also, as frauds become more complex and difficult to deal with, the requirements from KYC and identity verification will also start becoming more and more complex. One of the clear advantages of having a valid KYC in emerging countries is the reduction of corrupt activities as the identities can be traced back to an illegitimate digital transaction.

POS Systems

Retailers today use a POS system that is typically near the exit of the store or at the end of a particular section of the store, and these POS systems are fixed or stationary. The new concept which is gaining ground is having a POS solution on a tablet or a phone, and the billing could be done right there. This is helping customers have a "pay anywhere" experience while they are shopping. There is an increased focus from FinTechs toward enabling the customer to have a seamless payment at the point of shopping. In some cases, they are going a step ahead to eliminate the payment interface itself with the help of Internet of things (IOT). Examples of different ways FinTechs are revolutionizing the POS space are as follows:

1. POS systems from FinTechs are helping businesses in recreating an online shopping experience. FinTechs have helped transform the shopping experience by using an iPad, which has also helped the customer to choose from a wide variety of choices right there. Some of these FinTechs have also created a showroom within their office to showcase how the overall shopping experience can be transformed. They have an advanced analytics engine as part of the POS system to provide and generate reports. POS FinTechs are also doing acquisitions in multiple countries to expand their footprint globally.
2. Some of the POS FinTechs are facilitating online e-commerce transaction integrated with payments and also similar iPad solutions for even physical brick and morter stores. There are other POS solution providers who have also launched a Bluetooth-enabled credit card reader at POS terminals, especially to facilitate brick and mortar purchases.
3. Innovative POS solutions for restaurants have been integrated with apps from FinTechs that not only help an individual locate a restaurant registered with them, but goes a step further by linking all the orders placed by the customer to the bill. The customers can then pay the check directly through the wallet

application that is a part of the same app. Thus, a wallet integrated with the restaurant POS system indirectly helps both the merchant and customers alike.

FinTechs in the Lending Industry

Lending has been one of the most primary functions of money markets and banks. Investment firms and private lenders are the lenders in the financial services industry. A prospect typically approaches these lenders when he/she needs a considerable amount of money to be borrowed for a longer term and is often referred to as a formal lending. There is another form of lending that is common between friends and family for small amounts of money and usually over a short duration. This lending happens in the case of an emergency, crisis and in situations where the borrower knows he/she cannot reach out to established lenders for multiple reasons. The reason can be the lack of documentation, lack of borrowing capacity or any other reasons. This kind of P2P lending between family and friends is the most frequently done and is referred to as informal way of lending. On the basis of this, the entire lending industry can be categorized into formal and informal lending. Formal and informal lending can be further categorized as found below.

Formal Lending

This is the type of lending where the lender and borrower enters into a formal agreement to lend a certain amount for a specified duration. The borrower guarantees that the initial amount will be returned to lender along with a specified interest at the end of the agreed duration. The lending could be done either against a lien of moveable or immovable property or just based on a commitment from the borrower to return the loan without any lien on any property. In some of the Third World countries, lending is prevalent against livestock, and in extreme cases it could be even against a lien on a person. The formal lending in a more-organized market can be further categorized as below:

a. Lending to an individual customer
b. Lending to business corporations
c. Lending to government
d. Lending to FIs

There are other complex lending mechanisms including the lending by a consortium of lenders to a business group; but to keep the case simple, we will restrict the lending discussion to the above-mentioned four types.

The processes and software systems for formal lending have evolved over time. Every improvement in the software systems for lending has ensured there are less chances of committing fraud on an individual level. Additionally, there has been a radical transformation in software systems to carry out the due-diligence process regarding creditworthiness. This has helped to better predict nonperforming assets (NPA), i.e., the aggregate amount to which the borrowers will default on. In turn, lesser provisioning for NPAs has helped bring down the interest rates. The interest rates are typically calculated by estimating the cost that a lender incurs including the cost of funds. Lesser NPA amounts mean less provisioning for defaults which in turn means less cost of funds, thus ultimately bringing down the interest rate. To explain this further, let us take a hypothetical case in which 10 borrowers collectively borrow $100. Let us assume that the lender incurs a cost of about $7 and makes a profit of $3 for every $100 borrowed. Therefore, the net interest rate charged by the lender would be $10 for every $100 borrowed collectively from all the borrowers or $1 from each of the borrower. The basic assumption behind this calculation is that all the lenders will return the capital borrowed on time and in the agreed-upon installments. Now let us assume if two of the borrowers default on the loan taken out from the financial institution, then the next time the bank will end up charging $20 not paid plus $10 in expenses in total to all 10 customers. This would increase the interest paid by each individual borrower from $1–$3. Thus, the more borrowers default on their payments, the interest rates charged next time by the lender would be higher.

One of the advantages the formal lending process brings in is reduced default at the individual level. The financial crisis of 2008 has shown that it is the large corporations rather than the retail borrowers who have defaulted for huge amounts of money, consequently raising the cost of managing funds for lenders in the formal economy. The defaults have also brought in regulator and paperwork requirements for both the borrowers and lenders, further increasing the time to market and increasing the overall cost of funds.

In some countries, the state subsidies and writing-off of loan defaults have increased fund costs for lenders in the formal economy. The situation is ironical from an honest customer perspective, as after going through a tiring process of lending, they are not getting the benefit of a lower interest rate. Instead, they are getting penalized for somebody else's wrong-doing despite they themselves are being honest. Lenders rely on the credit scores by credit bureaus and credit rating agencies to determine the creditworthiness of retail and corporate customers respectively. Interestingly enough, the credit ratings improve if an individual borrows more and repays the same in time. Unfortunately, this system has a number of drawbacks:

1. It indicates how the customer has repaid in the past and is not predictive enough to determine the future paying capacity of an individual.
2. The system ignores people who might be paying by using their savings or cash and thereby having better creditworthiness.
3. This reliance from lenders on credit scores eliminates first-time borrowers with good creditworthiness.

Owing to regulatory processes and huge costs and time involved in transforming their monolithic systems, established and large lenders have stayed away from changing any process involved in determining creditworthiness. FinTechs, being agile and building their systems from scratch, have been able to define the disruption of determining the true creditworthiness of the individuals.

Informal Lending

This type of lending exists from a time before formal lending started. Informal lending typically involves low value transactions, but the frequency or number of times this type of transaction is conducted, is far higher than any other form of lending. This type of lending is also known as P2P lending. Lending between friends, family, acquaintances, etc. can be considered as this type of lending. Lending through quasi-governmental bodies, nongovernmental organizations (NGOs) and religious institutions can sometimes also be categorized as informal lending. Community lending amongst business communities to provide working capital assistance to one of their members can also be called informal lending. Additionally, lending to a fellow businessman to overcome difficult business conditions can also be termed as informal lending. Shopkeepers enabling customers to purchase items on the credit, to be paid back at end of a specified duration like month, is also a type of informal lending. This is one of the most common forms of lending in emerging nations. FinTechs through platforms like P2P lending, community lending and multiple other types of lending, have been very active in transforming the informal lending. Through their platforms, FinTechs are now able to provide a more organized mechanism to borrow, thus building transparency in the informal lending space. Additionally, FinTechs have also ventured into the areas of POS lending. This type of lending again is more prominent in the informal lending markets.

FinTechs Disrupting the Lending Business

The lending business is also closely associated, and sometimes have been interchangeably used, with the credit markets. The credit markets have the same formal and informal categorization. There are typically two types of credit systems—open-end and closed-end credit options. In the open-end type of credit, the credit is of a revolving nature, i.e., the amount of credit that can be borrowed each month and has to be paid back after a specified time period. Closed-end credit is a type of credit wherein a fixed amount of borrowed capital is returned in installments. When the installments are of equal size and paid back monthly, then the installments are called as equated monthly installments (EMIs). The customer continues to pay interest until the original capital borrowed (also called principal) is paid back.

The amount outstanding on credit cards is a typical example of open-end credit, and housing, car loans, etc., are typical examples of closed-end credit. There are multiple variations of credit. A special mention needs to be done for subsidized credit, wherein the government or an institution provides credit at a lower interest rate or with a relaxed return period. There is also a form of credit that people take from one paycheck to the next in a revolving manner to bridge the gap between the expense and paycheck. This is called a payday loan. In another variation, people borrow against insurance policies and sometimes against their retirement accounts. There is another form of mortgage that usually senior citizens avail of and is known as a reverse mortgage. In this kind of mortgage, a person borrows against his/her property, an annuity amount that will be settled with the property ownership being transferred to the lender at the end of the term.

The overall lending business is also dependent on the type of mortgage that is kept under lien for borrowing the amount. If the person borrowing against nothing except a guarantee to return the amount, then it is called as unsecured debt. Whereas if the debt/loan is taken against a movable/immovable property then it is considered a secured debt. There are more complex definitions and variations of the above-mentioned debt and lending terminologies, but we will restrict ourselves to the form of lending mentioned above. Please note for the remaining part of this book, we will be using the following words interchangeably—mortgage, lending and credit—since we are talking about the credit/lending industry as a whole and not about a specific process within.

After the financial crisis of 2008, compliance-related requirements to approve loans increased for established credit and lending companies. This resulted in their processes becoming more cumbersome and time-consuming. FinTechs emerged in this space. They were not only changing the prevalent business models, but were also ensuring regulatory compliance. Since they were agile, they could easily transform existing products or bring in new services/products that would address the huge opportunities that lay untapped in the informal lending space. FinTechs are offering multiple different types of lending which were not addressed by established companies owing to their being either informal lending processes or them being perceived to have insignificant transaction volumes. The different types of lending offered by FinTechs can be broadly categorized into the following types of lending:

a. P2P lending
b. POS lending
c. Online lending [B2C and business-to-business (B2B)]
d. Payday lending
e. Microfinance
f. Crowdfunding

Additionally, there are FinTechs that are offering platforms that are disrupting the businesses supporting/enabling the lending businesses. These platforms thus offered are either available as stand-alone offerings or bundled into the overall lending platforms. The customer journeys offered by these platforms have been quite disruptive and have not only driven their adoption, but also have been instrumental in making the entire process less time-consuming and simplified. "Cutting the queue," "loan approval under a minute" and "get the best loan offer" are some of the catchy phrases that have been implemented in reality by these platforms. The business functions that FinTechs are disrupting the most are listed below:

1. Origination
2. KYC
3. Aggregators for loan providers
4. Credit score providers
5. Loan/credit/mortgage counseling
6. Loan repayment schedulers
7. Loan enablers

FinTech disruption in the lending business is primarily centered around the following types of lending.

P2P Lending

In this form of lending, the transaction is done between individuals directly. The amount involved and the terms of payment are mutually agreed upon by the lender and borrower. This is one of the most prevalent forms of lending in the society. The reason for such lending is usually manifold.

1. It could be to earn goodwill from an influential person.
2. It could be to help somebody in distress.
3. It could be for somebody to make a most-desired purchase.
4. It could be done for somebody to earn profits.
5. It could also be done for multiple other reasons.

The profits that lenders make in P2P lending is usually much more than the formal lending system and therefore this type of lending is more popular. P2P lending has traditionally been done through informal mechanisms and is usually not encouraged by any established lender in the formal lending space. The interest earned on the lending is usually decided upon multiple considerations and the circumstances prevalent for the lender and borrower at the time of the lending or borrowing respectively. Some of the considerations that lenders use to determine what interest rates are to be charged are:

1. The reason for borrowing and its criticality.
2. The duration required by the borrower to return the amount.
3. The potential risk of default by the borrower.

The interest rates thus, are quite variable and in some cases the interest could be multiple times what is being charged in the formal lending system. In some countries, P2P lending as part of an informal system is considered illegal.

Though this is one of the most detested types of lending, it is yet very popular because it ends up providing just-in-time financial support. The reputation of the buyer and lender is the key for any P2P lending to take place. The reputation of either is known through references close to both the lender and borrower. Additionally, information gathered through word-of-mouth also determines the creditworthiness of the borrower, as well as the trustworthiness of the lender to return the mortgaged assets once the loan is repaid. In some cases, the lender physically verifies the mortgaged assets including gold, real estate, etc. before giving the desired financial assistance to the borrower. The recovery by the moneylender for the amount financed in the informal system is usually done in person and in cash. The lenders, in case of difficult or unwilling borrowers, typically employ the services of musclemen to recover the loan. This practice in particular has been criticized for being unethical and a kind of extortion or torture. In most of the humanitarian arguments against this type of lending, the borrower is considered of less means and it is difficult for him to return the loan taken.

All the above makes P2P lending a multistep, person-dependent and expensive alternative for borrowers. Consequently, P2P lending is usually resorted by borrowers when either the avenues for formal lending has been exhausted or denied to the borrower. In some cases, P2P lending is done if the amount involved is small and a large financial institution would not want to get involved in such a low-value transaction. While there are disadvantages of P2P lending, it is so popular because (1) it provides just-in-time lending, (2) the approval process takes less time, and in some cases, it is instant, (3) since the lender usually knows the borrower, typical borrowing prerequisites like KYC, on-boarding, etc. is eliminated, (4) the payment terms are quite flexible, (5) interest rates are quite flexible and (6) decisions like interest rates to be charged, loan tenure, EMI, etc. are taken on a case–by-case basis and usually done within a day itself.

In the last decade, multiple start-ups/FinTechs have brought in P2P lending platforms. These platforms blend the flexibility of informal P2P lending with the transparency and trust of formal lending. These platforms offer multiple features like:

a. The verification of lenders and buyers
b. Maintaining ratings for borrowers and lenders
c. Multiple calculators and auction engines for getting the best deal from a lender/borrower
d. Flexibility in defining the terms of the interest payment on a case-to-case basis
e. Enabling direct online payments and in some cases, direct debits
f. The lending marketplace for borrowers and lenders

g. Credit checks for borrowers
h. In some cases, guaranteed returns in case the borrower defaults
i. Easy to use interfaces for asset and collateral mortgaging
j. Differential interest rates and multiple different types of lending

The following is a summary of some of the ways P2P lending platforms have disrupted the lending space by blending the right flexibility with trust and transparency through use of technology. Some of these platforms have also introduced innovative ways of P2P lending and therefore, are quite successful and popular.

Most of the P2P lending FinTechs have created an Online marketplace wherein the borrowers and lenders can post details about their borrowing and lending requirements respectively. Then the members of the website can decide to participate in lending or borrowing in response to posts that are available on the site. This translates into potential lenders choosing from a list of borrowers depending on the interest rate offered, grade of the loan and the amount and purpose for borrowing the money. The process starts with borrowers applying for loans. The borrowers can apply for loans only if they meet a certain credit score requirement. Their loan then gets listed on the platform, and investors can browse through all the listed loans. These platforms verify their borrowers through a systematic verification process. Once a borrower is approved/certified, the loan is issued to the borrower if it is fully funded. The loan listed by the borrower stays for a certain specified time, and once it's approved, gets it within a very short time frame. The borrower then starts repayment of the loan after a certain specific number of days. The payment is principal plus interest on a standard amortization schedule.

In case of some of the P2P lending platforms, all the funds are queued on a first come, first serve (FCFS) basis. The money invested by an individual is then distributed to multiple borrowers at market rate. Therefore, a single investor could be lending to multiple borrowers and a borrower would be borrowing from multiple lenders. Each investor's investment is typically broken down into chunks of small amounts of the total amount invested. The borrowers are then categorized into a risk market based on various criterion like identity, affordability, employment and credit history. Every time a borrower repays the loan, the platform deducts the invested amount by the EMI paid and adds the interest to the lender account. The money in the lender account thus keeps adding up, which is then reinvested in lending to multiple other borrowers. From a lender's perspective, they are investing money for a specific duration and at an acceptable interest rate. Therefore, the platform keeps on reinvesting the amount at that acceptable rate.

In the past, P2P lenders have also experimented with the auctioning of loans to investors. The lenders on the basis of the loan amount, interest offered and borrower ratings and past history would be participating in the auction process. The auction would additionally drive borrowers and lenders to decide the best common terms of agreement for lending to begin. This mechanism has been quite effective in getting the best interest rates for lenders and borrowers together. Though as a downside the chances of default by borrowers or lenders participating in an auction becomes very high. Since the terms and conditions of the loan also gets negotiated, the auction can go on for a while before the lenders and borrowers agree on certain terms. Consequently, owing to the complexity of processes, many of the P2P lending platforms have moved away from auctioning loans.

Some other platforms cater to personal loans and provide a financial advisory platform along with managing loans. They even conduct onsite inspections to verify and recommend borrowers to the platform. There are franchise-based offline P2P lending platforms as well that are becoming popular. These platforms provide loans through offline channels. Some of the platforms are a mix of online and offline platforms. These platforms have partnered with offline lending services to provide offline loans and has a loan protection mechanism like many of the previously discussed platforms.

There are other customer to business platforms (C2B). These platforms identify projects and businesses worth investing in, and accordingly facilitate corporate loans through lenders investing in the platform. The business model, unlike investors participating in corporate debts, is actually reversed wherein the corporates instead leverage the investors' participation by reaching out to them using these platforms. For investors, these platforms offer alternate investment opportunities. Again, most of these platforms are very transparent in projecting their loan books, cash flow statements, etc.

Some P2P platforms enable lending to small businesses and entrepreneurs by creating a pool of money from small contributions of retail lenders. The platforms offer an online marketplace that helps lenders to invest small amounts. The platforms are an online platform wherein the lenders can lend a very small amount. A group of lenders investing small amounts end up creating a big pool of money that can be lent to borrowers for a decent return. Small businessmen and entrepreneurs are the typical borrowers in the marketplace. Before handing over the money to businesses, investors get to the check credit worthiness of the business, financial statements, reasons for the loan and expected returns on the loan. Some of these platforms do a due-diligence of the business before lending out to them and mandates that the business has been operating for a certain specified duration generating reasonable revenue with a prospect of being profitable soon. These platforms assign a rating to all the borrowers in a very transparent manner along with other information to the investors, so that they can evaluate risks and returns accordingly.

Some of these P2P platforms are veering toward getting a banking license and becoming a full-fledged bank, while others are clearly stating that they are not banks. The basic principle behind these P2P firms is the concept of sharing their savings with the borrowers and lenders. This is symbolic of the differentiation that FinTechs are bringing as compared to their established peers. It is also indicative of the transparency and trust FinTechs are bringing into the financial services industry. The platforms, in addition to facilitating lending, are also helping borrowers to get better interest if they have a good credit score. This is in contrast to the approach of a one size fits all approach of the established lenders. They use the credit score only to qualify or disqualify a borrower, but the interest rate they charge is the same for all the borrowers. Therefore, a good borrower pays the price for the payment not being made by defaulters. Additionally, unlike their established peers, most of the FinTechs do not let a borrower's credit score get impacted if they apply for a loan or enquire for a loan from them. A large number of P2P firms also publishes the gains made by investors and often provide a comparison of the profits investors would have made while investing in traditional financial instruments from banks and capital markets versus investing in their own platforms.

In P2P lending the chances are high that borrowers would default and therefore it is one of the key performance indicators for any P2P lending platform. Consequently to safeguard their investor's interest from a borrower's default, some of the FinTechs introduced a fund or notes. These funds or notes cover the investor's losses in case the borrowers default. Therefore, lenders are protected from a default risk. Most of the P2P platforms have also started rating the borrowers on a number of criteria before deciding on the rate of interest based on the risk category the borrower falls in. The loan pricing algorithm has therefore become a key factor for the entire system, and lenders have to agree to the terms laid out by the system before they start extending the loans.

These platforms make money by charging fees from borrowers or lenders, and some other platforms charge the fees from both, but the fees are quite nominal as compared to the established banks. Additionally, these platforms allow lenders to start lending from as little as few dollars to millions of dollars by individual lenders and large investment/lending firms. Every time a borrower repays the loan, these exchanges deduct the loan servicing fee for itself, deducts the invested amount by the EMI paid and adds the interest to the lender account. The money in lender accounts thus keeps adding up, which is then reinvested in lending to multiple other borrowers. As mentioned earlier, a large number of P2P lending firms are converting their loans into collaterals and derivatives that can be traded in the primary and secondary markets thus creating an additional source of income for themselves and investors.

P2P lending is now being adopted globally, including in China, where around half a trillion dollars worth of loans have been provided through P2P lending platforms. There are multiple platforms in China that have prospered in the last 5–7 years. Some of the P2P lending platforms in China are Tuandai.com, PPDAI.com, Eloancn.com, Touna.cn, Renrendai and Lu.com

Some of these platforms typically work like online exchanges that facilitate information and ratings for borrowers and lenders. These platforms have different interest rate plans based on the grading of the loans. Lenders can invest in them based on their risk capacity. The platforms also have links to social networks as it encourages lending to family and friends. It also relies more on these connections to impose social pressure and to reduce defaults. The most interesting thing about these platforms is they keep flashing the income earned by investors daily/monthly etc. and that drives more new investors to get into the platform.

A large number of P2P firms maintain a complete database of all the loans issued through them on their website. The database is available for analysis by request through the website. This is an entirely different level of transparency exhibited by FinTechs as opposed to large banks, which do not make their loan books available for scrutiny on this level. Consequently, these p2p lending firms have challenged banks by being transparent between lenders and borrowers and the commission it makes as a market place, which is much different from what large banking or lending institutions have to offer. Besides these P2P lenders, there is an ecosystem of data analysis platforms that can help analyze data about customers. The platforms typically include NSRPlatforms, lendingRobot and PeerCube. Some of these platforms even offer advice on how an investor should be investing.

This is a great example of how FinTechs are making inroads into the business functions primarily managed by large banks. Large banks typically do not want to give loans to small businesses as they believe recovery could be high risk. Instead they prefer to invest money in giving loans to moderate and low-risk businesses. Ironically, banks have lost huge sums of money to established businesses, yet they are reluctant to lend to small business. Additionally, owing to their large size, it is very expensive for large banks to evaluate the worth of small businesses and the subsequent servicing of the loans.

From an investor's perspective, banks (deposit and investment) have categorized investors into debt, equity or commodity investors and their hybrid products. There is no place for a low-risk debt investor to make more money by still being a moderate risk taker. This is where these lending platforms have made it simple for these investors and borrowers to come together and make investments on genuine borrowers. Additionally, since the invested amount is further split into fractional amounts across multiple borrowers, the investors make moderately higher returns by taking a fractional risk. This is different from what an investor would have made in a traditional banking or investment set-up. The different variants of P2P platform include:

- An aggregator for borrows and lenders and the primary focus is informative.
- A marketplace for trading to take place between lenders and borrowers directly.
- Invest on behalf of lenders to a specified group or kind of borrowers.
- Issue marketable securities on behalf of borrowers to be invested and traded like debt securities.

POS Lending

This type of lending is prevalent as a formal channel of lending in most of the established markets. In almost all other markets, this type of lending is existent as informal, ad hoc and circumstantial. The informal lending in most of the cases would happen at POS for the retailer, wherein one would want a loan to settle his/her purchases. The retailer would take into consideration the following factors before offering these kinds of loans:

1. How frequently did the customer visit the store and how loyal was the customer to the store?
2. What is the general economic status of the customer? This would typically be known as the borrower would be in the vicinity of the retailer.
3. Did the customer pay off the loan taken previously in a timely manner without coaxing?
4. The amount that was being typically borrowed by the customer. This was usually determined based on the capability of the customer to pay back his/her loans.
5. Finally, to maintain the transparency, the store owner would typically note all of this in a book as scribbled notes, which were time and again exchanged between the customer and retail store owner.

In a more formal setup point #1 would be replaced by KYC for the customer, points # 2, 3 and 4 would be equivalent to determining the creditworthiness of the customer and point #5 would be replaced by maintaining and reporting the account-related activities. This type of credit was traditionally offered to maintain customer stickiness (loyalty) and there was usually no interest involved. Though in some cases since the customer had less negotiating capability, because he was borrowing and there were not many alternatives, sometimes the retailer would charge for the purchased items at their will for a customer borrowing at POS. All these arrangements would be informal and would depend upon individual rapport that the customer has had with retailer.

Once the supermarkets started coming up, only the customers with enough cash to last throughout the month would visit them. Customers whose purchases or requirements for the month exceeded the amount they had, would still buy from their neighborhood stores on a short-term credit. Large retail store owners realized they were losing business and customers by offering no credits, and therefore they soon brought in a credit facility that would now be availed at the point of purchase by swiping their credit cards. The credit taken by the customer on credit cards could be paid back in 21 days, while the store owner would get the payment within 3–4 days. This continued to be a great solution that was adopted until people started realizing that the experience of using and managing credit cards was getting out of hand. Also, the credit card companies were not offering loans on individual items purchased. Instead, they would provide loans on the entire credit card balance or an individual would have to avail a separate personal loan.

Owing to exploitation and ballooning disputes, multiple governments brought in compliance and regulatory checks on these loans, and in some countries even declaring this practice illegal. All of this led to less businesses authorized for issuing POS loans, and the cost overheads including the regulatory compliance led to increasing the overall interest rates charged for these loans. The customer experience was more person-dependent and very few firms employed professional practices in offering loans and managing account statements. During this time, multiple e-commerce businesses emerged and within no time, a large part of in-person purchasing shifted to online purchasing. Though online purchasing simplified the purchasing process, but the POS lending was still missing. Credit cards offered loans, but that was offered at a very high interest rate and the eligibility was dependent on credit scores. Additionally, this kind of loan would be treated more as a personal loan and would not have any relevance to the purchases made or the stores from which purchases were made.

Therefore, looking at potential opportunities, FinTechs started making POS lending a formal process. Initially it was PayPal and then a host of other companies like Affirm, Klarna and Zest started becoming popular in this space. The potential of this market is assumed to be half a trillion dollars.

While FinTechs were transforming POS lending, the technology disruption in POS systems was transforming the customer experience at checkout counters. The earlier-generation POS systems would typically be placed at the store exits, and there would be a large line of customers waiting to get their purchases billed. The attendant on the terminal would be struggling between cash, card, redemption coupons and loyalty cards. These systems were difficult to operate in some of the operations like deleting an already-scanned item or reversing any purchases. In recent years, the POS systems have changed radically. A substantial part of that has been made online as well, thus changing the experience for online customers as well. In some of the stores, a customer can select an item and then scan the same using his/her mobile phone and complete the billing and payment right on the spot. Therefore, he/she does not have to stand in checkout lines. Some of the e-commerce sites like Amazon now provide devices that monitor your washing powder level and reorders automatically after the stock levels have been depleted.

There has been a major shift in terms of POS technology as well. Now the POS systems are movable, as they operate on SIM cards as opposed to the wired connection they were earlier using. Some of the POS systems actually take in your mobile number and send bill and payment confirmation details directly to an individual's mobile or email system. The software also is usually hosted on the cloud, thus simplifying loading upgrades and infrastructure requirements by a retail mart. The systems are also directly connected to an e-commerce solution, thus enabling an individual to order through a website. The customer can then collect the purchases in-person and then pay for it at the POS terminal in the stores.

Some of the large retailers and e-commerce giants are changing the experience by having no checkout lines. In this model a customer logs into the physical store by tapping his phone at a terminal and then picks up groceries from shelves and walks out. The store software based on sensors and machine learning is able to identify the items that the customer has picked up and lists them in his/her mobile application. Once the same has been done, customers can checkout and make payments from his/her mobile device without going through a physical checkout counter.

Retailers now have their own wallets and this makes the entire POS processing much simpler and straight forward. Now the customer does not have to take out a different card for making the payments as well. The best POSs sold in the market currently also have a 24/7 customer support system for their products. Most of the POS systems have virtual e-learning courses and trainings to train the users to manage their systems.

Another trend that is happening in POS systems is providing an in-store experience. There are systems available that help you to screen products using a digital kiosk or a mobile device, thus facilitating the customer for a faster checkout. The sales person has been elevated to an advisory role, wherein he/she helps the customer in selecting an item and at the same time enables them to do the checkout there and then itself. This type of selling has a personal connection and reduces the time a customer spends screening products and then stand in line to finish the billing for the same.

Social media itself has now become a great POS system in the new-age customer experience. Some of the applications are now using media platforms like Facebook and Twitter to do checkout and billing. Most importantly, these platforms are also being used to provide customer service. Most of the POS systems are integrated/integrating with social media to provide information on order processing and then being able to provide billing confirmations. The latest POS systems enable a customer to make a payment by just tapping his/her card or through a wallet that is integrated in the POS system. Some of the good POS systems also provide guidance in terms of overall store layouts, and provide offers and recommendations based on the customer purchasing patterns. All the above has made it possible for digital lenders to provide on-demand lending for most of the customers.

One of the biggest experience changes that is believed to be transforming the entire POS experience is eliminating the payment stage in the overall shopping experience. Since it has been observed that most customers doing purchases online drop out at the payment step owing to the complexity involved in the payment process. Therefore, eliminating the payment step increases the customer conversion for the online e-commerce websites. A similar service by Amazon 1-Click does the same thing but this works only for Amazon. There are FinTechs that are transforming the entire POS experience by merging the areas of payment and POS lending, thereby creating a completely new business process. Some of the key characteristics of POS lending platforms introduced by FinTechs are:

1. They are facilitating purchases and in some cases, actively involved in the purchasing decisions for the user, besides enabling the payments.
2. A large number of these POS lending platforms approve/disapprove funding instantly either by using the standard credit score or by using proprietary credit scoring mechanisms.
3. Despite a credit score check, most of the lending platforms do not impact credit scores at the point of a check, unlike established banks or card companies.

4. Most of the POS lending platforms usually charge a very nominal fee, but their main income source is the late fee received owing to defaults by the users and the commission from merchants and card companies.
5. All the POS lending platforms provide flexibility in the terms for repayment and charge interest rates and late fees for delayed payments.

Using these lending platforms, a user after ordering from an online website initiates a payment using the payment platforms provided by these FinTechs. These platforms, after doing an adequate credit check, pays the bill to the merchant and then sends a monthly or quarterly bill to the user. The user can decide to pay the bill using a credit card/debit card, bank checks, etc. If the user defaults on the payment, it will impact his/her credit score. Additionally, they charge interest to customers on delayed payments, and offer facilities to pay using a debit card. This mechanism to enable payments using debit card allows them to pay lower commissions to the card company while they charge the same fees to the merchants. These FinTechs charge fees to the customers and merchants for the credit service it provides to the customers. Some of the platforms use government-issued IDs to carry out instant KYCs.

One of the interesting things that these FinTechs offer as part of POS lending is a facility whereby a customer can decide to pay back in installments. They, therefore, provide a complete end-to-end payment and lending experience transformation. The consumer feels secure as he/she does not have to provide any credit/debit card information. Additionally, they would have to pay only if the goods are acceptable and they can consolidate all the purchases into a single monthly invoice. Though the customer pays monthly invoices, these FinTechs pay the merchant immediately after the customer has bought the item. Therefore, from a merchant's perspective, this is a win-win as well, since immediate payouts to them helps keep cash flow running, especially in the case of small business owners.

In the United States, one in three purchases are made online, therefore lending at the checkout for online purchases becomes more of a necessity than an option. More often than not, most of the consumers, while making expensive purchases for a deal on an online website, may or may not have sufficient money on their debit/credit cards. This is where POS lending becomes very important. There are FinTech credit platforms associated with wallets that facilitate payments during the checkout after completing the online purchase.

The customer is registered with the credit platforms after providing relevant information required for registration. Some of these platforms do a due diligence from a credit viability perspective after the registration application. These platforms may ask customers to provide their date of birth (DOB) and the last four digits of their social security number. If the same is authenticated, the customer walks away with the purchases and the approved customers can then pay the bill by mail (check), phone or online. These credit finetchs provide a certain amount of time to repay the amount in full for any purchases made through them. If the consumer does not pay within the stipulated time, then the customer is charged an interest rate from the date of purchase. This helps customers with a revolving line of credit and at the same time, stops them from using a specific credit/debit card, thus transforming the overall payment and lending experience in its entirety. This is also now being widely accepted by most the retailers.

FinTechs are not only transforming retail consumer lending, but they are also transforming the way purchases are being made for more-expensive items like airline tickets and healthcare. There are multiple loan options available for healthcare and vacation needs for an individual. FinTechs are creating a disruption to standard loan models by getting involved in the decision making of an individual for a dream vacation and then funding the entire trip. The consumer can then repay back the ticketing and lodging expenses through equal installments before the trip is actually made. Using the platforms provided by these FinTechs, an individual can identify his dream destinations and then search through travel sites to find the appropriate combination of bookings to be made for the vacation. He/she then sends his/her searched results to the FinTech platforms. The platforms then, based on certain criteria, determine the eligibility and creditworthiness of the individual. Accordingly, they sanction the funding for the vacations and issue payments to different entities involved to complete the vacation. The user can decide and agree on payment terms with these platforms before the payment is actually done. Therefore, the user can define terms like the initial deposits to be made, the number of installments for repayments, etc. Some of these platforms do a credit score check, whereas others do not, before approving/sanctioning the funding for an individual user. These platforms usually charge the customers a fee and may have commission-based charges for tie-ups with airlines, hotels, etc.

Interestingly, in addition to being a consumer-lending firm, these platforms help individuals realize their dream vacations. If a person is aspiring for a trip to Paris, and because of multiple other priorities has never been able to save for it, then these platforms are the most appropriate option for him/her. With these platforms, they can ensure that all the amounts being accumulated is directed toward fructifying this vacation. Therefore, it is not only transforming the way booking, payments and lending is done, but instead it is moving a step closer to realizing individual's travel dreams which he/she might have considered too difficult to save for. In case the customer is not able to pay before the trip or trip gets cancelled, the payment he/she has made after the initial deposit gets credited for a future trip. Some of these platforms have been able to integrate themselves into robust travel search engine(s) and tie up with FIs so that they can help people design and pay in installments for their entire vacation. The good thing about these platforms in contrast to other travel loans is an individual would have surely repaid the entire debt before he/she goes on the vacation and therefore can travel with a peaceful mind.

Healthcare lending is another cost where FinTechs are transforming POS lending. Consumer lending in healthcare has been prevalent for a long time and specifically at the POS, in this case at the hospital. In the hospital, people have to make emergency decisions on high-cost medical operations to be performed on patients. In the current scenario, an individual has to go through a complicated loan application system to apply for any healthcare emergency loan. But with healthcare P2P lending FinTechs, the customer can apply on their platform online and get access to various lenders who are ready to lend to these individuals. The borrower can then decide to repay the amount in equal installments. These lending firms either charge interest rates or a one-time processing fee or both from the borrower and lenders alike.

In yet another interesting combination of payments and consumer lending, the consumer, after purchasing an item usually on an online e-commerce site, can opt for using one of the wallets as the payment method during checkout. The interesting part is that the customer does not get charged immediately, instead his credit/debit card as set up in the account gets debited with the amount in multiple equal installments. Thus, the customer gets to keep more money that he/she would get as per his/her eligibility on the credit card. Moreover, the payment in installments ensures that the customer is not charged the penalty for the entire amount, but only for one installment and the merchants get paid immediately.

An example of such a FinTech would be Afterpay. Afterpay, a provider of installment services online and in-store, is a FinTech in Australia that is making news and is liked by consumers. It is evident from the 100K+ likes and 100K+ followers on their Facebook page. They are liked by most consumers because they have again merged payments and consumer lending and have come up with an entirely different, yet interesting concept. During the checkout process, the consumer can opt to use Afterpay as the payment method to confirm the purchase. The interesting part is that the consumer does not get charged the full amount immediately; instead their credit/debit card as set up in the Afterpay account gets debited with the amount in 4 equal installments every 2 weeks. Moreover, the payment in installments ensures that the customer is not charged for the entire amount upfront, but only for one installment. The merchants are paid upfront, rather than waiting for all the installments to be made by the consumer, and Afterpay assumes the risk of nonpayment by the consumer. An individual needs to be 18 years or older and have a credit/debit card to open an Afterpay account. Afterpay does not charge any fees to the consumer if payments are made on time and there is a transaction fee structure for merchants. Afterpay takes all the precautions to ensure the customer is not taken by surprise, including reminders by text messages and email. If payments are not paid before the due date or automatically processed on the due date, Afterpay charges a late fee and again gives 7 more days to pay back the outstanding amount before an additional late fee is incurred (source: www.afterpay.com).

Therefore, FinTechs in POS lending are not only impacting how people interact with lenders, but they are changing the process entirely and venturing into the space where big banks (investment/savings) did not even think to venture before.

Some of the FinTechs are getting merged and others are not able to become profitable, but the ones with a robust business process and customer reach are definitely causing disruption.

Online Lending (B2B/B2C)

The digital channels have revolutionized the entire online lending space. Unlike most P2P lenders who act as merely a marketplace that facilitates lending by enabling investors to lend directly to the borrowers, online lenders use their own funds to lend to either businesses or consumers. Depending on the regulatory requirements, almost all of these online lenders have their own banking or financing arms. These lenders use digital technology to onboard, process and finally approve loans. Also, they have some very well-defined processes for funding and underwriting these loans.

After the 2008 debacle, it was evident that banks were finding it more and more difficult to provide loans to businesses and consumers. The established banks also lagged behind in providing a compelling digital experience. This is where some of the FinTechs like Ascend Consumer Finance, Avant, better.com, Earnest, Kabbage and OnDeck have chosen to grab the opportunity available. We will talk more about how FinTechs are transforming the entire experience around online lending using digital channels.

In the U.S. loan market, an individual with a low credit score would have a greater likelihood that his/her loan application would be denied by most of the established banks. This would mean that millions of customers' loan applications would be denied. This includes people who would want to take out a loan for a rainy day. All of these such cases, in all probability did not get the loan as they would already be in debt at that time, consequently impacting their credit scores as well. This is where online lending FinTechs provide an opportunity for credit-worthy borrowers to borrow from them, despite low credit scores at high interest rates. The loan process in a traditional set-up could mean customers going on multiple trips to branches of a bank or a financing company. The entire experience is time consuming and could be quite frustrating for the customers. Additionally, the verification of an individual for loan eligibility and the interest rate being charged is not a transparent process. In contrast to the established banks and financing companies FinTechs, through proprietary machine-learning algorithms and their online partnerships are able to complete most of the process entirely online and in a transparent manner.

There are websites by FinTechs that offer a list of quotes with the best possible repayment terms. Based on the search criteria provided by an individual, these sites offer multiple alternatives available with fixed and adjustable interest rates. Since FinTechs encourage transparency they differentiate between the options that have fine print or predatory lending options versus the ones that state their terms clearly. The user experience is also transformative with most of these FinTechs while searching for different loan options. Some of the FinTechs, besides aggregating and showing multiple options, usually are lenders themselves or they have a tie-up with an established lending agency/firm. Therefore, they are able to provide a seamless experience for the user's to choose from different available options and then completing the entire lending process to finally issuing the money to the user. Some of these FinTech firms can display all the options in less than a minute and the entire loan processing can be done in less than an hour. Therefore, the process that used to take weeks/months to complete the loan processing, and was considered as one of the big milestone in one's lending life, now takes about less than an hour to decide. For a customer, this is an out of the world experience and illustrates how online lending FinTechs are transforming the lending space.

FinTechs are not only changing the experience for their customers but also are changing their spending behaviors for a better future for them. In contrast to the established banks who are perceived to have caused hardships to average Americans, the FinTechs are being perceived as saviors for credit-worthy borrowers. These borrowers have been traditionally good borrowers, but cannot get loans in their hour of need owing to multiple defaults and high debt already, thus FinTechs are helping these borrowers in managing their finances. Additionally, they help the borrowers lower their interest rate by implementing a good fiscal discipline monitored by proprietary algorithms that helps a borrower in achieving a good fiscal discipline. Some of these platforms go as far as monitoring the fiscal behavior of most of its customers. Some of the behaviors tracked are lowering the overall debt level, restructuring the credit card debt and the ability to build emergency savings accounts.

Some of the other FinTech platforms guide customers on managing their credit score and debt repayment. Using gamification and a rich user interface, the user can manage their interest rates viably through the platforms provided by FinTechs. Therefore, it goes on to convey that FinTechs are not only there to make money, lest be quick money, but instead, they are bringing services and opportunities to people and helping them achieve their goals as well in some cases becoming the advisor-of-choice at affordable rates.

Some of the other online lending firms are transforming customer behavior in the online lending spaces by rewarding people for good repayment behavior. The reward is not in the monetary form, but instead, raises the level of customers to a privileged status. What it does is if a borrower has taken a loan out under a certain category, and if the borrower makes timely repayments, he/she will get upgraded to the next level, meaning that borrower is eligible to borrow more at lower interest rate. In the journey, an individual reduces his/her interest rates and increases his/her loan eligibility by making prompt payments. This fact correlates to a credit score, but is applied completely differently. This in turn induces good behavior among borrowers, thus making the entire financial industry trustworthy.

Besides lending to people who are salaried or with a certain source of income, FinTechs are involved in loaning to students as well. These FinTechs are changing the potential multibillion dollar student loan industry that is envisaged to grow further. They are doing it differently by recognizing an individual as an individual rather than a simple "credit score." This has made them favorites in the student and investor community as well. Some of them are helping shape careers and are becoming the guiding light for their job search. If we picture any big banks doing all of this, one can imagine how many changes they will have to make. They will have to begin by changing the approach of their relationship managers and probably end by carrying out a number of technology changes. Thus, FinTechs, are "thinking for we (the customer)" rather than thinking to make more money for themselves. Some of the different ways these FinTechs are facilitating student lending are looking beyond at the current needs of the student and betting on the promise of the future.

These FinTechs have their own proprietary algorithm to evaluate a person's full employment, education and financial profile, thus, enabling them to provide loans to students and professionals who do not have a good credit score by a credit bureau, yet they are creditworthy. Using analytics and data science to the fullest extent, the platforms are able to assess the potential risk regarding the repayment capacity of an individual. Hypothetically, let us talk about Sam who was admitted to a top university for their prestigious baccalaureate program in computer science, but because he is a student, he will not have a good credit score to borrow money unless he has a co-borrower. This eventually makes the student take a high-interest loan. This in no way reflects the potential of Sam earning much more money in the future and being able to repay the loans as scheduled. This is where the FinTechs evaluate the potential, and provides a loan that is on par to a good credit scoring customer. Thus, they are able to serve the students aspiring for loans in a better way. Since the evaluation is based on a host of parameters, the amount is usually capped to few thousand dollars, therefore the overall default rate for such loans is very low. This helps in bringing down the interest rates charged to high-potential students and young professionals.

Some of the other FinTechs are offering loans to students based on their potential return on investment (ROI). They consider each loan as an investment they are making on an individual student. One of the big problems with giving student loans is that repayment by the student is possible, only if his/her skills are compelling enough to secure a good job. To ensure students are deployable into getting jobs after they graduate, these FinTechs are working with colleges and schools that provide the right kind of training besides the standard education at affordable costs. Thus, giving loans to students from those schools that were spending less on marketing and infrastructure and instead focusing more on ensuring the students are deployable. These FinTechs have also partnered with schools to reduce the amount of loans the student has to pay back if they are not able to a find a job after graduation. This is a clear example of how some of these FinTechs are redefining the entire lending practice by not sticking to the standard credit scores. At the same time, they are helping by connecting various stakeholders in the lending chain to offer a win-win arrangement for all.

FinTechs are also disrupting the business model by determining the creditworthiness of a student through proprietary algorithms and parameters. Based on the outcome of their evaluation, they provide loan at a lower interest rate to credit-worthy students. The FinTechs are going beyond providing loans and instead are helping students become part of the community that offers networking opportunities, career support, hosted dinners and many other events where prospective employers could hire potential individuals for jobs.

FinTechs are also revolutionizing the online lending for homes and auto mortgages. Through online channels they are reducing the huge amount of paperwork involved in the lending process. Interestingly, they have been able to pass the savings on cost to the customer either in the form of low interest rates or low commission fees.

One of the most inspiring stories is of a bank in Brazil that had been trying to overcome the financial crisis created because of the big financial meltdown globally. The interest rates for nonsecured debt in Brazil's postfinancial crisis was hovering around 58% and in some cases for credit card loans it was hovering around 178%. The FinTechs found an innovative opportunity and they became the lender of choice for most consumers. These FinTechs started a service through which they would convert the unsecured loans of most of the customers into structured and secured loans. They did this by backing each one of these loans with a house or vehicle as collateral, thus decreasing the interest rate or in some cases extending the loan duration. This has made most of the loans affordable for a normal Brazilian household as not only are they out of the constant interest payout's vicious cycle for credit card, etc. loans, but they can repay the loan at their pace.

It was not as if these channels were not available for most of the established Brazilian banks. But for them to do something like this, it would mean they would have had to do the following: (a) take regulatory approval to introduce a new product line, (b) ensure all the bank employees are trained for the same and (c) the decision making would have had to be decentralized. This would have been a huge risk for traditional banks. Additionally, they would have to change their technology systems to fit in this kind of arrangement. This clearly says that FinTechs are already challenging the systems, infrastructure and processes banks have built up over the years. These FinTechs charge about 20% to 30% against home or auto equities. Also, these FinTechs have fewer branches and most of the processes are automated. Most loan applications are self-help applications, thereby reducing the infrastructure and manpower cost. Like most of the other FinTechs in the United States, these FinTechs also try to profile their customers using their custom algorithms. Consequently, it enables them to offer differential interest rates based on customer profiles.

Until now we have looked at how online lending is changing the consumer lending business. Let us also take a look at how online lending is changing lending for businesses around the world. It has always been a catch-22 situation when you are building your business, and I can relate to that because my wife had the same set of problems when she started her own start-up. The problem was that without money on the table, downstream businesses were not ready to offer any business deals. Banks were not ready to lend unless you have a sustainable balance sheet to show for at least a number of years. The small FIs that were ready to lend, were lending at about 24% to 36% per annum interest rate. The prevailing interest rate in India is about 9% to 11% for commercial loans. All of this despite you having a brilliant business proposal to work upon.

Therefore, the only alternative left is borrowing from friends or family to start the business until it becomes stable. Additionally, as with most fast-growing businesses, the available working capital gets exhausted in fulfilling the orders and there is very little left to run the operations and replenishing the stock. Therefore, the lack of working capital could even lead to shutting down the business. The processes involved in getting working capital or start-up loans from established banks or lenders could take weeks and months and is subject to a very high level of scrutiny. Instead of focusing on business growth, the entrepreneur spends more time convincing the banks and finance agencies how their business is creditworthy. This sometimes could lead to the closure of good start-ups at an early stage. Some of the FinTechs sensed the opportunity and started financing small business start-ups and their working capital requirements. This type of financing when coupled with online lending is also known as B2B and C2B lending.

Business lending FinTechs provide loans for as low as a few thousand dollars to a million dollars at a nominal interest rate with repayment terms extending from 3 to 5 years. The loan-approval process depends upon the credit score of the business or individual. Again, like in consumer lending, the scoring mechanism could use the standard scoring mechanism available for the industry or could be done using some of the proprietary platforms by their respective FinTechs. The eligibility for a loan application could range from a newly started business to businesses that have been in existence for more than a year. Thus, a business that has recently started can go in for additional capital or a working capital loan from them and the process is quite fast. Since the lending is done through automated loan processing mechanisms, the entire processing in some cases can be done as fast as in 1 day. This clearly indicates that all the documentation mess that was involved in loan processing with some of the large banks is now replaced by a fast processing algorithm by these FinTechs. One of the key features that customers like is that returning customers can avail low interest rates and waiving off of the origination fees—clearly identifying a loyal customer, which most large institution seems to miss out on.

Most of these lending FinTechs are making small business borrowers' lives much easier by:

a. Provide financing for small loan sizes.
b. Do credit checks that many a times is done on parameters associated with an individual's capability to repay, rather than the credit he/she has taken in the past.
c. Processing the loan quickly, thus making the money available when the business truly needs it.

    d. Providing flexible repayment terms usually customized to individual businesses.
    e. Provide a mobile app that could make the entire process from application to approval to payment quite simple.
    f. Make the platform available to third party for integration with the desired APIs.

Consequently, these FinTechs are hugely popular and are being used by most of the small businesses for their working capital loans and short-term capital requirements. These Fintechs being fast in processing comes as a real help for most of the entrepreneurs as against applying to conventional institutions, which would have taken weeks/months to process the same. FinTechs with more than a billion+ dollars worth of loan processing is an example of how small business lending FinTechs are disrupting their established peers.

Payday Lending

Payday lending is an unsecured loan of a small amount of money with a very short payback period, and the payback is usually deducted from the next paycheck of the individual. People would largely take these loans to meet financial commitments like paying for car insurance, etc. The financial commitments for an individual seeking payday loans typically do not have enough cash available, but there is a fixed date for paying out the commitments. The individual is confident that if he/she takes a loan to pay-off the immediate financial needs, he/she would be able to pay the same back from his/her next paycheck. Payday lenders usually in most of the cases verify that the person is employed and is expected to get a next paycheck.

    The process in a traditional set-up works with an individual visiting a payday lender and getting a cash amount as payday loan. In return, the customer gives a post-dated check to the lender. At the decided date and time—usually within a month's time—the borrower pays back the money and takes his/her check back from the lender. But in case the borrower is not able to pay the loan back in time, then the lender cashes the check and then goes after the borrower for the interest payment. In the digital age, the same is done by the borrower applying through online channels, and then the lender crediting the borrower's account with the said amount. On the due date, borrower's account is debited with the amount equivalent to the borrowed amount or the predecided EMI amount. The average borrower for payday loans according to a study by leading analysts is indebted for about half of the year. Payday loans are usually availed by the low-income and unbanked persons to meet their living expenses and the interest rate charged by traditional lenders is usually very high and could range from 30% to 50% annual percentage rates (APRs). There are country-specific regulations to limit the interest that can be charged for low-income and unbanked persons, but more often than not, it is the informal agents that are making such lending expensive and in turn, making the low-income communities poorer.

Though interest rates for most payday loans may seem extraordinarily high, studies have proven that the average payday lender is making less profit margins than players in the traditional lending space. Less profits can be attributed to high operational costs involved and high default rates involved in the entire business. The high operational cost is also because of multiple entities involved. Though pawnshops and credit unions have tried to make new avenues available for most of the payday borrowers, the success has been mixed. Some of the large banks and FIs tried entering into payday loans using multiple channels including SMS text from mobile phones, but owing to regulatory pressure, have scaled back their operations. A large U.S. bank also offers its version of payday loans. It is a service that works primarily on the same principle as payday loans with a substantial high interest rate.

Besides credit unions, there are FinTechs around the world that are transforming the payday lending space through multiple different propositions. The P2P lending platforms described earlier has also been actively used by payday borrowers and lenders. Additionally, the entire arrangement for payday lending has been made simple and is more convenient for anybody to now become a payday lender. With increased lender availability and low default rates owing to proprietary AI-driven algorithms, the overall operation costs have also come down. This is enabling most of these lending companies to charge lower interest rates, thus making the entire proposition financially appealing for most of the stakeholders.

A large number of payday lending FinTechs are disrupting the entire lending industry through some of the alternative business models mentioned below.

1. Since payday lending involves lending to people who are not able to save enough money to address financial contingencies until he/she receives their next paycheck, the traditional credit scoring mechanisms to identify the creditworthiness of an individual is not very helpful. A large number of FinTechs have therefore built their own proprietary risk assessment platforms that analyze the profiles of customers who have defaulted in the past and accordingly indicate the probability of default by the applicant (borrower). The profiles of customers are also analyzed by enriching the same with inputs from traditional credit scoring mechanisms as well as from social media. These FinTechs use data available for processing to predict the repayment capabilities of the borrowers. Some of the FinTechs have been able to achieve a 90% accuracy with their platforms and have had the highest repayment rates even during the peak of the financial crisis. Consequent to low default rates, these FinTechs have been able to manage profitably even with increased loan applications.

2. A large number of these FinTech targets are tech-savvy young professionals who are salaried and have a decent payback capability. These people earlier were borrowing from banks and did not have enough money available on their credit card balances as well. The main need for borrowing was to payback an unexpected bill or a financial emergency.

3. Some of the other FinTech companies are using machine-learning algorithms to underwrite customers like millennials. The traditional underwriting systems, owing to millennials not having good credit scores, would have not qualified them for a loan. These platforms, built for creditworthy payday borrowers, has now evolved as one of the standards for credit ratings. FinTechs are making these platforms available to others through APIs for using the same in their lending systems. Consequently, these FinTechs have been quite successful in partnering around the globe with banks and FIs to provide credit scores for borrowers, especially for the short-term borrowers with no credit scores, but having a better repayment capability.

4. One of the alternative business models some of the other FinTechs are adopting is to allow anyone to borrow from them as long as they have a checking account with their employer. The salaries are typically paid at the end of the month. They enable a borrower to withdraw his/her accrued income for that month to pay for a short-term emergency before their actual pay arrives at months end. The entire process is similar to any payday lender, but what makes it interesting is this mechanism does not require any credit checks nor needs sophisticated machine-learning capabilities to assess the repayment capability of the borrower. Since the salary account is available to the lender to withdraw money automatically, the chances of default are also very low. Some of the FinTechs have made this more interesting by not charging any fees for the loan, but instead run through voluntary donations or tips. Since this helps the salaried community a lot, they are more than willing to give a donation or tip to such a service.

A payday lending firm named Kadki is revolutionizing the payday lending space. Kadki is a company based in Pune, India that bridges small finance requirements for individuals. Kadki was started by young entrepreneurs who were primarily doing informal P2P lending to their friends and family. Soon they realized that there were lot of young salaried individuals who wanted an easy way of borrowing and refunding, to bridge their expenses until the months end. Therefore, Kadki helps such borrowers provide payday loans to these individuals. The customers who were earlier borrowing from friends and family now do not have to take these loans, and instead can borrow using the Kadki platform. A customer usually gives a request by providing very basic information through Kadki's website. representatives, then contact these individuals and then the loan application procedure begins. The service-level agreement (SLA) for Kadki representative is to complete the loan application process, verify the process and credit the requester's account in 48 hours. The overall processes are paperless and very quick. They approve/disapprove loans based on the repayment capability of the individual and evaluating related factors like employment records, etc. In comparison, the established banks and lenders in India would typically take about a week to deliver personal loans. If one wants to borrow smaller amounts, usually the effort is not worth it. These are one of the many reasons they have been quite popular (Source: www.kadki.in).

Microfinance

In most of the emerging nations like China, India, Brazil and Bangladesh there are people who could not get loans through normal banking channels. In these countries, FinTechs have emerged in the last 10–15 years, that are running their business as a profit/nonprofit organization, with a motive to alleviate poverty. Recently this has become a lucrative business opportunity for large banks as well and they are planning their own ventures in this market segment. Microfinance start-ups are getting the unbanked into financial systems, thus encouraging financial inclusion. Before microfinance companies existed, the poor would usually take the loan from moneylenders and would be left at the mercy of the moneylender for the interest rate and the collection frequency. What microfinance companies do differently is they have a standard process for lending and there is only a certain amount that they prefer to lend, thus ensuring lower default rates. Some of the microfinance companies would increase the amount being lent based on the repayment capacity of the borrower. In developed nations, primarily the United States and Canada, most of the microfinance companies are nonprofit organizations and they help the unbanked. Microloans in the United States are categorized as microfinance or microcredits and are loans up to $50K.

Most of the microfinance companies involved are not only dealing with micro-credit and finance, but also are helping crop insurance and other micro-savings. In fact, some of the microfinance companies have ensured limited default by lending against micro-savings. Though on one hand, this principle has helped poor people save and build a kitty for themselves for a rainy day, it has been misused by some to buy household utility items like televisions, refrigerators, etc. than saving or borrowing for emergencies. Thus, this has increased poverty instead of reducing poverty. There are technology solution companies that have been providing platforms/solutions for microfinance companies to use.

One such company in China provides microfinance solutions to other microfinance institutions (MFIs). There are financing companies that have also played a key role in making capital available for MFIs. Since MFIs in most countries are private institutions, their funding is usually perceived to be a high-risk debt market. Therefore, big FIs are not willing to put a lot of capital into MFIs. There are companies acting as intermediaries that have created financial products enabling the funding of MFIs. The products thus created are creative enough to reduce risk weightage of high-risk debt through stringent audit and risk management features, consequently increasing the inclusion by enabling MFIs to give loans to unbanked creditworthy customers.

Microfinance institutions have various challenges to overcome, specifically in the developing nations. One of the most common challenges faced by microfinance companies globally is to identify a user and prevent frauds from false identity creation. Most of the microfinance companies have built a team, culture and trust between its customers and within its employees which prevents such frauds. Additionally, some of the microfinance companies have used biometrics, usually fingerprinting, to ensure frauds in the space is prevented.

In some sections of society, gender bias is quite prevalent, especially in rural areas. The bias is prevalent even in the homes where women are the only bread earners for the entire family. Therefore, it is very important that MFIs as a social cause should help women get loans to overcome emergency and financial needs. Unfortunately, in most of these cases, there are very little documented evidences that indicate the earning or repaying capability of women. This becomes one of the key challenges for lenders to lend to women. Social restrictions in rural areas in some countries do not allow agents to talk to women. Therefore, in such cases it is difficult for a field agent to have an in-person discussion with the women borrowers.

There are multiple such problems that FinTechs globally are trying to resolve including:

1. High default rates owing to fraudulent practices.
2. Complexities in reaching out to the eligible borrowers due to the vast geographical spread of the prospects and low-technology penetration in these areas.
3. The high operation costs arising out of the need to have face-to-face interactions with the borrowers.

FinTechs in emerging nations like India and South Africa, are trying to make customer onboarding free from frauds using their mobile platforms. The platform captures all the customer details like business income, livestock holdings, any secondary income, etc. digitally. It also helps the field agent with any previous loans taken and default history by the customer. There are checks and balances built-in as part of the platform itself. The platform indicates if information provided by a borrower is correlated or not. In case the information is not correlated, there is a high probability that the borrower is a fraud. This coupled with other information is used to analyze if the loan sanctions can be provided to the customer. In most of the cases, the loan approval/denial decision is provided to field agents very quickly. The timing is of essence here because a field agent may visit a rural area possibly once a month or once a week. Usually the loan requirement is urgent and of a small amount. Some of the MFIs have been enabling loan provisions in excess of $1 million. The interesting fact in some of the FinTechs' financial models is that they charge the customer based on a success fee model and not a license model. In this model, the FinTech bringing in the platform gets paid only if the loan has been given to a customer, rather than just on the usage of the platform. This is another example of how FinTechs are using technology to bring in social reforms through financial inclusions. They are also betting big on the success of their business model and implementation, rather than just being a technology company.

Some of the other FinTechs in African countries and Indonesia are run by volunteers with no offices and a handful of permanent staff. Again, most of these FinTechs run using an entirely digital platform and helps microlending to low-income entrepreneurs in these countries. A large number of these platforms work like a less complex P2P lending platform, wherein once an applicant is registered and puts across his/her business case or borrowing need, the lenders lend the money at very low interest rates. The lenders are safeguarded for non-repayment to some extent through a reserve fund created either by charging the borrower at the time of getting the loan and/or charging a service fee to cover conversion costs. Since these companies are run by volunteers, consequently the operational costs are really low. Therefore, the end loan offered to most of the customers is at rates that are comparable to secured debt interest rates and is way lower than the 35% to 70% interest rates typically charged for such debts globally. Similar to other FinTechs in other domains, a large number of Fintechs in MFI domain also filter out fraudulent applications using machine-learning algorithms.

A large number of these FinTechs are nonprofit organizations and some of them besides helping individuals are also building platforms that help minorities, low income entrepreneurs and students globally. These FinTechs, besides providing technology platforms, are also helping connect people and facilitate lending to the needy, thus attempting to alleviate property. A large number of FinTechs are either themselves MFIs or they have partnered with another FIs to facilitate lending. Therefore, FinTechs who have partnered with other FIs get their loan processing done through field partners. The field partner can be a MFI, social business, school or a nonprofit organization. There are also FinTechs that are primarily a digital platform that enables loan facilitation using digital platforms like PayPal or mobile payments. It is a platform that brings both the borrowers and lenders together wherein lenders charge very low interest rates or sometimes no interest at all from the borrowers. The borrower puts his/her story/business case on these platforms and then the lenders, including MFIs and charitable institutions, help these people get a loan at a very low or sometimes 0% interest rate.

Crowdfunding

In crowdfunding, a number of investors or lenders contribute financially toward the expenses that a project has incurred or would be incurring. Also in crowdfunding, the amount of contributions and the desired outcome varies across investor and lending communities. Crowdfunding has a long history of existence and has been done in the past for multiple religious and social causes. The biggest examples are building a temple or planting a community garden. Crowdfunding for the most part of last century was informal and typically recognized as a partnership. Crowdfunding has seen a large upswing since the financial crisis of 2008 as faith in the banking system eroded and investors and borrowers were looking for avenues to invest more as a partner and/or help the cause they always wanted to fulfill. Crowdfunding is also closely related to donations but unlike a donation where the only outcome expected is emotional satisfaction, in crowdfunding the expectation is for material gains, in addition to emotional satisfaction from goal achievement. If we eliminate crowdfunding done for donation activities, then crowdfunding is used for funding some of the following causes:

I. Funding for equity
II. Funding to build an innovative product
III. Funding for a research project
IV. Funding for emotional reasons

Out of above, the most common causes are for crowdfunding are #1 and #2. They are primarily driven by contributors who are interested in a business concern or building a product that will address an opportunity gap. In fact, most of the FinTech companies themselves are a big benefactor of crowdfunding. Contributors who encourage entrepreneurship or are interested in seeing a new product launch, start contributing toward corresponding projects. One of the reasons why some of the contributors contribute is because of the co-achievement feeling associated with something path-breaking happening. Crowdfunding has also been extensively used for funding artists, publishers and works of art. The coverage of the topic in this book will be focused around different operating and business models adopted by crowdfunding platforms rather than on the causes of crowdfunding. In some of the crowdfunding platforms, the royalty from the publishing of a work of art/innovation is shared among all the investors as well.

Crowdfunding platforms usually charge either commission for the entire fund received or service fees for enabling an investor transaction.

Crowdfunding helps investors, since the crowdfunding platforms charge very low transaction charges and the platforms help find the right opportunities easily to respective investors. These platforms enable to invest small amounts of money and are accessible to a larger audience. Therefore, it helps small investors to invest in opportunities which would typically be available to only large investors like venture capitalists (VCs) and fund houses. Crowdfunding platforms, beside facilitating the funding for the fund seeker, helps get an early feedback on their projects or product by engaging with investors and getting their views on the same. In some cases, the product owner benefits by discovering features that would be key to the user. In some cases, such discussions also lead to bringing up-front some features to keep the prospects engaged. All these interactions help promote the product before the launch, through word-of-mouth and without spending on commercial marketing and communication media.

Though crowdfunding faces regulatory issues in multiple countries, it is one of the best forms of partnering with entrepreneurs, artists and innovators. Therefore, the platform capabilities in crowdfunding are usually restricted to the regulatory compliance and allowable causes they can support and encourage. It is estimated that billions of dollars have been raised globally using crowdfunding.

Some of these platforms help innovators, artists and entrepreneurs to ask for funding on their platform. These platforms have been funding hundred of thousands of projects globally, aggregating to multibillion dollar propositions. The fund-raiser defines his/her project, the funds required for the same and then sets up a deadline for achieving the funding goal. The fund-raiser in some of the FinTech platforms can post his/her video explaining the project as well. The investors on the website start committing the amount they can contribute for the cause or the project. If the fund's goal is met, funds are collected from investors. Until the funding goal is met, none of the investors are charged. A fund-raiser could define what the outcome of the project could be and how the investors will get rewarded for the same. The reward could be a thank you note or a guarantee to send the preview version. Some of these FinTech firms charge a certain percentage of the total funds raised. The fees charged is usually a very small percentage of the total funds raised. Besides the fee charged by these platforms, the investor and fund-raiser will have payment processing charges deducted by the respective payment provider from their contribution. These platforms have identified a set of rules to be followed on their websites for the work of art as well as other projects, including providing a physical prototype for an engineering product. All these guidelines and monitoring of the projects uploaded has made these platforms less prone to being misused for promotions and campaigns. Also, these platforms are taking measures to ensure that it does not become a buy/sell site for actual products by scrutinizing the projects being uploaded. These platforms help fund-raisers get visibility and publicity through the investors on the platform and word-of-mouth publicity.

There are equity crowdfunding platforms that are more of an online marketplace that connects start-ups with early-stage investors. The platform, unlike other platforms, is not open for all but instead open to only accredited investors. To ensure the investors on the portal are valid, the FinTech platforms employ different techniques, including making phone calls to the investors upon registering, to determine if they are accredited investors. Some of the platforms could have a mix of accredited and non-accredited investors, but despite this, these platforms are far from being open to all and access to them is restricted to a certain verified group of investors. Some of the equity crowdfunding platforms are on a registered dealer-broker platform, thereby helping investors and fund-raisers to legally sell shares of the company that wants to dilute its equity holding. The FinTech firms that do not have the valid licenses for operating as dealer brokers will have to go through a brokerage or a third party to sell/buy equity within a company/project being invested. Some of the large social media giants have raised funding using the crowdfunding equity platforms.

There are other platforms that are open to all and people can post multiple projects, and there have been success stories from these platforms as well. These platforms have enabled small investors who can get together to create something meaningful, artistic and innovative. Unlike established banks who would always look toward evaluating a business case, the crowdfunding platform enables investors to evaluate the business themselves. This also helps these small investors to ascertain the risk based on their judgment and then can contribute accordingly for the project they think is the right one. Crowdfunding also helps the fund-raiser by enabling them to get funds quickly from investors on the platform as against a lengthy process with large established banks.

FinTechs in a Wealth Management Industry

The wealth management industry has been the third industry after the lending and payment industry, that has been disrupted the most by FinTechs. The FinTech disruption in the wealth management industry has been centered around the financial management and wealth advisory functions that were usually performed by the investment banks. The typical customers for most of the traditional advisors were the baby boomers. In the last decade, this generation has witnessed the emergence of complex products like derivatives and have seen a couple of boom and bust phases of the economy. This generation was also the most active in terms of learning the basics and advanced techniques of investing. This is also one of the few generations that have witnessed more than one recession in their lifetime and also have seen skyrocketing inflation at times.

In the 21st century, the emergence of technology has made more things accessible to most of the customers, but at the same time they have made things more complex. The millennials who would soon be getting into the employable age have been brought up in a digital age. They are more comfortable operating digital devices, especially for playing games and using social media on these devices, than the baby boomers. In one of the research studies it was shown that these millennials would have more faith in advice given by Facebook and Google than a qualified advisor from a bank. Millenials are spending more time on devices and mostly talking to a mobile device. The implication is millennials are trusting devices more than humans. Consequently, the millennials are more likely to believe in advise given by a machine than a qualified advisor. FinTechs, with their technology advantages, are well positioned to utilize this opportunity. Additionally, since most of the FinTechs are agile and lean teams, they would prefer to connect virtually than in-person to reduce the overall operational cost. Moreover, FinTechs are start-ups and have less upfront expenses, therefore they can have customers with investments as low as $1 up to larger sums. In contrast, large investment banks cannot have customers below a certain minimum amount due to their overheads. Lastly, FinTechs have tied up with regtech companies to address the regulatory compliance-related requirements. Regtechs are the technology start-ups that address regulatory compliance-related requirements for different industries. Though some of the large banks have also started collaborating with regtechs for the same, but owing to their large monolithic technology set-up, it is challenging for them to integrate regtech-related offerings. Thus, FinTechs with their low charges, less initial investments and through digital interfaces have enabled the large middle-class population to be a part of the wealth management industry. We will be discussing some of these FinTechs who have disrupted the wealth management industry, though a large part of the FinTech disruption is centered around robo-advisors and financial planning. The business functions impacted by FinTechs include the following:

a. Financial advice
b. Automated investing
c. Socially responsible investing
d. Investment-related research

Financial Advice

Established investment banks would typically offer financial advice to only high networth individuals (HNI), i.e., individuals with a certain basic minimum corpus, usually thousands of dollars and above, available for investing. Increasing wealth of the middle class globally and multiple avenues available for financial literacy including the Internet, has resulted in dramatic increase in the new generation of investors. FinTechs have been able to capitalize on this increase by using digital channels for financial advice and planning instead of luring investors through a face-to-face meeting that most established investment banks do. One of the interesting things about such tools are that they help you manage your long-term finances. A salaried individual would typically be planning from month-to-month or in some cases for an entire year as well. To have a long-term goal planning that spreads over multiple years including retirement usually requires a tool. The tool would typically help a person to keep updating his/her financial situations and goals as life situations evolve. Additionally, using these digital platforms over the Internet and mobile devices, FinTechs have been able to keep their operational costs low. The same is reflected in low joining and maintenance fees for the investors from these FinTechs.

Some of the FinTechs are using a mix of digital tools and personal advice for an individual to help him/her do financial planning. These companies also provide targeted financial advice for individuals registered with them. Once an individual has registered with them, they ascertain a score for the individual based on the financial information provided by the user. The score determines the financial dependency and the possible risks an individual would face while achieving the goal. The platform also helps an individual to define the financial goal, provide targeted advice to improve the same and keep track of steps taken to achieve the same. All these platforms provide a dashboard where one can see how his/her financial actions are updating the scorecard, and track their progress for achievement of the targets. Regular advice from these digital and personal financial advisors enable an individual to assess if he/she needs to continue pursuing the same set of financial steps or tweak/change the same. Some of these companies have also built gamification elements as part of their product portfolio. Using gamification to help millennials and young investors understand financial planning makes their platform more engaging as compared to only providing financial advice. Therefore, the FinTechs are transforming the manner in which financial advice and planning is done using digital channels and gamification.

Some of the other FinTechs are revolutionizing the entire digital financial advice space by providing financial advice on mortgage management. The idea of helping somebody to manage their mortgage is in itself quite innovative. More than two-thirds of the world is currently under debt and they would want a digital solution that can help them look at how different mortgages could be handled properly. Additionally, there are people with disposable incomes who are not servicing their debt in the right manner. Inadequate financial literacy is making the same further complex. These FinTechs have a personal advisor algorithm that calculates and lets a customer know how they can handle their mortgages. Besides this, they have the option wherein you get financial advice over a phone or in person. Since they use a digital platform for providing the advice, the money they charge is also not significant. Using API, these platforms have made this functionality available to other application developers who can integrate the platform capabilities in their applications.

There are other FinTechs that are changing the way financial management is done for the common man. These FinTechs have made their applications available as an online application and a mobile app as well, thus enabling financial planning as a self-service. The most innovating thing about these platforms is they link all the financial accounts of an individual and monitors the same in real time. The financial accounts could be checking accounts, retirement accounts, etc. Another interesting aspect about some of these FinTechs is that they give free consultation from a financial advisor either during the trial period or within the free versions of their application. The financial advisor provides portfolio recommendations by looking at an individual's investments. In the paid version, they additionally manage the personalized portfolio as well as advise. They have very reasonable fees which range from 0.5% to less than 1%, and the same is quite nominal as compared to large investment firms. Additionally, these firms have multiple tools and utilities that help do retirement calculations and manage daily budgets. These platforms have digitally aggregated all the silos of financial data for an individual and provides real-time analytical recommendations for managing his/her goals, finances and investments. One of the most tiring exercises for a mid-level earning individual is to manage tax implications across his/her portfolio of investments. A large number of these FinTechs uses different tools to analyze the tax implications for an individual and then recommends possible ways to regroup the investments. The regrouping of investments is done to provide the maximum benefit to an individual by reducing the overall tax liability. Almost all of the financial advice platforms do a risk balancing and scoring across portfolios and provides a track of investment goals being achieved or not. These platforms also manage users expenses and income, and additionally provides alert from time bound financial activities like paying EMI, paying other bills, etc. Besides helping in financial management and budgeting for goals, they additionally provide free credit score monitoring. Interestingly, some of these platforms use gamification elements to showcase factors that are impacting the credit score for that individual.

Some of the above-discussed platforms, with the information and advice coverage they provide, are slowly becoming the go-to financial advisors for most of the earning individuals. These products provide the platforms, toolsets and advice desired by most well earning middle-class populations who have small amounts to invest and get advice/alerts for events that require decision making.

Automated Investing

Automated investing is more commonly referred to as robo-advising in the wealth management industry. Robo-advising is done by robo-advisor platforms or automated investment services that use computational algorithms to manage customers' investments. There are multiple different types of robo-advisor platforms depending on the extent of automation they apply to manage an individual's investment. The typical robo-advisor platform is categorized as (1) completely automated, (2) guided, (3) a hybrid or (4) a minimalistic automation. There are multiple advantages that robo-advisors provide over the conventional financial advisors. One of the most important advantage is to be able to reduce the overall transaction costs for trading. The automation of operational processes using computational algorithms drastically helps reduce the expenses incurred by wealth management companies. Additionally, the interface provided by most of these companies is quite user-friendly, which in turn is driving adoption for the same among young and tech-savvy investors. In most of the robo-advisor platforms, once the user has defined his/her risk-taking capability and linked his expenses and budgeting, the computational algorithm therein keeps on picking up stocks based on the profile provided. The algorithm also does rebalancing and stock churn as when required. A robo-advisor platform is the right choice for financially well-off individuals who do not have enough time to spend in picking stocks and managing their portfolios. These are typically mid- and high-income salaried individuals who are not able to provide enough time for investing even though they know that they could make more money if they transact in stocks and equity markets rather than in fixed interest rate government securities. Lastly, research has indicated that a great deal of high net-worth investors are also most likely to have considerable portions of their portfolios run by robo-advisors. All these factors and the increased participation from all the different kinds of investors increased the total assets under management for robo-advisors. In the last couple of years, the overall share of investments from robo-advisors have increased dramatically. Most of the robo-advisor platforms have been launched during the bull market and therefore the returns have been quite good, yet they have to be proven during a downturn scenario.

Robo advisor companies depending on the level of automation achieved have multiple different variants. Most of the robo-advisors either offer an entirely automated solution while others offer a mix of manual advising and robo-advising. We will be discussing some of these types of platforms and multiple different automation and financial advising models they are adopting. Most of the robo-advisors are available from FinTech/start-ups. Large and established investment organizations like Vanguard also have their own robo-advisor platforms. We will be discussing some of those platforms as well.

A large number of robo-advising platforms automate investing for customers through goal-based investing techniques. They typically categorize an individual's goal into multiple buckets like (1) retirement, (2) contingency, (3) children's education and (4) major purchases. As per their recommendations, each of these goals would have a recommended minimum and maximum stock allocation, anticipated term and certain cash-out assumptions. An individual investor can tweak these allocations based on his approach (aggressive/conservative) for every goal type. Once a user has defined this, he/she is pretty much on cruise control until the investor does not intervene himself/herself. The platform also monitors the portfolio and continuously rebalances it so that the plan identified by an individual is on track and the risk taken is also not very high. The interesting part of all this is, the entire process is automated to suit a particular goal type. In case of a retirement goal, there is an accumulation phase wherein the portfolio could be 90% stocks in the individual in his/her 30s and then can gradually come down to 50% stocks in the portfolio as the individual comes closer to retirement. These platforms enable investors to start their portfolio from as low as $1. Additionally, they also help investors in saving taxes. In fact, saving taxes is one of the things that most of the robo-advisor platforms are able to do effectively.

These platforms typically charge annual fees less than a percentage of the account balance depending on the type of account, and they do not charge any other fees like trading fees and transfer fees. The charging model varies from one FinTech to another. Some of these FinTechs provide free portfolio management for a certain time period, others provide the same for a certain qualifying amount and there are others that provide these free services for a certain proportion for the AUM. There are FinTechs that offer free services across a combination of previously discussed different conditions. The free service primarily includes the advisory services. The fees for these platforms are essentially a fraction of what financial advisors from large investment banks would charge for doing a similar kind of work.

Some of these platforms even provide free management of an individual's portfolio up to a certain amount, if the individual has referred a certain number of customers to the platform.

The traditional financial advisors (individuals/firms) make money by either charging the commission directly or from the products they sell to their clients. Therefore, the advisors would look to meet their interest and objectives ahead of client interest and objectives. Consequently, they would be more interested in selling products to clients that benefit them and may or may not benefit the customer, thus, letting down the entire purpose of financial advising which should primarily be focused around how I/we can help customers make more money. The advisors would typically benefit by getting commissions from the product they recommend and therefore the bias would be to sell products that provide maximum commission. Instead, if the platform or individual advisor charges only the fees from customers for managing their portfolio, automatically the advisors focus would be to make more money for their customers. Still, a better alternative would be if advisors not charge any fees or get a commission from the product, yet provide a selfless advisory service. Consequently, there are some FinTechs who have introduced platforms keeping the same vision, that neither charge any fees nor are making money by taking commission from the fund houses for selling the products, yet manage the portfolio of the customer efficiently like a regular advisor would do. One of the obvious questions that everybody would have is how do such FinTechs make money if they do not charge any fees or they are not recommending an investment product from the point of view of the commission they get? These platforms therefore have categorized their services as basic and premium services. According to them, they offer most of their platform services for free and then there are a set of personalized services they offer to their customers that are chargeable. Though they have these services available at a certain fee, according to them they do not pester their customers to buy any of these services. They ask questions to individuals to determine their preference as an investor and then build the recommended portfolio. They have a complete automated process of investing an individual's fund, monitoring its progress and then reinvesting dividends wherever required.

One of the most common types of investment techniques used by these FinTechs is using the modern portfolio theory (MPT) which in summary states that an individual can reap more benefits if he/she diversifies funds across multiple risk-weighted categories instead of concentrating on a single stock.

There are a group of FinTechs that are revolutionizing an entirely different investment class, primarily the 401k(s). A 401K is a pension account in the United States with defined contribution every month/year and is tax-exempt. The funds in the 401k(s) are further invested in multiple investment plans and funds. A large number of robo-advisors manage all the retirement funds and do not focus on managing 401k(s) only. 401k(s) are one of the most important financial instruments that every salaried individual is automatically invested into. Despite this, most of the salaried individuals do not pay enough attention to the way their 401k(s) are being managed. Consequently, they are in most cases not able to make optimal use of the 401k(s). These FinTechs charge a nominal fee for personalized advice to look into an individual's 401k plan and suggest changes accordingly. Interestingly, the customers do not have to engage them for an entire year, as 401k(s) do not tend to be quite dynamic and only needs pruning once in a while. Therefore, the charges are usually monthly and can be availed for the month when somebody wants personal advice on them. Their investment strategies include looking into the existing portfolio and eliminating the funds that do not make sense, and instead aim for index funds. They occasionally use actively managed funds as part of 401k(s). Once all the funds are identified and their targets allocated, they run an automated algorithm to select the ideal investment portfolio depending on fund returns and the fund managers experience, etc. They then cross-reference the recommendations to the allocated funds. They continuously monitor the account for any changes in fund or account preferences and periodically rebalance the portfolio. An individual can start an account as low as $1 as an initial investment amount.

Large investment firms like Fidelity and Charles Schwab also offer their robo-advisors with a different names like FidelityGo and Charles Schwab Intelligent Advisory. These robo-advisors primarily focus on building automated portfolios for their customers. Some of these automatic investment platforms also offer a hybrid model, wherein they can get advice from a professional face-to-face or by telephone, or they can opt out of robo-advising. Some of the platforms mentioned in the financial planning and advice sections also operate as robo-advising platforms.

Socially Responsible Investing

It is an investing concept that believes that financial return and social good can go hand-in-hand. The concepts that define social good typically converge upon the following areas: environment, social justice and corporate governance. This kind of investing could be divided into two approaches: (1) only scanning the investing options for their adherence to social good using automation and machine learning or (2) taking a more socially interactive approach comprising of proactive practices like impact investing, shareholder activity or community investing.

Social investing has a long history, but has taken center stage in last decade with people becoming aware of social issues globally. Amidst increasing concern for the environment, society and self-governance and with information available on the Internet regarding corporate social responsibility (CSR), government initiatives and initiatives launched by nongovernmental organizations (NGOs), a large section of the investing community is opting for investing in funds with themes addressing one of the areas of socially responsible investing.

In most countries, there are corporations, NGOs, government and pseudo-government bodies like railways, insurance companies, etc. that have a large corpus of funds to be invested for social causes. The capital invested by these corporations often makes them eligible for tax deductions. A large number of the citizens are now becoming aware of these provisions and therefore, would want these firms to invest responsibly for social causes. It is estimated that the U.S. socially responsible investing (SRI) industry is a multitrillion dollar industry.

SRI can be done in multiple ways that include eliminating the non-socially responsible companies from the portfolio of securities/products and instead include only socially responsible companies stocks. Another mechanism which most of the funds do is eliminating securities and portfolios that are against the principle of SRI, for example, moving capital away from funds investing in tobacco companies. One of the recent trends in social investing has been impact investing, wherein people target only certain companies/funds that intentionally target certain social initiatives and monitor their performance. Thus, making good financial returns coupled by the desired social change is considered to be more effective than purely philanthropic activity. One of the other investment themes that is picking up recently is investing directly into companies that are responsible for alleviating the social good of communities. This type of investing is also called community investing.

There are quite a number of platforms that have ventured into SRI. In addition to offering capabilities of a typical robo-advising firm, these platforms rank companies in the order of social causes they support and to the extent they support the cause. The platform then sorts out companies that do not match a particular investor's values. It then offers a product that is the best in terms of the financial returns and meeting investor values. This ensures that an individual does invest only in those companies that match their values, thus driving a social change. These platforms require a minimum investment amount and charge a nominal annual fee for managing the assets that are way less than the 2% fees charged by most of the similar financial advising and investment management firms. Investing in these firms starts with an individual specifying the social values he/she cares about. Some of the issues addressed by some of these platforms are: (1) not investing in companies known to have been causing direct health issues like tobacco and alcohol, (2) investing in companies that are supporting the right social causes like LGBTQ, abortion, etc., (3) not investing in companies that support the exploitation of nonrenewable sources of energy, (4) divesting from the corporations driving or encouraging deforestation, (5) investing in encouraging women participation at the workplace, (6) investing in companies supporting eradication of poverty and unemployment, (7) divesting from companies that are encouraging or supporting gun violence in any form, (8) divesting from companies that are not complying to carbon emission norms and causing pollution and multiple other issues. Accordingly, a diversified and transparent portfolio is built around the values that an investor cares about. The platform has a dashboard to track and monitor the progress of an individual's portfolio and how the portfolio is helping the overall social cause. Additionally, they enable an investor to directly participate in the change by ensuring that their opinions are being discussed with the respective management of the companies.

Equity Research FinTechs

Equity research in the investing world is summarily defined as researching about equity and associated products like mutual funds, etc. to provide a buy/sell recommendation to an investor. Though the term indicates research related to equities only, in the real world the same has been extended to multiple other elements like commodities, real estate, etc. Until the last century, most of the research was limited to the work being done by research agencies, which were usually hired by the corporates or by investment banks. In most cases, the transparency of research reports owing to the influence either the corporations or investment banks had on the reports published was always doubtful. These corporations, investment banks, investment agencies and research agencies hire highly-paid analysts and expensive research teams to carry out research and publish the same. These institutions in most of the cases pass on the hefty charges paid to these analysts and research teams to the end-customers. The charges could be passed on in the profit and loss account, through a balance sheet or by charging customers a subscription fee to get access to these reports.

A host of research-related websites emerged in the last decade that specialize in providing analyst reports at a nominal fee or free of charge. Some of these websites were linked to freelance analysts who would provide personalized recommendations for stock selections for nominal fees. Over time, multiple such websites emerged resulting in a huge quantity of information available for each and every investing subject. Processing this information and judging the credibility and authenticity of information started becoming a challenge for avid investors. Some of the start-ups have grabbed the opportunity and have created apps and applications that publish the reports only from vetted analysts associated with their platform. Other start-ups, though, continue being an aggregator for reports, have restricted their association with only certain qualified websites. These apps/applications are transforming the way people access and understand research reports regarding multiple different types of financial instruments.

These aggregators provide a host of charts and tools to analyze financial information of an equity or mutual fund. They have a database of a large number of companies and funds with multiple years of history. These platforms send data alerts and stream news about a stock/fund. A large number of these platforms provide information that is useful for further analysis, but does not itself provide any advice to the investors. Thus, these platforms provide the necessary data and analytics required by an analyst to provide recommendations. Consequently, besides being a useful tool for analysts, these platforms are also turning novices into experts in stock trading through graphical utilities like 200-day moving averages, etc.

There are multiple other FinTechs that are equipping advisors with the much-desired global analytics and research. These firms provide investment research and analytics services besides a host of other services. They are usually employed by corporates for valuation of their companies or the companies they are interested in acquiring. They help their customers in valuation of IP portfolios of an organization.

Alphametry is a company formed in 2014 that believes itself to be transforming the equity research world in a manner similar to what TripAdvisor has done to holidays. It has tools and utilities that help bundle all the research reports together, search for the right research and collaborate with teams globally. It also helps linking analysts with investors globally to make all the research available. (Source: https://alphametry.com/)

FinTechs in the Insurance Industry

There are primarily two types of insurance, –life and nonlife insurance. The major difference in both types is the coverage duration. The coverage for life insurance usually spans over multiple years, and in most cases, usually over decades. For nonlife, the coverage is usually of a shorter period ranging from few days to about a year. Though premiums in both types of insurance is paid at periodic intervals as per policy terms, the coverage in the case of life insurance is valid for a longer duration as defined in the coverage terms. Regular premium payment ensures the policy is in effect. In the case of nonlife insurance, the policy has to be renewed at a periodic interval as defined in the policy terms. Also, the ways in which payouts and benefits are accrued differ widely between life and nonlife policies. From a financial perspective, managing the operational expenses in life and nonlife policies also vary. The costs are usually less for managing the life policies, whereas for most of the categories within nonlife policies the costs of managing those policies are high.

Life and pension insurance includes all kinds of life insurance and pension annuities; often medical insurance is also categorized under life insurance. The nonlife category is host to multiple different variants of insurance and they typically vary based on demographics, country, region, etc. Most often following types of insurance are combined into the nonlife category—auto insurance, marine insurance, travel insurance, property and casualty insurance, corporate insurance, etc. In the nonlife category, the insurance that is serviced by the insurance industry is primarily auto and property and casualty (P&C) insurance. The most widely accepted and known insurance formats are:

a. Life insurance
b. Medical insurance
c. Auto insurance
d. Property insurance

The insurance industry works on a principle of sharing risk among its member participants, assuming that only a few will be able to claim at any given point in time. Therefore, it is key for the industry that they maintain a healthy pool to stay afloat. At the same time, it is necessary that the trust is maintained between the claimant and the insurance company to honor the claims raised for any eventuality. The insurance industry in earlier days and specifically during the industrial revolution was quite simple wherein a group of people, usually in the same business, would pool their money with a neutral entity. An individual from the group would make a claim if they met with an eventuality for the risk being covered by the pool. In most of these cases, a majority from the pool would have had to agree before the claim was honored. Between the 19th and 20th centuries, governments globally asked most of these neutral entities to register themselves and incorporate as insurance companies. Most of the insurance companies were owned by promoters. The interest of promoters in making profits started becoming the prime objective of most of these insurance companies.

The profit for an insurance company at a specified date =

excess of premiums collected until the specified date

+ the investment profit from premiums already collected

– the claims made and the operational cost until the specified date.

This prompted a large number of insurance companies to start denying claims or collecting excess premiums and sometimes creating their own measures for extracting more money from the members. The overall faith in the system started going down.

In order to establish the trust back in the industry, governments globally started coming out with regulations that would govern the insurance industry. Some of the key aspects that were put together as part of the governance was to have an initial capital pooled in by promoters, and the minimum contribution from promoters was also stipulated by the regulator. Additionally, there were restrictions on how the overall investment structure of most of the insurance companies needed to be in place. An example of the regulation was that insurance companies could only invest 5% of their total capital in equity. The regulators also started looking into the claim ratio that was maintained by each insurer.

The claim ratio is the ratio of the amount collected in premium versus the amount that has to be paid in the claim. Claim ratio also started becoming a de facto measure for judging an insurance company's performance. This also ensured that most of the insurance companies honored claims more diligently, thereby reducing a conflict of interest between insurance companies and its members. But on the other hand, this prompted a lot of insurance companies to push their sales people to get more insurance policies done. Consequently, it led to the misselling of insurance policies. Governments again intervened by formulating a regulation that would make insurance companies to be held liable for any missellings.

All of the above helped build trust in the industry and to some extent increased the overall insurance coverage in terms of the number of individuals insured and the insurance amount per person. As a side effect, all of these regulations increased the number of processes in the insurance industry, and the entire industry started responding only to regulations and ignoring the demand from the people. Also, since the insurance industry moved from one regulation to another over the years, their IT systems started looking like patchwork and this made them to some extent less agile. Soon start-ups and FinTech firms also referred collectively as InsureTechs emerged in the insurance industry who were transparent, quick, responsive, had a human touch and most importantly cost effective. Multiple new business models started emerging that could help address the above issues by using the latest technology. These business models were reshaping the existing business processes to address different expectations of the digital-savvy generation including the below-mentioned expectations:

- Delivering transparent and collaborative insurance products
- Offering personalized and on-demand insurance
- Providing a seamless multichannel customer experience
- Charging low premiums with increased breadth of risk cover
- Enforcing a social change

In order to address the changing demands of the customer, insurance start-ups have introduced personalized insurance for insuring assets and property. An individual can customize the coverage based on different items he/she wants to insure. Thus, individuals can insure only specific valuable items while ignoring others that he/she may be willing to lose in case of an emergency. Another area FinTechs are disrupting is aggregating information related to multiple insurance offerings, and associated coverage from different insurance providers in the industry. Thus, equipped with information available on the aggregator websites, it is much simpler for customers to look at the various options available and then make an intelligent decision on the insurance products one needs to opt for. Digital technology is enabling customers to apply for a policy or cancel a policy with a few clicks on a website or on a mobile app, within the free-look period provided by insurance companies. Some of the FinTechs are disrupting the health insurance industry by providing an end-to-end support including primary care to get an individual connected with the hospitals in case of an emergency.

Ushering in the New Age of Collaborative Insurance through P2P Insurance

The financial working of the insurance business can be simplistically outlined as below:

- The base capital for an insurance company is organized by contributions from promotors and pooling in premiums from its members.
- It further assumes that a certain percentage of the members will claim compensation on meeting with the eventuality of the risk insured.
- The company then invests the unused capital left after reimbursing the claims in various financial instruments and movable and immovable assets. The different instruments and the ratios in which the insurance companies can invest is constrained by regulatory authorities.

■ The yield from these investments in addition to the different transaction charges levied by the insurance company is used to make up for the different costs and expenses incurred by the insurance company on account of running its operations.

■ Any excess amount remaining from the above is declared as profits or earnings of the company. Therefore, insurance companies may either delay claims or raise transactional charges for making more profits. The transactional charges are usually competition driven, therefore makes it difficult for insurance companies to raise the same unilaterally, thus limiting them to charge as per the industry standards for the same. Therefore, the only alternative insurance companies may delay claims processing in order to have a larger pool available for investments and more yield, leading to a larger profit for the insurance company.

There are FinTech firms that are transforming the insurance industry by eliminating the conflict of interest between the insurance companies and customers. The conflict of interest primarily stems from the fact that if insurance companies' payout all the claims in a timely manner, they would be reducing their profits and consequently, there could be an inclination to delay claims from insurance companies to maximize the profits.

Interestingly, some of these FinTech firms that are trying to eliminate the conflict of interest between insurance companies and customers have been registered as a public benefit corporation (corporations with their primary goal is to seek benefit for people in addition to corporate goals of maximizing the overall profit). The platform is available to customer as a mobile app or a Web application that facilitates the customers with a shared cause to come together to pool in their premiums. These platforms charge a certain nominal amount as a fee for managing their operations. The fact that they distribute the remaining pool of money after honoring all the claims for a charitable or a public benefit clause, ensures they are not making a profit by rejecting the claims. Thus, the only source of income for these firms is the fees that they charge for this kind of arrangement and they do not keep any surplus. Besides, ensuring that the company is not making profits by denying claims, it additionally helps people to get a "feel-good" about the entire insurance thing as they are also helping the society through the giveback of the surplus for public benefit at the end of their tenure. In some of the FinTechs, the give-back option is given as a preference for the customer to opt in. The concept, therefore, is quite disruptive and works for the social good of the society. A large number of these firms are digital-enabled firms and one can buy insurance through a website or an app on a mobile device or even through a chat session. The chat sessions are typically handled using a chatbot. These chatbots will ask a set of questions to the prospect like what type of insurance does one need?, how much coverage does one expect?, etc. and accordingly provides the right insurance plan to the customer. Offering its services through a digital channel instead of brick and mortar branches helps these firms keep the expenses and costs low, thus delivering a win-win proposition to all the stakeholders – the customers, themselves and the society.

Though some of these firms may appear to be a P2P insurance company, they are more of a traditional insurance company that makes money from fees and do not really make money from interest/investment payouts from the premiums collected. A true P2Pinsurance company would be a group of like-minded people pooling their money to insure themselves for a certain risk, and if a member of the group meets with an eventuality of a risk insured for, then he/she is paid out from the pool. A true P2P model can only prosper and have substantial membership if the agency making the entire arrangement is trustworthy. Thus, a P2P insurance provider will have to build in transparency, efficiency and non-profiteering goals as a key to the overall business performance. Additionally, the agency should ensure that the costs are kept low and the payouts are fast and unbiased. FinTechs owing to their digital-only models and by charging only the transaction fees are enabling P2P insurance. With the use of technologies like digital, mobile, cloud and AI, FinTechs can keep the systems transparent and low cost. There are different P2P insurance business models that exist in the insurance industry.

One of the most common forms of a P2P insurance business model is the insurance broker model. In this model, the policyholders form a small group among themselves and keeps a certain portion of the premium paid by an individual member as part of the pool. The remaining premium amount is used to buy regular insurance, usually from an established insurance provider. Money is drawn from the pool in case of minor damages; for larger damages, claims are routed through the regular insurance. The amount left from the pool at the end of the year is refunded to members or may be reinvested for the next year. If there is more money demanded than available in the pool, then the claims could be routed to regular insurance. This type of insurance helps the participant get a quick claim settlement as a group. The settlement is usually done over a meeting of the authorized members with very limited documentation. The authorized members themselves or through a third party can assess the loss and provide immediate support to the individual in need. This is convenient for the member as well, since he/she gets the monetary help immediately instead of going through a time-consuming insurance process within traditional insurance companies.

One of the other more commonly used models is a variant of the insurance broker model. In this model, as in the insurance broker model, a group of members come together to form a group and then pool money that serves as an insurance. In some cases, the peer group is formed by insurance companies themselves. These peer groups in turn reinsure themselves with a larger reinsurer to accommodate the claims that are beyond what the group can handle. Most of these companies charge a fee for processing claims and servicing the customer. They do not make any money from the premiums collected making the entire P2P insurance business non-conflicting. The insurance companies' expenses and profits are covered solely through processing claims and servicing the customer, consequently benefiting the customer in the long-term with low premiums.

FinTechs are encouraging good social behavior while at the same time being profitable, by engaging a group of people to have pooled insurance. They offer discounts to all the members of a group like in any traditional group insurance. Additionally, they offer incentives for the risk-free behavior of the group as a whole. This encourages each individual in the group to monitor and ensure good behavior for the others in the group, thereby keeping the premiums low for all the members in the group.

There are FinTech companies that have established P2P insurance in reality. Policy owners with the same insurance needs form small groups and a small amount of their premium is paid into a pool. The pool is utilized for settling smaller claims that arise within the group. If the group does not make any claim within the agreed duration, then the amount available in the pool is distributed back in a predefined proportion to all its members. If there are claims, the cashback to individuals is reduced by the proportionate amount. This arrangement yields the best results for members if they know each other or they are friends. The belief is that friends would not encourage fraud claims or cheating among themselves, and also they are less likely to make damage claims that are very small in nature. The friends can sign up together as a group or can find each other on the application/app from the insurance company and then form the group. A part of the premium money paid goes into the pool as described earlier and the remaining money goes into paying the premium for insurance companies to settle large claims. If there is insufficient money in the pool to cover for an anticipated claim, then the same is covered by the insurance company to which the member group has been paying premium from their pool.

There is another P2P FinTech that is offering car insurance with an innovative twist to the way car insurance business works. Like other P2P insurance platforms, it enables customers to pool their money in order to lower the collective premium, and refunds the unclaimed amount from the pool back to the customers. Interestingly they have this innovative feature where you can be invited by a family or friend on social media to be a part of the insurance pool. One can also create a pool for specific groups comprising of only family and friends. They encourage family and friends to join mutual groups that in turn reduces the collective premium. Groups also have a message board to discuss their claims and make discussions collaboratively. In case an individual does not have a friend or family who could be part of this group, then the firm will suggest the most relevant pool for an individual to be a part of based on the risk profile, location, etc.

In Europe, a large number of people use bicycles to commute between different places. The damages happening to the bicycles can range from few euros to entirely replacing the bicycle, and sometimes this could be an unnecessary risk that no one wants to take. Also, people need theft protection since most of the time bicycles are parked at open and unmanned parking lots. Though most of the automobiles have a good theft protection system, bicycles have very limited theft protection. In many instances, an individual would pay out of his/her own pocket for bicycle repairs or theft instead of going through the insurance. In order to raise a claim with traditional insurance companies that offer bicycle insurance, one has to follow lengthy paperwork and multiple meetings/discussions with insurance company representatives before the claim is even considered valid. Therefore, since the claim amount is usually not a very large amount, an individual prefers to pay the same out-of-pocket.

Insure A Thing, rebranded as Laka, is a company based out of the UK that specializes in providing bicycle insurance and they have simplified the entire process by providing a mobile first Web app. The most innovative approach that is being adopted by the company is, they do not charge fixed monthly premiums as is the case of traditional insurance policies. Instead they send bills at the end of the month, with premiums reflecting only the claims notified during the period. This is entirely opposite to the way traditional insurance companies work by creating a pool and then honoring the claims from the pool, while accumulating the capital as a buffer to be used later. Laka operates in a P2P model. The individual signs into a homogenous or like-minded group of people, i.e., they group similar people with a similar mindset for an increased risk profile, and his/her policy immediately becomes effective. The customer does not have to make any payments at the time of purchasing the policy and there is no fixed premium. Instead Laka waits to see how many claims have occurred in the pool over a month and then splits the cost by number of people. How the same works financially is that Laka borrows working capital from a partner, which they use to settle claims immediately. At the end of the month they ask all customers to contribute to recover the claims expenses (paid out of the working capital). Ultimately they pro rata the contribution of each customer to adjust for different levels of insured value. At this stage, only customers contribute to the claims expenses as they all collectively benefited from it. The premiums therefore are a reflection of actual expenses incurred because of claims made rather than a predictive value of the number of claims that might occur. The latter mechanism of calculating is used by most of the traditional insurance companies. Since the entire thing works on the claims being initiated, the providers also have an insight into the funds spent and they are entirely covered by the funds spent. This makes the entire industry a cost-plus model and reflective of actual claims made in this kind of insurance, rather than collecting amounts in advance and then relying more on the pool. In case there are quite a lot of claims, there is a possibility that customers would end up paying heavy premiums. Laka protects its customers in such instances by capping what customers pay and the rest is covered by insurance carriers. The insurance company they work with also provides the initial capital injection, thus providing for the claim settlement until the time, the same is not reimbursed by the next month's premium. This ensures that the monthly premium payout for most of their customers is within a certain range and customers can budget their payouts. At the same time, customers save big time if there are very limited claims in a month.

Laka started by providing insurance on bicycles. The concept can be effective in low-risk insurance as the customers raising claims would usually be less in numbers. The more membership a start-up like this has, the broader would be the risk spread in this kind of insurance. This model, though at a nascent stage, has the capability to shake the entire insurance industry as the premiums today are decided predominantly based on the prediction of the possible number of claims in a year and pricing of a similar product by competitors. The concept of determining a premium by actual claims made in a month, there is less scope of competition-driven pricing. Thus, the competitors would end up competing on a timely response and customer satisfaction. In turn, this would drive more customers to such insurance providers over time. Thus, further lowering the risks and increasing the throughput, leading to a cyclical effect. This is entirely against the perceived notion of the industry wherein it is presumed that both the customer and provider are fighting for the same pool of money and therefore the customer service takes a toll.

Laka uses mobile phones to ensure raising a claim is effortless and the customer can narrate the incident or accident conveniently over the phone. After raising the claim, their teams would immediately get cracking on the same. They currently insure bikes for theft, damage and loss—competition (unless Tour de France level) and travel is included. They have plans to rollout further products in due course. As mentioned on their website, they do not have any fine print clauses and they do not provide cover for professional racing (Tour de France style) and wear and tear (Source: https://laka.co.uk/).

There are multiple P2P insurance platforms worldwide that are transforming the insurance space in their geography and globally—A P2P insurer, based out of Paris, operates a Web-based P2P insurance platform that allows users in a group to reduce their premium collectively. There are some other insurance companies that are using the power of Bitcoin to provide a real-time P2P insurance platform. It allows a group to deposit money into a Bitcoin wallet, which can be claimed only if a majority of team agrees for the claim. If the majority agrees, then each individual teammate's share is deducted to honor the claim. It also provides user control on every aspect of insurance like rules, premiums, claims and reimbursements.

PEERCOVER in New Zealand is taking insurance to a new level. One can subscribe to it by simply paying a certain one-time subscription fee to become a member. If any member has a personal crisis, he/she can start a donor campaign. The members who decide to donate for the need or cause will have a certain proportion of their money deducted from their respective subscription amount. The member should belong to a certain risk club and if they want to exit the club they have to make their balance run down to $0. PEERCOVER charges a $1 fee to cover its operational cost and expenses of running the website. This also enables inclusion by facilitating insurance for the poor at affordable costs and in a transparent manner. Peercover automatically matches crisis campaign donations, i.e., donations from friends and family are topped by the club. (Source: http://www.peercover.co.nz/)

Some of the other FinTechs are using P2P insurance to bring about a change in people's behavior and helping societies. The customers pay a fee for getting themselves enrolled into the platform. The same money is then pooled and the pool is used to pay for the claims made by the members for an eventuality. If at the end of a specified period money is left in the pool, then the same is returned back to the customers in appropriate proportions. This is what other P2P insurance companies are also doing. The difference with these FinTech companies is that they are providing insurance for social issues like divorce, child kidnapping, abandonment of parents, etc. These are some of the main concerns that impact individuals and are related to the society directly. Since these platforms are a P2P platform, the members within the group, which primarily is a close-knit social group try to resolve the issues related to marriage, child safety, etc. and thus help avoid the eventuality in any of these areas. This in turn helps keep the contribution low for individual members and at the same time helps benefit the society as well. In Asian countries, it is usually family and friends who intervene to counsel in case if they have to protect a marriage of a fellow family member or friend. The same group would proactively participate in finding a child who has been abducted. Some of these informal measures timely taken are more effective while authorities are perusing the same at their own speed. On similar lines, these FinTechs are providing a platform with consular access and advises on how the social issues can be managed. They also provide a similar platform to provide financial and other assistance to the aggrieved parties. Thus, they are doing more than what a traditional insurance company would do to transform the society and insurer goals by participating in social issues and not only focusing on making profits.

On-Demand Insurance: Insuring only When One Wants It

On-demand insurance is altering the way the insurance business is being conducted. Until recently, one would buy insurance for a specified coverage period. The period would typically be a year for nonlife policies or 60 years and/or until death for life insurance policies. Insurance companies were offering fixed-duration policies because they were dependent on the insurance calculations working on basis of yearly calculations. Accordingly, business and operational processes were aligned to these concepts and involved immense human intervention. Additionally, over time, due to the lack of innovation, the technology systems and business processes had become highly complex. Any transformation would mean high upgrade costs for transforming the technology systems. It would also translate into a time-consuming process of transforming the culture of an underlying workforce as well. FinTechs with the help of new age technology and owing to their agile and lean set ups were at an advantage to innovate and transform quickly as against their traditional peers. Therefore, they could offer a digital-only, multichannel customer interface. Secondly their processes were built in a configurable manner to address the fast-changing business dynamics, thus enabling them to transform rapidly to the changing market demands. Lastly, they were using more automation and artificial intelligence, thus minimizing the human intervention required. Consequently,

FinTechs were more agile, innovative and flexible to address the changing customer demand to have on-demand insurance coverage instead of fixed insurance coverage.

In a typical on-demand insurance, the user does not take an insurance coverage for the entire year or lifetime, but instead takes it only for the duration that he/she needs it. Something similar to travel insurance, but the advantage here is just-in-time. To make this a reality, what is required is a rapid response system that generates offers the moment a customer puts in the type of insurance he/she needs and the duration for the same. This kind of just-in-time has also been referred to as the "Uberization" of insurance. It is believed that in the future, people will adopt this kind of insurance service more than any other kind of insurance services. An example of such an insurance would be a driver of a car subscribing to insurance only when the car is really being driven from one point to another by the owner, family member or a designated driver. It is very likely that the driver would be using the car for only 3 months a year and therefore ends up paying only for the 3 months the driver is using the car. In a traditional insurance policy, the driver would still end up paying insurance for the entire year and more or less the premium would be equivalent to what would be typically paid by any other customer who pretty much drives the car every day of the year. This would mean overcharging the first customer by mandating him/her to subscribe for a fixed duration policy and subsidizing the second customer by compensating his/her real contribution into the pool through an excess contribution from the first customer.

On-demand insurance thus helps to fix this anomaly by enabling customers to only buy insurance when it's needed and the same is made feasible by using technology options like mobile devices. By using the mobile device, a customer would now be able to start and stop a policy whenever he/she wants by setting a toggle button on and off. Though it is simple to implement a customer interface for the same, the real challenge is the flexibility of backend processing systems to adopt to these just-in time requests and near real-time responses. In a traditional insurance set-up, achieving this is almost impossible, but since most FinTechs are building the system from scratch, it is easier for them to build this level of configurability using the current tools and products. Besides the technology challenges faced by traditional insurers, they also would face a big challenge in underwriting the risks and then calculating the premium since there is very limited past data available for on-demand insurance and the premium calculations could vary based on multiple factors like the timing of the request, behavior of the individual, etc. It is difficult for them to fix a premium amount for a particular risk during the specified duration. FinTechs have been innovative in solving this problem by using information gathered from social behavior and device sensors like on-board diagnostics to gather data points. They have also deployed technologies like AI and machine learning to analyze the data points generated from social media and Internet of things (IOT) devices. Thus, when these technologies are applied on the gathered data, they are able to derive multiple conclusions on driver behavior, time of asking for the insurance, social habits of the insurer, etc. Therefore, FinTechs have been able to transform the insurance processes to suite the customer's requirements. Some of the FinTechs that we are discussing in this section have used some or all of these features to make on-demand just-in-time insurance a reality.

The insurance FinTechs are ushering in a new way of insuring electronic items on-demand. In the last decade, the electronics utility devices industry has been on a major uptick. There have been new products/models being released of different electronic items like mobile devices, headphones, smart watches, etc. every 3–6 months. Consequently, a large population, primarily the youth, is purchasing more devices every day in order to own the latest device with the most current technology trend. Since most of these devices with high-end technology are expensive, this has resulted in individuals incurring losses, owing to the devices getting damaged, lost or stolen. Sensing an opportunity in this space, FinTechs have started insuring these items, thus compensating for the loss incurred on these devices.

Interestingly, unlike other insurers wherein an individual agrees to pay a premium for a fixed duration for a fixed coverage, these FinTechs enable an individual to specify only the items he/she wants to insure instead of taking an umbrella insurance. The customer can insure the items merely by taking a photograph. Additionally, the individual can select/deselect (toggle on-off) an item to be insured from the list of items specified, thus enabling an individual to seek coverage for a specific item and only for the desired duration instead of taking coverage for all the assets for a fixed duration, therefore offering a complete on-demand insurance and facilitating the same by providing an interactive app and website. The digital enablement of the whole process has made the claim process also very convenient for a customer, as a customer can even raise a claim through a text message. The feature of enabling claims through text messaging is also redefining the customer experience. It is easier for a customer to initiate a claim using a text message rather than a long process involving huge documentation. One can insure phones, tablets, laptops, televisions, monitors, appliances, headphones, speakers, sports equipment, musical instruments, cameras and gaming equipment using these platforms.

Some of the other FinTechs are offering insurance to cover for liabilities incurred in case of accident/damages caused by friends or drivers other than the owner, going on a trip. These FinTechs additionally offer insurance to protect an individual against damages that might happen during a visit to a stadium for an event like a football match, an election campaign, etc. The damages could typically be more severe if there is a stampede of people that have come to watch the event or participating in an event. These platforms additionally secure an insured person's luggage and equipment from any theft or damage. They also ensure that coverage is provided against any accidents that happen at water sports, cycling, golf or at many other sporting events. They provide on-demand protection from any liabilities that a person may incur because of damages caused by flying debris. If you are sharing a car between multiple drivers, it protects you from any liability caused to the car by drivers other than yourself as well. Usually car dealerships that offer their cars for test drives have to take the normal protection that an individual car driver would purchase and could be expensive as the same covers any damages to the car for a fixed duration caused by any driver. These FinTechs therefore provide an insurance that is specific during a test drive and the driver can opt for the purchase using their mobile device or through an online application, consequently reducing the overall premiums and providing timely insurance. This also provides peace of mind to drivers taking a test drive as it covers them in case there is damage while they are test driving a car through a dealer or even in case of individual sellers. They also have insurance products that the customer can activate just in time to cover himself/herself for an accident in a foreign country or during a voyage abroad. They also cover for any losses due to missing a flight, if the flight was missed because of a delay or problems with a connecting flight. As a claim compensation, they provide a settlement for the next part of the journey. What is more interesting is they even cover family and children for one-off events that may happen at school. Thus, one can opt for one or multiple insurances using their app or through an online portal. After registering on the app or through an online portal, a customer can then choose the product he/she wants to get insured for and then define the running time for which the customer wants the coverage to be applicable to. It could be from hours to days. One can buy the insurance product for oneself or for other people like their friends, families or for somebody they care about and believe are under the risk of meeting with the eventuality of risk. Once all the products are selected and added to the cart, one can now move toward making the payment for the coverage purchased and completing the process of buying the insurance.

There are other FinTech companies that are focused on disrupting the traditional car insurance market by providing on-demand car insurance. These firms essentially build on the concept that one should pay the insurance only when they are using the car and not for the entire period. The insurance is primarily designed for infrequent drivers who probably commute to work on trains, but use a car only once in a while. In this kind of model, the individual pays for basic coverage when his/her car is idle and is protected for damages caused by everything that could happen to a stationary car in a traditional policy. When one is driving, he/she can increase the insurance with a specific amount for a limited duration to ensure all the available risks are covered as part of the short-term insurance purchased. One can register the car details through an app or online website, thereby getting the desired insurance immediately. They also provide a separate learner's insurance that helps cover the driver and car for the duration they are learning. One can take learner's insurance which would become applicable only for the hours when one is learning to drive using a family or friend's car. The same is activated by just providing car details on the app from the insurance company. The interesting thing about this insurance is any coverage claims made by the learner does not impact the owner's insurance. Most of the other terms and conditions are similar to a traditional insurance policy, but through the platforms offered by these FinTech companies it is now more responsive and on-demand than a traditional insurance policy. Using these platforms, if eligible, one would get no claim bonus as in the case of most of the traditional insurance policies. They also have a community of fellow members wherein one can discuss questions related to the industry, their feedbacks, etc.

There are other FinTechs that are offering a moment-based protection plan, definitely a kind of on-demand insurance that most people are seeking. The most innovative thing about the entire concept is that one has to pay a very small premium for insuring themselves for those moments. The insurance premium could start from less than a dollar per hour for moments like a daily commute. Almost all the traditional insurance companies do not provide coverage while playing sports or they would charge hefty premiums to provide such a coverage. Therefore, these FinTechs provide insurance coverage for the moment when a person is playing the sport, covering him/her from any accidents that might occur during the same, including any damage to the sports gear as well. The customer can purchase insurance for a specific moment or for a group of moments. Some of these platforms have made their functionality public through APIs that can be used by other platforms to build in these contingencies.

Some of the other FinTechs have taken the on-demand insurance to the next level by offering pay-per-mile insurance. In this kind of insurance, the customer is charged with a fixed monthly amount referred to as base rate and then customer tops the same with a certain fixed amount for every mile driven. The base rate in such an insurance is usually a small amount and even the top-up amount is usually in small increments. At the end of the month, the insurance bill one has to pay is equal to the base rate plus the miles one has driven times the per mile rate one has subscribed to. The base rate and per mile rate are dependent on multiple factors as in the case of traditional insurance. This is one of the most hassle-free customer experiences with the most innovative business proposition for an on-demand insurance. These platforms have a device that plugs into the car and measures the mileage covered. It additionally helps locate the individual's car in a parking lot with the help of a mobile app. The insurance is available 24/7 and provides all the features of a traditional insurance like emergency roadside assistance, personal injury protection, etc. The interesting thing about the app is unlike other on-demand insurance, the customer does not have to worry when to start the insurance and shut down the same. With the embedded device, the distance is automatically calculated and the bill is sent at the end of the month to the customer based on the usage. This is similar to the utility bills where customers are charged a basic rental and then charged based on usage. This is of prime importance in metropolitan areas where most of the people take their car to the nearest train/public transport stations and commute to work using the public transport available. Their car, for most part of the day, is parked in the parking lot and they are additionally paying for a commute by train while paying full insurance for their car. If they would be using on-demand insurance services like this, they will be charged only for the commute they have been doing, while being charged at a base rate for the remaining part of the coverage.

Typically, most of the life insurance policies have a fixed premium to be paid quarterly, half yearly or yearly for the entire schedule of the policy. Some of the FinTechs have taken an innovative concept for servicing the life insurance policy.

According to them, life has different stages and insurance needs are different at different stages. An individual would typically have more insurance needs as his/her children are growing up and the same will reduce once they are earning or becoming independent adults. As against traditional insurance, with these FinTechs, an individual using their application/app can easily opt for a different coverage at multiple times in their lifespan. Therefore, it would mean that they can increase or decrease their coverage depending on the stage in life they are in, thus giving an individual flexibility to alter his/her premium based on the life stage he/she is currently in.

Reducing Healthcare Claims through On-Demand Consultation

In traditional medical insurance, one purchases health care insurance by paying premiums annually. The typical pay-out arrangement for a claim in case of eventuality like hospitalization, surgery, etc., is split in different ratios between the insurance companies and individuals. The ratio could at times be about 30% of the co-pay, even for a consultation visit, and then there are follow-up visits, etc. Additionally, getting appointments from doctors could usually take weeks and could be at a faraway location. This may lead to an ailment getting aggravated or may drive people to a more dangerous approach of self-medication or trying to get an alternative pseudo-medical help. In turn, this could further worsen the patient's condition thus causing a lose-lose situation for all the stakeholders. The policyholder ends up paying a large amount as a co-pay due to emergency and repeated visits, the insurer ends up paying a bulk of the expenses as the ailment becomes an emergency ailment and the hospital ends up spending more on helping the patient. All of this can be prevented if the patient gets timely medical consultation.

There are telehealth companies that are revolutionizing the healthcare business and helping insurers with their innovative approach. A patient initially gets primary care if not well. Otherwise the patient has an option to go to emergency care by paying an extra amount, either through insurance or from their pocket. In most of the noncritical cases, the patient typically gets an appointment after 2–3 days of asking the request. If the patient is not able to explain the underlying symptoms properly, it is very likely that within 2–3 days' time an ailment may become critical. This is primarily because of the limited number of specialty doctors available within a locality. In all likelihood, all the specialty doctors are associated with very few hospitals usually at faraway locations. The telehealth platform from these FinTechs companies connect patients to doctors over a video call through a mobile app. The application enables 24/7 healthcare support across multiple locations and connects to the first available doctor. The app charges a certain fee for the appointment with the doctor. The same could be reimbursed through insurance in part or in full. These platforms ensure that there are availabile doctors 24/7 to attend any critical care request. All the doctors associated with the platforms are licensed and certified physicians. An appointment with the doctor on the platform may result in a direct diagnosis or direct treatment. The doctor could prescribe the medication as a result of the diagnosis or treatment. The patient gets a text message that contains the notes from the appointment and the instructions or follow-up care prescribed. The doctor in some of the cases may recommend an in-person visit, depending upon the condition of the patient. The entire process is handled through secure interfaces to ensure security requirements related to user information are met, and associated medical history data is available only to authorized users. Interestingly some of the platforms offer multiway video capability to have a video/audio conference between the patient, doctor, a specialist, a caregiver or even a language translator. Patients can schedule an online and an on-demand appointment for critical care. Otherwise they can schedule an appointment at a later date or time with the doctor based on his/her availability using the calendar utility of the framework. The doctor using this platform usually has the patient details like the patient's history, duration and periodicity of critical care requirements, etc. available on the mobile device while the doctor is attending to the patient. Through APIs and webservices, these telehealth platforms are also able to integrate data and information from various doctors and hospitals. Thus, the platform, besides helping doctors and hospitals to set-up virtual practices, also has enabled doctors to provide timely assistance to the patients. Consequently, this has helped the overall insurance industry by preventing the deteriorating conditions of patients and thereby reducing overall claims.

There are other FinTechs that are transforming the way medical insurance is being handled. Telemedico applications provide the options to consumers meeting a doctor over a video call, though a large number of such applications do not guarantee seeing the same doctor the next time on the app or for an in-person meeting the second time. Some of the FinTechs have taken a very innovative approach to find a solution to this problem. These FinTechs have a group of doctors assigned to an individual who provides the desired consultation and are available 24/7. Therefore, continuity if not with the same doctor but with the same group of doctor remains and all the medical advice is messaged to the group. Therefore, the patient builds a relationship with the group and gets the entire team to care for him/hers. An individual patient creates a case within the app elaborating his/her symptoms and any relevant medical history. The communication thereafter is done using one of the media like email, messaging, photos, phone calls or videos depending on the ailment and criticality of the medical condition. The length of communication and need to stay connected to the team of doctors for the ailment would be dependent on the type of ailment. It could be days, months or until the patient gets better that he/she can continue seeking the advice. The doctors available on the platform are full-time doctors and they would have all the necessary qualification for the required ailment. If the doctors are not sure about the condition of the patient, the priority is given to have the patient visit face-to-face, though in some cases a physical examination may be required. But in most cases, test results and imaging information can be uploaded through the app and the doctors are able to make a diagnosis.

More important is staying connected and being advised throughout the recovery process. In case the patient needs to be seen in person and there is no doctor available locally, they recommend an in-network doctor. In case one has to visit a specialist, they ensure that the specialist is aware about a referral and their consultation report is shared with the member. There could be cases where one has to visit a hospital for a major procedure. In this case, the regular insurance for the patient kicks in. Though the medium used is similar to what most telemedicos do, these FinTechs provide more of a relationship-based healthcare. A patient more often than not values relationships. The first major step in effective health consultations is about trust in the doctors. They charge a monthly fee and an individual can get consultation through digital media. According to some of these FinTechs, a customer using their platform does not reach out to a traditional insurance company for a doctor visit or consultation more than two-thirds of the time.

Introducing New Ways of Customer Engagement

In the traditional insurance set-up, customer engagement primarily comprises of quote to sell, policy servicing and claims management business functions. FinTechs are transforming the experience around all of these processes by introducing flexible yet cost-effective ways of doing the same business.

Quote to Sell

This is the first business process that the customer starts to interact with after registering with an insurance company. The process typically starts with customer providing various details like name, age, gender and smoking/nonsmoking. Using this information, the insurance company comes back with different quotes for recommended products. If the customer identifies a product and is okay with the offered price, benefits and servicing criterion then he/she buys the policy and associated insurance coverage. The insurance company then takes the payment, associated documentation and issues the respective policy to the customer, after receiving the consent regarding the same from the customer. A large number of FinTechs are transforming the entire quote-to-sell functionality by aggregating insurance products from multiple established players. Some of the ways in which these FinTechs are transforming the business function are as follows:

- Enabling customers to do business with a broker of their choice through an entirely online/digital platform.
- Acting as a marketplace for insurance by aggregating online responses to a quote request from the customer.
- Creating an online insurance comparison platform for different kinds of insurance products.
- Offer quotations from various insurance providers based on the requirements posted online.

- Using AI to identify the condition of an item based on image information of the item and thus providing a personalized insurance. They have also made the API of their platform public so that other insurers can use the same as well.
- Offering platforms that helps people search policies that fit their needs and act as a recommendation engine helping individuals to purchase policies under affordable healthcare plans. They also help the user by identifying and letting them know upfront the penalties and consequences of the nonpayment of premiums, etc. It helps one recommend an insurance policy that can optimally cover doctors and prescription fees.
- Help recommend policies to customers based on their needs through licensed advisors who provide unbiased insurance advice. They claim to have agents that are salaried and do not have commission-basis sales targets, thus minimizing the conflict of interest between an agent's motive to sell a policy and what the customer actually desires.

Policy Servicing

Once the policy is issued to customer, then there are aspects like updating the profile of the customer, reminding the customer for the premium payment, providing a platform for the premium payment and enabling an individual to alter some of the policy terms. All of these functions together are referred to as post-sales service management. Therefore, policy servicing business processes encompass all of the post-sales service management functions. In the policy servicing segment, the usage of social media and chatbots by FinTechs have transformed the traditional policy servicing business function. Some of the ways in which FinTechs are transforming the policy servicing space are as below:

- Offering an insurance app that acts as a one stop shop for an individual's policy servicing needs. The app offered by these FinTechs are extremely customer friendly for a user to file a claim, change his/her premium, change his/her address and/or any other information. Besides providing an app for easy policy servicing, these FinTechs also provide individualized guidance on all the policies a customer holds and finds out gaps based on what a person's need is. It also has recommendations on how one can improve his/her insurance coverage.
- Offering a platform that caters to small businesses and enables an individual to manage his/her plan monthly through an app. Since the paltform caters to small businesses, it has identified risks for different business types and claims to even cover the risks associated with digital businesses. A large number of these FinTechs handle their own claims. There are other FinTechs that also provide platforms for better customer servicing by consolidating all the policies in one place. These FinTechs help transform the overall policy servicing experience, by using state-of-the-art technology.

In addition to the above, there are multiple technology start-ups that are offering policy servicing solutions out of the box that could be readily deployed within an insurance company.

Claims Management

This is the most critical business function of the customer engagement for all the insurance companies. Most of the traditional insurance companies do not have an appreciative feedback from their customers for this process. Once an insured member has met with the eventuality of the risk, then the claim process starts. The claim may involve providing all the associated documentation and details of the eventuality. The claim is honored after verifying all the associated conditions. The customer is paid the compensation as per the insurance coverage mentioned in the insurance policy issued. A large number of FinTechs are also revolutionizing the entire claims business FinTech by using:

   a. The digital technology to enable customers to file a claim and upload accident photographs immediately through the mobile application.
   b. Using analytics and IOT interfaces to get the actual details from the accident site, thus reducing fraud in the claims process.
   c. Providing quick-claim settlements by the use of new age technologies like AI, etc. as compared to traditional insurance.

The claims process in cases of traditional insurance companies ends up being a time-consuming process, as it involves coordinating across various entities to validate a claim. The entities involved are surveyors, underwriters, providers, etc. The process involves validating and quantifying the claim to avoid frauds, and is usually done manually. Though this being a right step from the perspective of insurance companies, it is inconvenient for the customer to wait for weeks and months before his/her claim is settled. FinTechs have been able to reduce the time elapsed in claims process dramatically by using digital technology. The entire cycle of surveying, adjusting, etc. is now done in days instead of weeks and months. Companies are ensuring fast claim settlements through extensive usage of AI and data as well. In fact, all the FinTechs in a claims processing business have some flavor of innovation around claims settlement.

Technology Reshaping the Insurance Industry

The digital technology and devices are now available in the hands of customers, surveyors and agents. Using these devices and self-help online tools, the customer is able to understand and compare various insurance alternatives, leading to a smart purchase decision. IOTs and cameras on devices have helped the insurance companies understand behavioral patterns and capture event details for the eventuality, thus making claims simpler and fraud-free. All these technologies coupled with analytics have made the operating expenses for the industry minimal. All the above-mentioned technologies and sensors are getting better over time, thus enabling start-ups to provide on-demand insurance and the flexibility to build and monitor an insurance portfolio to cover different types of risks. Start-ups in the insurance industry are referred to as InsureTech and they are already disrupting the $1 trillion insurance industry globally.

Some of the devices like drones, on-board diagnostics and health bands are helping insurance companies to keep track of the liabilities their consumers may incur in case of an eventuality, thereby offering the right kind of insurance as well as changing behavior for their overall well-being. Additionally, they are also offering assistance by connecting with services like road-side assistance, emergency services, etc. Therefore, technology changes have improved the performance of the insurance industry across all the major key performance indicators (KPIs). New age technology is enabling FinTechs in:

- Reaching out to a large section of people within the target segment by providing the relevant customer experience.
- Eliminating fraud by increasing the ratio of valid claims to overall claims made.
- Lowering operating expenses because of sales and service by using the digital technology.
- Raising awareness among people to buy insurance through social media.
- Offering on-demand and flexible insurance products using business intelligence and analytics.

FinTechs are also offering an out-of-the-box telematics solution, thus helping traditional as well as other insurance start-ups with the data they need to provide on-demand insurance coverage. These platforms additionally provide behavioral analytics on automobile driver behavior that in turn could help in building a score which can be used to determine the variable insurance amount one can charge for different drivers. Using this data and information, FinTechs have innovative approaches for engaging drivers and changing their behavior using gamification. Their platform also helps insurers to create campaigns that seek to create the right driving behaviors and rewarding the best of the drivers. Using these products and platforms, insurers and other FinTechs can be informed about driver progress and monitor all the parameters of their driving patterns. One of the interesting facts is they point out instances of over-speeding as well. All these start-ups are creating the right kind of ecosystem for encouraging better driver behavior as well. Thus FinTechs, by providing more data and information about an individual are enabling insurance firms to offer personalized insurance to their customers.

There are other application platforms by FinTech firms that are committed to ending distracted driving, which is primarily considered as one of the most common causes of accidents among drivers. These FinTechs have an app that needs to be downloaded by drivers. The app then measures the score for each and every driving instance that has been enabled by the driver to be monitored. It additionally offers suggestions on how an individual can improve his/her driving behavior. The most interesting thing about the app is it even helps identify instances when a driver was distracted while driving due to reasons like dialing, texting, etc. on their phones. The app also helps track the whereabouts of the family and their driving habits.

Accuscore is a FinTech company that is transforming the auto insurance space by predicting driving risks related to a driver based on analysis of data received for individual drivers. This helps insurance companies to correct behavior of erroneous drivers, thereby reducing the accident claims and improving the profitability for the insurance company. Accuscore declares itself to be a data processing company that has a scoring platform that can determine how drivers behave and creates a multidimensional profile that accurately ranks a driver on aggressiveness, distraction, general driving tendencies and specific risky driving events. Accuscore captures a wide range of data and information of driver behavior to come to a more definite scoring engine and can use information provided through smartphone devices, telematics devices like on-board diagnostic devices or JBus devices and video solutions. Caruma Technologies, Inc, the Intelligent Connected-Vehicle Platform™ company, will be integrating Accuscore's driver risk scoring engine into Caruma's intelligent vehicle platform for providing an accurate driving score. The platform has a Caruma cam device mounted on the windshield of a vehicle that collects high definition video and data and stores it to a cloud. Using AI, the data and video stored is analyzed for driver behavior providing early warning signs for driving issues like drowsy driving, etc. The information thus gathered is provided to Accuscore's scoring system, resulting into accurate identification of driving risk. This further enables insurance and fleet management companies to accurately underwrite and carry out fleet loss prevention initiatives (Source: https://accuscore.xyz/).

There are other FinTech companies that are a mix of insurance and technology companies that are transforming the way surveyors capture details about buildings and properties. They have software platforms enabling insurers, surveyors or third-party agents to capture, organize and analyze data of buildings and properties. These platforms have software for drone-based building and property inspections. The software platform provides a score that helps you to decide if a closer look with drones is required. Their software helps coordinating between various influencing agencies and natural parameters before the inspection is actually done, like weather, consent of authorities and flight plans, etc. Once the flight is scheduled, then photos and flight logs are downloaded from the drone and uploaded to a cloud storage system for processing into advanced outputs like orthomosaic maps and 3D models. The details thus obtained are analyzed by a specialized set of SMEs aided by AI-driven machine learning algorithms and provide actionable insights. An interesting thing about the software is it ensures that the process is followed for flights undertaken and in capturing image data to prevent any compliance issues or to trace back in case of future litigations. Additionally, some of these firms provide training to new remote pilots, exams for certification and feedback tools for evaluating flight skills.

Therefore, through the use of technology (in this case drones) these FinTechs are helping inspection done in a safer and fraud-free manner. There are multiple other FinTechs that are providing the desired technologies to insurance companies to provide the right kind of assessment and ensure coverage/claims based on the facts.

Insurance companies provide data collected through IOT devices, sensors or other data-gathering devices to the technology platform from FinTechs. These technology-centric FinTech firms use data analytics and machine learning to provide meaningful conclusions of the structured and unstructured data received back to the insurance companies. As an example, the platform analyzes the information and let it know if the chances of damage in a particular area has been higher than the other areas. Insurance companies use this analysis to further determine if premium for a particular coverage needs to be different across different areas. They could then charge higher premiums for the routes and locations where there are more accidents as against routes and locations where there are less issues.

There are multiple companies that are providing chatbot solutions that enable insurers, brokers and online sites to talk to customers. Some of these companies have developed their own chatbot solutions or they use existing chatbot solutions from Facebook Messenger and Skype. Allie is an online assistant available from Allianz, Mia is a customer support chatbot solution answering insurance queries from a co-op bank. Nienke is a chatbot solution that speaks in Dutch talking to NN's customers about insurance. There is a solution that is offered from SPIXII that can be integrated into any of the insurance provider's solution. Digital native generations are expected to be more familiar with chatbots than having an in-person discussion with agents.

Leading Innovation in Nontraditional Insurance

There are multiple insurance start-ups that are offering innovative products for nontraditional insurance. Nontraditional insurance is rarely offered by established players owing to perceived limited ROI and regulatory compliance. FinTechs, having an advantage due to their low-cost structure and agility, are bringing in new products that address a customer's requirement for these kinds of insurance. Interestingly a large number of FinTechs are bringing in products that are also driving social causes like the abandonment of pets, donations for a cause, etc.

Some of the FinTechs have started offering pet insurance. Though there are multiple traditional insurance companies that offer policies for pets, these FinTechs have taken pet insurance to the next level. They have multiple insurance products for pets which are unique in their configuration.

1. They have products that offer an individual to pay fixed insurance premiums for the entire life of the pet. Traditional insurance companies change premiums based on claims made or as per the age of the pet. But these policies ensure that an individual pays the same amount throughout.
2. Then they have policies that give back a certain percentage of the premium if there is no claim made.
3. There are other products that cover preexisting diseases, thus bringing in pet owners within the ambit of pet insurance who have not covered their pets yet and now want to cover them as well so that they do not incur huge medical liability.

Since the traditional insurance companies do not cover preexisting diseases for pets, this usually leads to owners abandoning their pets, due to lack of insurance coverage. Therefore, it could be summarily said that FinTechs are doing social good while transforming the pet insurance industry.

There are other FinTechs that are transforming the insurance industry by bringing in an element of charity while choosing an insurance provider. These firms while issuing an insurance policy from the provider encourage people to make some part of their premium as donations to charity. The way these FinTechs work is they have tied up with insurance providers that are willing to give away some amount received as premiums from customers back to them as donation credits. The customers can then choose to donate these credits to a cause of their choice. This way, while a customer is safeguarding his future, he/she is also donating to make somebody else's life better. Thus, by bringing in the aspect of a noble deed in the form of donations, these FinTechs are attracting well-off customers wanting to share their wealth. Once a customer is on board and he/she has purchased an insurance, these FinTechs either charge fees for the same or get commissions out of the same and that is how they run their operations. Thus, a very innovative way of making a win-win situation for everybody and at the same time encouraging donations to help others.

Cyber risk is often recognized by most traditional insurance firms, but for them a more challenging task is to quantify the damage it may cause. Additionally, estimating the damage and paying the claims is also challenging for the insurance companies. There are complexities like past data, valuation of IPs, etc. that the traditional insurance firms have not been able to put their arms around. Understanding the impact of cyber risk and developing a financial model around the same is also difficult for most insurance companies. The challenge is to analyze the data points that could get impacted by a cyber-attack.

It is under similar circumstances FinTechs have come up with innovative insurance products that addresses the changed circumstances. Since the new product meets the customer's requirement in the changed business landscape, it is therefore quickly adopted by the customers and more often than not can drive profitability for the issuing companies as well. There are FinTechs that have generated an economic model out of the underlying cyber risk. The model is able to quantify the predicted impact of a cyber risk by employing data science, analytics and elements of cybersecurity. This information is then used by the insurance industry to create new insurance products that help provide coverage to underlying assets. The models therefore can be used by insurance companies to identify the risks, assess risks and understand the associated financial risk. Accordingly, they can manage their risk portfolios and accumulations and bring new insurance products to the market. Their models are evolved through a combination of people, process and technology. The cyber risk world is quite complex and therefore modeling the risks require a deep understanding of technical, economic and behavioral factors at play. One of the most critical factors that need to be considered while assessing the risk is the rapid transformation in the overall technology landscape thus making it difficult to define the probability of something happening in the near future. Therefore, the technology changes and its impact needs to be monitored continuously for occurrence of such events. This further leads to tweaking of the risk portfolio and weightage of individual risk parameters.

In the late 20th century there was a mad rush of people to own things, presuming they would get rent and appreciation at the same time. Twenty-first century millennials do not believe in owning things and instead believe in sharing things. This is more cost effective and nature friendly. The social media success is a clear sign of the intent of millennials to share. This concept of sharing has led to the creation of a new kind of economy called a sharing economy. In this sharing economy, people are sharing their apartments, automobiles and many other things. The biggest risk in the sharing economy is damages caused to the asset by people other than the owners who are sharing the asset. We have discussed automobile coverage that can be now be extended to family and friends sharing the automobile on a temporary basis, thanks to FinTechs. What has not yet been covered is coverage to home property that is being shared by multiple people. In fact, most of the homeowners sharing their home are under the impression that they are covered by their home insurance, or by renter's insurance that traditionally covers the renter's liability for a property. Unfortunately, this could get into a debate and the guest/tenant may deny to own up to the responsibility of the damage and not pay anything themselves or through their insurer. Additionally, the homeowner's insurer may not pay for the damage since the issue is caused by the guest or tenant. This could leave the homeowner high and dry.

Some of these FinTechs are developing insurance products for start-ups engaging in the shared economy. Some of these platforms are using blockchain as the underlying technology platform to conduct unique transactions. The distributed ledger approach for insurance helps in coordinating the provision of products between counterparties in near real time, thus radically cutting the cost of coordination. Using this technology, these FinTechs are launching new insurance products to protect property owners from losses and thefts caused by tenants. These products, besides covering the homeowner with the traditional insurance, also cover the guests and any damages caused to the property during the stay of the guests, but not caused by the guests. This last inclusion is very important as in the event of the guest not owning up to the damage caused by him/her, the property is still covered. These FinTechs are therefore becoming the torchbearer of innovations for nontraditional insurance including insurance in the new age sharing economy.

Chapter 3

Technology Disruptions Enabling FinTech Innovations

After the financial crisis of 2008, the financial industry was rebuilding itself by ensuring compliance, regulations and leveraging new ways of doing business introduced by FinTechs. While the industry was discovering new business models to delight its customers, the technology world was evolving in parallel. After the introduction of desktop computers, there was no significant disruption that impacted the financial services industry for a long time. In the late 20th century, multiple technology disruptions started redefining the way business was done. One of early disruptions was the introduction of the smartphone and its capability to receive and transmit media content.

Since smartphones required a large amount of data to be received and transmitted, the telecom industry started exploring ways to increase data transmission speeds. As a result, the data speeds leapfrogged in a decade from providing the GPRS- (general packet radio service) -based (50 kbps transmission speed) connection in the late 1990s to 4G connections (100 Mbps to 1 Gbps transmission speed) in last couple of years. Having mobile devices and data connectivity at the most inaccessible/remote locations increased the demand further for the availability of interactive applications on these devices.

The computing power of processors was increasing at a tremendous pace and their sizes were also reducing with the same speed. This transformation coupled with the capability to transmit data at high speed enabled the proliferation of mobile devices at a tremendous pace. The high-speed data made available at affordable prices coupled by the small size of mobile devices due to the advancement in technology resulted in the mobile device penetration growing to an all-time high of being estimated at two times the population of the earth. The devices connected to the Internet are identified through a binary device identifier, often referred to as an Internet protocol (IP) identifier for the device. In the telecom world, where devices were connected over a telecom network, the phone number of the SIM embedded in the device soon became an identifier of the device/phone itself. The increasing computing capability of devices coupled with the ability to transmit data at high speed changed the way people were using applications and the data therein. The capability to text across devices had also transformed the way individuals could interact with a business as now a large chunk of information could be accessed through a very low bandwidth text message as against navigating through multiple user interfaces (UIs) to access the same data/information over data/phone lines. This further changed with a drastic change in data storing and transmitting capacity of mobile devices and telecom networks, thus making it possible to transmit and receive large content on mobile devices.

In the initial days, mobile devices were restricted to cell phones, and subsequently they evolved into multiple devices like tablets, e-readers, etc., and were now available in all forms and shapes. Now a majority of content could be consumed on the small screens of smartphones, and the content that would need a bigger screen could be consumed on tablets, which had a screen size between a laptop and a smartphone. This helped the customer view content on the correct screen size on relevant devices, but from a developer's perspective, it meant that the developer was required to create multiple versions of the same application so it could adapt to the different screen sizes. At the same time, due to Internet proliferation, a large part of the enterprise and consumer applications were being developed as browser-based applications. Since most of these applications were to be adapted to multiple screen sizes of mobile devices and desktops, creating multiple versions of the same application across screen sizes would have been very expensive. Therefore, developers developed the concept of responsive Web design wherein one could have the same user interface page adapt automatically to different browser sizes or screen sizes, thus starting an era of developing multichannel, cross-browser responsive applications.

Mobile devices are built to handle content offline and online, therefore it was prudent that they have resident applications that are secure and available to only the user of the phone. This was possibly due to the availability of App Stores from device manufacturers like Apple, Google, etc. App Stores are centralized distribution systems where a developer can publish his/her app and the consumer can download and use the same with respective authorization. Any of the applications installed that were not available in App Stores (centralized and enterprise), were flagged as "not secure" and had limited capability to interact with other applications/data on the device. The App Store brought in technology entrepreneurship, as most of the entrepreneurs could now launch their business idea through mobile devices at a relatively low cost. Additionally, through App Stores they were able to reach out to a large number of customers globally as App Stores are available globally to all mobile device owners. Since the application published in the App Stores are custom made for the device, they have a much different and appealing customer interface than the traditional websites.

The enhanced computing capability on mobile devices helped large applications run on small devices that would only run on machines with good processing capabilities. This capability, when coupled with high network speeds, made a federated execution of applications on devices possible. FinTechs, or financial technology start-ups, were able to understand and anticipate the potential of mobile devices. They clubbed all the capabilities of mobile devices to provide a disruptive customer experience in a cost-effective way. This also meant that they had a back end processing system capable of handling the flexibility and ease of use provided by the mobile applications. FinTechs were able to deliver that as well, since they were building their back end systems from scratch and using new age configurable tools and technologies. In contrast, the traditional established players were stuck with their monolithic systems built over the years and were able to take only limited advantage of the new capabilities unleashed by the mobile devices.

In parallel, the technology with sensors was improving on an everyday basis and some of them were getting embedded into the mobile devices. All of these sensors inside the mobile devices and in other devices were equipped with better performing processors and high-data transmission speeds. Therefore, these devices could talk to each other, transmit information over Wi-Fi and the data generated by them could be analyzed to derive patterns and predict future actions. Sensors were also making smartphones very powerful devices with capabilities to track movements, understand speech and take photos and videos. The data thus captured by mobile devices and sensors would in most of the scenarios be transmitted to the servers hosted at a centralized location. The media transmitted by these devices in the form of text, audio, video, photos and multiple other formats required computers with high-computing capabilities and a high-performance database with a vast storage capacity to analyze the data, derive meaningful trends and predict probable outcomes.

One of the possible alternatives for having a high-performance and high-capacity database was to use Big Data solutions that were under development in the 1990s, but started being tested and implemented in the early 2010s. Interpretation and analysis of the existing data was helpful in building trends and reports that could convey and understand the past better, but its real use was when the same could be utilized to understand what could be future predictions. Artificial intelligence (AI) combined with the high-computing capabilities of modern day computers could derive existing trends by scanning through huge amounts of data stored in Big Data and then extrapolate the same to provide predictive analytics.

Using high-computing capabilities, large data storage and the ability to make applications available to millions of customers world-wide required heavy-duty infrastructure to be setup. In the last couple of decades, high infrastructure costs were a major deterrent to build such a setup. In the last decade though, cloud computing brought in the desired disruption by enabling the sharing of hardware and software costs with multiple users at the same time. This brought down the cost of owning the hardware and software and transformed the industry into a pay-per-use model. The model also converted the huge initial setup cost which was primarily the cost of buying the entire infrastructure and owning the same, to renting the infrastructure, thus resulting in only the rental cost. Cloud computing also helped entrepreneurs to automatically scale up and down their infrastructure during peak and off-peak time respectively. A similar change was happening through the App Store, which was transforming the customer's' behavior from owning the content to renting it. The impact of all this was reducing the initial setup cost drastically for the entrepreneur and reducing the cost of owning the software for customers as well, thus enabling the emergence of FinTechs and causing one of the biggest disruptions in the financial services industry. Now a start-up/FinTech could start his/her business with very low seed capital and then expand elastically, i.e., renting more hardware and software capability on-demand whenever the application becomes popular or is being used by more users at a particular time. Keeping the costs low helped the FinTechs compete with established players in the financial industry.

The mobile devices were soon becoming hand-held computers with embedded sensors, resident applications and high-computing capabilities. But more than that they were now becoming an essential accessory. Besides being able to make phone calls, smartphones could be used to start a car, pay bills, act as a remote, etc. Phones were now not only a calling device, but had become more of an essential utility for every individual. Soon, mobile devices were equipped with capabilities to access bank accounts and make payments at a point-of-sale (POS). This was one of the most critical technology (hardware and software) disruption that took the customer experience for making payments through a mobile device to an entirely new level. With this capability, the customer was now able to pay by tapping the card or bringing the mobile device to a close proximity to the point of sale system. This transformed the entire payment industry as now paying by physical means like cash or a card was not user friendly, thus fueling e-payments for financial and non-financial applications. In fact, payments and lending were one of the first business functions that FinTechs disrupted. Disruptions in payment and POS technology has been instrumental in enabling financial technology start-ups to bring about new and innovative ways of doing payments.

Compact sensors, enhanced processor capabilities and high-data transmission speeds were bundled together into a single device called an embedded device. Embedded devices capable of communicating over the Internet were called smart devices. Examples of embedded devices are smart-sensing devices in utilities like dishwashers, ATM machines, routers, point of sale (POS) terminals, etc. Ecosystems of embedded devices connected over the Internet is referred to as Internet of things (IOT). FinTechs employing new age data storage and analytical tools use the data/information emitted by theses embedded devices to understand the customer behavior and as well drive preventive and corrective actions. FinTechs were able to introduce innovative business models using data/information and content gathered from mobile devices, embedded devices and social media. Analyzing the data gathered, they were able to determine the paying capability, understand the damage caused by an accident, remotely diagnose patients and in some cases even paying tolls at toll booths automatically.

All of the above resulted in low initial seed capital, sharing of infrastructure and reach to a global customer base for the FinTechs. Additionally, since all the FinTechs were building their platform from the ground up, they had the flexibility to tweak or transform the business processes supporting a business. All these together not only made them innovative but they soon started disrupting the traditional financial services business. Since FinTechs were innovative, customer friendly and also economical, in no time they were quickly adopted by the user community. Soon enough the governments and regulators realized that they had to make the environment conducive for these start-ups to be successful.

Traditional businesses in the past have had a complete monopolistic control over customer data, therefore, to share bank account-related information with a financial planner, one would have had to take a physical/soft copy of the relevant bank documents shared by the banks to the financial planner. The financial planner would then interpret these statements manually or through a tool and then come up with the appropriate financial advice. There was no way for the customer to share his/her bank related information online with any trusted third party despite consenting to share the information. The possible reasons that stopped traditional banks and other businesses to share the information could be:

1. No clear guidelines from any of the government entities to own up to the liability in case of fraud or failure.
2. Technically complex and expensive to build such interfaces with no potential for direct benefits.
3. Fear of the customer getting stolen by competitors.
4. Lowering revenue from commissions, as the data owner would only own a part of the transaction.
5. The perception that a cumbersome and time-consuming process for sharing would indirectly ensure customer not going away to other banks.

Therefore, to enforce data sharing by traditional banks and to encourage entrepreneurship, regulators created the provisions in the legal setup mandating traditional businesses to share information and data. To offset the infrastructure cost and ensure the right level of security, traditional businesses started sharing the information in a secure manner over the cloud. Information and data available over the cloud helped start-ups consume the information and data after proper authentication. The entity publishing the data/information is referred to as a provider and the application consuming the data and information is called the consumer. The information and data sharing is achieved by the provider developing and publishing interfaces, called application programming interfaces [APIs]) on the cloud and the consumer calling these APIs runtime in his/her application. The entire process of publishing the API on cloud is collectively called as API-fication.

The process of API-fication involves bundling the respective business functions into a defined number of interfaces. These interfaces are then exposed using certain protocols and products on the cloud. The consuming application calls these interfaces to extract the information and initiates the next part of the logic. It is very likely that the provider of information may charge a considerable transaction charge to the consuming organization depending on the business criticality of the information. Regulators and governments globally are bringing in rules regarding the monetization of API, to regularize the transaction charges that can be levied by the provider to the consumer for sharing the information. Therefore, API-fication has been one of the most important technology disruptions for FinTechs. Since they now have access to customer details directly from their established peers, they can focus entirely on creating their own innovative offerings without worrying about managing and maintaining customer details. They could get the information they seek by paying a nominal fee for the same. FinTechs are also leveraging API-fication to monetize their intellectual property comprising of innovative technology and business functions offered by their platform. In some cases, they are also monetizing the innovative customer experience built by them by exposing the same using API. Therefore, the monetization aspect of API-fication by the provider and consumer has led to creating an entirely new economy, referred to as an API economy.

In addition to the above-mentioned technology development, there was a parallel advancement happening in the field of cryptography to make the entire environment responsible for conducting financial transactions, secure and hackproof. During the financial crisis of 2008, a new technology, referred to as blockchain, for conducting financial transactions was introduced. Blockchain can be understood as a distributed ledger containing chains of records. Any addition, update or deletion to the ledger happens only through a consensus mechanism. The chain of records is called blocks and each block has a pointer to the previous block. The blocks represent a transaction and are unique because of the timestamp information and the blockchain algorithm. Lastly, all these transaction blocks are linked and secured using cryptography. Blockchain has disrupted the entire financial market by bringing in a new currency that is truly global in nature and is not monitored/managed by any country, government or central bank. Instead, it is controlled and managed by all the individuals on the chain.

The currency introduced by blockchain is known as "Bitcoin." Bitcoin has still not been recognized by a large number of governments or central banks globally as a valid currency to carry out business and retail transactions. Irrespective, it is being widely used as valid currency for transactions on e-commerce sites and currency exchanges. Since there is no physical currency printing involved in Bitcoin, it can be termed as a true digital currency. Some of the FinTechs/start-ups have mainly focused themselves on developing applications that would transact using Bitcoin. Wallet applications, currency exchanges and Bitcoin-payment providers are some of the types of applications being developed by FinTechs for Bitcoin. Bitcoin can very well be the currency of future and is challenging the traditional hypothesis of monopolistic control of governments on currency. If Bitcoin gets accepted as a valid currency globally, then it would break the last bastion of a controlled economy and would lead to a more-open economy with regulatory control.

While there are ongoing debates regarding the possibility of Bitcoin becoming a currency of the future, the power of blockchain is leveraged by FinTechs as a distributed ledger, enabling transactions based on a consensus of multiple parties involved. As mentioned in one of the whitepapers, a blockchain can be considered as a ledger that is distributed and decentralized in nature, and is unique and cannot be altered retroactively without altering all the previous blocks only through a consensus mechanism between all the parties involved in the transaction.. In more simple terms, blockchain enables the creation and management of unique records in a multiparty system. This is very significant in the financial industry, as all financial transactions are recorded as unique and nonmodifiable. Any modification to an existing transaction is usually recorded as new transaction. This helps in providing a complete audit report of the transactions that happened. The same is true for records maintained by the government and associated agencies. Since in these organizations the trail of the transaction is very important, therefore they would want the unique set of records to be maintained for any transactions being done. Additionally, they would want all of them to be collectively managed by the authorized stakeholders for owning and modifying the documents. Thus, blockchain can also find significant use and application with the government agencies.

Blockchain can be considered a database having transactions and blocks. Each block can have batches of transactions that are hashed and encoded into a tree. Each block includes the hash of the prior block and the linked blocks form a chain. This mechanism ensures that the transactions are tamper-proof, since anybody wanting to alter the transactions maliciously will have to impact all the previous block transactions back in time. The same is not feasible, and therefore blockchain is being considered as one of the most secure way to make a transaction by business and government entities.

FinTechs were quick in adopting the blockchain concept and building solutions based on blockchain. Transactions like cross-border trades, originations, currency exchanges, trade finance transactions and many others that require multiparty involvements, are being built using blockchain. Blockchain offers an efficient workflow in such scenarios, since using blockchain all parties can view the same copy of the transaction and provide their changes incrementally. All amendments can only be accepted if there is a consensus between all the authorized entities. Therefore, a multiparty transaction in a traditional setup would have meant multiple communication exchanges, taking weeks to be completed. The same can now be done quite seamlessly using blockchain. FinTechs are employing the blockchain concept for multiple other financial business functions like multiparty lending, wealth management and advisory, etc. A detailed overview of some of these applications for blockchain is elaborated later in this chapter.

Together, all these transformations have created a perfect storm for a digital future, and FinTechs have been the torchbearers of the disruption to conventional ways of conducting financial business using technology innovations. In later sections of this chapter, we will be taking a deeper look into each of the above-mentioned technology areas and see how the same has impacted the financial services industry.

4G and 5G Networks Fueling FinTech Opportunities

The first and foremost technological change that disrupted the financial industry was the capability of the telecom industry to transmit information at high speed. This enabled sending and receiving content at lightning speeds across devices. The telecom network responsible for transmitting data and information is referred to as the cellular network. They have evolved through several generations. The first-generation networks, often referred to as "1G networks," were analog telecommunications standards. In 1G networks the voice signals were only modified to a higher frequency and there was no data transmission as we understand today. The radio signals used were analog and not encoded as digital signals. The initial mobile transmission systems used a single channel for sending and receiving, therefore only one person could talk at a time. The user had to push a button to enable transmission and disable reception and vice versa. Soon the systems evolved to a dual channel system, one for receiving and other for sending. Now there was no need to push the button, as one channel could be used for sending and other could be used for receiving simultaneously. 1G networks are based primarily on analog communications, meaning that the information is transmitted more as seamless waves of frequency transmissions like in the case of certain types of radio channels and not as "0" or "1" binary signals, often referred to as digital signals.

1G Networks

1G cellular networks were introduced in the 1980s, and the main concept was to divide a geographical area into multiple cells, all of these cells would be served by a single base station. Since the cells were small, the frequency could be reused in nearby cells, but not adjacent cells. Thus, with 1G networks, more users can be supported in the same geographical area. Also, since the cells were smaller, they required less powerful, cheaper and smaller devices to transmit and receive information. 1G networks brought in the terminology cellular networks and cellular phones.

Cellular phones were later abbreviated to "cell phones." The first cell phones and cellular networks were introduced in Japan and the Nordics countries, and over time, spread worldwide. 1G analog cellular phones were not secure as anybody with an all-band radio receiver could easily listen into the conversations.

2G Networks

2G networks are based on digital transmissions and commenced soon after the introduction of 1G networks. In 2G networks, besides transmitting information in digital mode, the conversations were encrypted and therefore more secure than their predecessor. Since 2G systems enables the phones to share the channels dynamically, therefore 2G networks were more efficient in terms of sharing the network between multiple phones within a single cell, thus allowing for a further increase in density of phones within a cell. Consequent to the high density of phones within a cell, the handsets could work with low radio power as well, thereby reducing the handset size and addressing health concerns as well. Call-drops and not getting signals in weak signal areas were the downside of a large number of devices sharing the same bandwidth, as handsets confused low signals with end of call. The 2G networks required that more cells be placed in an area as compared to 1G. Consequently, handsets were required to emit less radio power resulting in the reduced size of handsets and addressing health concerns as well.

Data services for mobile phones started with 2G networks and the initial service offered was short message service (SMS) text. Soon other data services like email were introduced as well. A global system for mobile communications (GSM), a 2G technology, operates at a data rate of up to 9.6 kbps and has been one of the most popular 2G technologies. The GSM phones could also be used as a modem for computers. Another network type in 2G networks is a code division multiple access (CDMA) network. In CDMA, each user is assigned a unique code that differentiates one user from another as against time-division multiple access (TDMA) used by GSM wherein each user is assigned a time slot. Therefore, in CDMA the frequency reuse is very high and many more users can be supported as compared to TDMA.

2.5G networks, also known as general packet radio services (GPRSs) and enhanced data rates for GSM evolutions (EDGEs), build packet-switching systems on top of existing 2G systems to improve data rates significantly. GPRS is a service developed by GSM carriers which overlays a packet switching network on an existing circuit-switched GSM network. This enables support for a packet-based data service, resulting in higher data rates and a constant "virtual connection" without the need to dial into the network. This capability of being "always on" on GPRS networks meant that for transmitting and receiving data, one need not dial a server again and again. Since the Internet works in a request-response mode, i.e., when user requests a URL or does an action on the website, the server responds back with a response. Therefore, GPRS networks are the most ideal for Internet-based content. GPRS ushered in a complete new set of features that could be used on mobile phones like Web browsing, email and file transfer between phones. This was the turning point in the mobile network evolution. Entrepreneurs used this feature to use mobile phones as not only a telephony device, but a more complex data transmission device. Following GPRS and before the introduction of the 3G technology, telecom networks used the technology called EDGE. EDGE uses 8 phase shift keying (8PSK) modulation that allows a much higher bit rate and can deliver data rates up to 500 kpbs.

3G Networks

3G, a third-generation telecom network, complies with the International Mobile Telecommunications-2000 (IMT-2000) specifications covering services like voice, Internet access, video calls and television in a mobile environment. 3G systems typically support bandwidths in the range of 144 kbps to 2 Mbps, depending upon the network coverage in the area and mobility of device. The most important characteristic of 3G networks has been to support access to Internet over a larger geographic area. In 3G networks, since data is broken down into smaller packets, the packets can travel in parallel on different channels, thus increasing the data rates significantly. Also, since the same is transmitted in a connectionless communication mechanism, the user can stay online throughout and yet not be charged for the time spent online. Explained more simplistically, even though a 3G handset is always connected to the network, it uses the bandwidth only when needed. When not using the bandwidth, it is shared with other handsets. This was a very big enhancement over 2G networks where the connection was dedicated to the callers and was not available to anybody else while in use. This improvisation was the main reason to not only increase data speed over telecom networks but also dropping of data charges rapidly. This made it possible for a common person to own a mobile device and use all the services on his/her phone like the Internet. This change also facilitated multiple start-ups to manage their workforce in the field effectively as they could now use email and video-conferencing to talk to a person while he/she was on move. 3G networks significantly changed the connectivity options for an individual. Users were now able to communicate using text message, email, video communication, audio communication and chat using social media applications. Social media applications on 3G networks started becoming successful and were being adopted widely. FinTech and start-ups latched onto this upgrade in capability of telecom networks and mobile devices to transmit information at low costs. Consequently, this enabled them to reach a wider customer base globally. Additionally, the services helped them to communicate with their customers in a cost-effective manner. Since the data service charges were also nominal, the customers were also not incurring hefty charges on consuming the information being delivered by FinTechs. One of the main drivers for the success of FinTechs was the ability of 3G networks to transfer multimedia messages, i.e., videos, photos, etc. besides text using the multimedia messaging service (MMS).

4G Networks

4G networks, the fourth generation of wireless standards, specified data transmission speeds up to 100 Mbps for high-mobility communication zones (in cars, etc.) and 1 Gbps in low-mobility communication zones (in offices, etc.). A 4G mobile system is an all IP-based network system, i.e., it should integrate all the wireless technologies to give seamless connectivity across multiple technologies, thus providing a seamless and continuous interface to all mobile users for using multimedia applications. This is possible by having a core interface between the core network and all other radio access networks and mobile users, consequently creating a single network across all the users within the network. There are two technologies that are popular with 4G networks, long-term evolution (LTE) and worldwide interoperability for microwave access (wiMax).

5G network,s also known as a fifth generation mobile network or fifth generation wireless system, is a terminology used to talk about the anticipated next major phase of mobile telecommunications. It is expected that it builds a true wireless network to provide a Worldwide Wireless Web (www).

Various countries have adopted 4G networks very quickly and this has enabled a large number of multimedia transfers over phone services possible. In the last decade, what would have been a network of computers became a high-speed network of devices for phones. The capability of 4G networks encouraged people to use mobile devices for activities that they would have usually done with a computer over a Wi-Fi connection. This change in adoption of mobile devices to do business transactions unleashed opportunities for FinTechs/start-ups to build business applications on mobile devices. Additionally, the capability to transmit multimedia messages helped FinTechs interact with their users using video/text. High-speed networks fueled the FinTech revolution by enhancing the capability of phones to conduct business anywhere at any time.

Mobile Applications and Smartphones Reshaping the Customer Experience

As discussed in the previous section, the telecom network evolved from being a single channel service to a 4G/5G service. A similar evolution happened in mobile devices. The walkie-talkie used in World War II can be considered to be the first mobile phone. Ericsson's Mobile System was the first partly automatic mobile system for automobiles. Phone models introduced by Motorola between 1983 and 1989 could be said to be the first generation of mobile phones that we carry today. One of the first phones to use GSM technology was introduced by Motorola, and subsequently, IBM introduced the phone that could be considered as the first smartphone as it had a phone, fax, pager and a PDA all rolled into a single device.

It had a touchscreen and Qwerty keyboard. The StarTAC phone from Motorola in 1996 was the first clamshell pocket size phone.

The Nokia 9000 Communicator could be considered as the first smartphone in the true sense as it had a LCD screen and Qwerty keyboard and the processor in the phone was quite powerful, almost like a minicomputer. The Nokia 7110 provided content over a wireless access protocol (WAP). WAP as a technology was providing text content in a more-organized manner than simply sending text messages. J-SH04, built by J-Phone in Japan in 2000, was the first smartphone to have a camera built inside the phone. It could transfer pictures using Sha-Mail (picture mail). It could also be termed as start of the MMS. In 2002, the Sanyo 5300 was the first camera phone in America.

In and around 2002, the PDA revolution started and one of the leaders in this field was Microsoft's Pocket PC phone. It combined the capability of managing contacts, calendars, emails, etc. while integrating voice and data capabilities. Thus, with this phone one could browse the Internet using Internet Explorer. Palm's Treo 180 running Palm OS was another phone that combined a PDA with phone services. In 2002, the BlackBerry came up with a series of executive phones that were quite secure and could be used for doing email communication, instant messaging and had a very basic browser. It soon became one of the most desired devices for it being a status symbol. It also enabled instant messaging which was named as BlackBerry Messenger (BBM). It had a Qwerty keyboard and around 3–4 lines of LCD screens that one could browse to get to the desired application.

In 2005, Motorola's ROKR E1 was one of the first smartphones that had the capability to store and play music. In 2007, Apple introduced the first touchscreen phone in the true sense called the iPhone, which revolutionized the entire smartphone industry in many ways. The first and foremost thing the smartphone changed was eliminating the keyboard that was always available. On smartphones, the physical keyboard replaced the virtual keyboard that could be operated through a touchscreen. Additionally, one could make the keyboard appear and disappear on-demand. This led to applications that were less intensive on keying input but more intuitive to display information and click through actions using only one or two fingers. The iPhone, besides providing the touchscreen, also had a camera and music player inside the phone itself. Thus, the iPhone was a phone that bundled all the possible media formats into a single phone and had the capability to not only store the media information but also transmit and receive media content over the phone using 3G services.

The most interesting part of the iPhone was it combined three great features:

1. You could make calls, receive calls and do all the functions a phone was expected to do.
2. You could now run the applications on the phone. The application could be a music application, a video application, etc.
3. The phone could transmit information as data streams.

It is the last feature of the mobile phone that has really caused the biggest transformation in the overall technology industry. With data bytes being able to be transferred from one device to another, which was only possible over a local area network (LAN) or a wide area network (WAN), which was a closed or semi-closed network, it was now possible to create an open network with devices being connected through telecom providers. This capability was complemented by the telecom networks capability to enable high-speed transmission of multimedia content. The iPhone was the right phone at the right time. It became hugely popular and was fiercely adopted by the consumer. In fact, there were lines of buyers outside an apple store to purchase the latest iPhone models, the day these models were launched and the same trend is visible even as of the last iPhone Launch. Soon after the launching of the iPhone, multiple other device manufacturers introduced their own smartphones spanning over multiple operating systems (OSs) including android, BlackBerry and Windows. The entire smartphone market was racing to provide more secure and more content-rich capability in the most compact hardware.

While the hardware for mobile devices was getting upgraded, network speeds were getting enhanced and mobile phones were getting transformed into smartphones. Simultaneously, there were multiple other technological breakthroughs happening in the areas of hardware and software. It is difficult to say which change was the first one to cause the disruption, but to a very great extent we can say the transformation in the telecom industry coupled with an increase in computing capability of processors in mobile devices triggered the new era of financial disruption.

FinTechs Making Life Simple by Using Embedded Sensors

Multiple sensors were being embedded in the mobile device to enhance the hardware capability of smartphones. FinTechs were able to accentuate the mobile device capability by leveraging the embedded sensors to offer an exemplary user experience to their customers. Below is an explanation of how different FinTech firms have been able to leverage these sensors to offer a unique customer experience.

Accelerometers

Accelerometers are the most commonly used sensors and is used by the mobile applications to detect the mobile device movement. This sensor has been available since the first generation smartphones, but the real business-use has been put into practice in last 5–10 years. FinTechs and start-ups supporting the financial and insurance industry have used this sensor to get information like driver behavior, track movement of an individual, etc. The sensor is also used in fitness apps on mobile devices and fitness devices to understand the health-related movements of an individual such as for distance traveled and the speed of walking, etc. There is another sensor that detects the number of steps traveled more accurately. This will be discussed later.

Gyroscopes

A gyroscope is used with an accelerometer to detect the orientation for phones and also which direction the phone has moved to. Most of the FinTechs have used accelerometers and gyroscopes in tandem to provide virtual reality and gamification-like solutions to their consumers. It also helps mobile applications switch their orientation mode into either portrait or landscape mode.

Magnetometers

A magnetometer is a sensor used to detect magnetic fields and is used in compass-like applications to detect the North Pole. Though it is of limited use in financial applications, the same has been used again in tandem with an accelerometer and gyroscope to determine in-store navigation which ultimately leads to "no checkout lines."

Barometers

A barometer is a sensor used to measure atmospheric pressure and can be used to determine how high the device is placed above sea level. The sensor along with other sensors can provide GPS accuracy specifically to insurance providers, associated emergency assistance services, etc.

Thermometers

A thermometer sensor is built into the smartphone, but is used primarily to detect the temperature within the device and to detect if the device is overheating or not. The same has been used by mobile insurance start-ups to detect the state of the device before it became unresponsive, which can then be used by them to provide appropriate compensation for the claim made for breakdown of mobile devices.

Air Humidity

The air humidity sensor detects air humidity and is useful in health applications to understand if the user is in a comfort zone or not.

Heart Rate Monitor

A heart rate monitor sensor is used to detect the minute pulsation of blood vessels inside a person's finger and has been used in multiple health insurance applications to get an indication of heart rate.

Fingerprint Scanners

A fingerprint scanner helps detect a fingerprint and is one of the most extensively used sensor. This sensor has been used by FinTechs to transform the customer experience relating to authentication. A large number of financial applications use this sensor to authenticate biometrics information of the registered customers and to directly get access to most of their account information. If there is a pre-populated know your customer (KYC) data base existent that is linked directly to fingerprint data. It is possible to get the entire onboarding of the customer done in minutes using the data from this sensor and the biometrics information being made available through APIs from the KYC database.

Radiation Level Sensors

A radiation level sensor detects radiation levels in an area and has been used in health applications to prevent the exposure of an individual to high-radiation areas. This sensor is used in very few smartphones.

Cameras

A camera is used to capture images and video and has been the most extensively used sensor in all financial applications. In customer onboarding applications, a camera is used to capture images for identity, address proofs and many other application areas. In check deposit applications, a camera is used to capture the check information. The captured check image is then interpreted using an optical character recognition (OCR) software. There are multiple other software that help convert the free-text information in images like licenses, etc. into digital information. The camera capability has also been used by FinTechs in insurance applications to capture images of an accident. They are also used for making an instant claim or to get immediate roadside assistance.

Microphone and Speakers

Besides being used for talking and speaking a microphone and speakers are now being used in financial applications to authenticate a voice footprint and also in some of the financial applications to prefill forms using speech-to-text conversion with tools like Siri, Alexa, etc.

Smartphone Operating Systems

While the mobile device manufacturers were upgrading the hardware and the computing capability of the devices and the telecom providers were equipping the devices to communicate faster and more efficiently, at the same time, the OSs for mobile devices were also getting enhanced over time. Mobile OSs are the operating system software that help mobile devices carry out the basic operations like starting up, connecting to Bluetooth, setting up SIM cards, etc. The software developers leverage the operating system of mobile devices to launch their applications and perform corresponding device-related operations. Since the mobile devices are movable devices, they may or may not get a charging station at a specific location. The most important aspect about mobile device OSs is to offer optimal performance while consuming low battery. The purpose becomes more challenging because unlike laptops and desktops, the devices have to operate optimally while ensuring they consume low on device memory, ensure availability of all the embedded sensors, provide access to Wi-Fi, communicate using Bluetooth, operate touchscreen on-demand and offer the ability to operate many other such features. A large part of this evolution in mobile OSs happened in the last decade. Initially there were multiple phone OSs that were launched, but during the last 4–5 years, the following mobile OSs with a majority of the market share are existent.

1. The Android OS was developed by Google and has a maximum number of handsets using this OS. The Android OS is a free and open-source software. Different mobile device vendors have either adopted or extended the OS to suit their device needs and the corresponding versions developed by the device vendors have typically been proprietary.
2. Windows 10 Mobile is one of the recent OS versions available from Microsoft and the devices are manufactured by Nokia, Microsoft, HTC and Samsung.
3. BlackBerry 10 is an OS introduced by BlackBerry and is used in all the BlackBerry devices. Besides the OS, BlackBerry also provides one of the good mobile device management software as BlackBerry Work and Access.
4. iOS is a mobile device specific OS from Apple Inc. for phones manufactured by them. It has the second largest installation base on smartphones. It is a propriety OS and is based on open source Darwin OS.

In recent times iOS and Android OS have become the two most popular OS systems worldwide, and it is foreseen that they will be in use for a long time.

FinTechs Transforming the Customer Experience Using Social Media

In late traditional technologies, application capability was limited to the extent of managing the hardware associated with the computers. Because of computing capability increasing on mobile devices, the application capability was amplified by the use of various sensors on the devices like cameras, accelerometers, etc. This brought in the possibility of an entire new set of functionalities like one could take a photograph of an address proof and attach it to a bank account opening form. This was in contrast to the traditional setup, wherein the same would have been done by entering the details on the online form through a computer and then scanning the photograph and attaching the same on the computer. Therefore, many such functionalities being enabled using enhanced features within the mobile devices resulted in the applications on these devices becoming more complex than the traditional desktop applications.

In addition to increasing computing capability, the associated hardware was reduced in size, thus the phone device which was bulky got transformed into a pocket device with a computing power closer to what most desktop computers would offer. Since the devices were small, their casing was also concise and could be carried to remote locations. One of the technology innovations that was impacting the hardware world was the enhanced capacity and reduced sizes of the battery required in the mobile devices. Increased computing capability, reduction in hardware size and increased battery capacity, when coupled with high speed and affordable data rates enabled business to host complex applications on mobile devices that could even operate at the remotest locations. The most complex applications like the banking and insurance application were now available to individuals on mobile devices including the places where brick and mortar branches could not be built. This disrupted the entire banking and financial world as what was once only possible through an in-person transaction could now be done remotely and without interacting with a person. The immediate impact of this was that now anybody could build a relationship with a customer base as long as they have an application that serves the customer and there is a process/system that manages all the back-office activities.

Mobile devices started getting adopted in a big way in the last couple of decades. This was the time frame the digital native generation was getting raised using these devices. This generation started having a strong dependency on using these platforms. Most digital natives are now earning adults, and for them mobile devices are similar to what microwaves and washing machines were for the baby boomer generation. The baby boomer generation was awed by the microwaves and washing machines, which has now become an inseparable part of the same generation and they would feel out of place if they did not have access to these machines. Similarly, the digital natives would consider mobile devices an inherent part of their life and would get lost if they did not have these devices around. FinTechs and start-ups were quick to realize the opportunities arising because of these devices and started building products that were suited to the new generation. They had all the elements of making an engaging product either through gamification, price competition, brand adoption and brand discarding.

Digital natives are used to communicating using these devices, even if they are sitting next to each other. The dependency on devices is also catching up with other generations as well. Start-ups leveraged this to let their product be known to a wider community using peer-to-peer (P2P) communication and social media. This word-of-mouth publicity and advertising their product through social media helped companies not only to save on advertising costs but also addressed issues and concerns of people more effectively. Now they were able to address the issues at point-of-impact, as the customer could convey and communicate the dissatisfaction with the product right there and then. Start-ups were able to save costs on setting up high-end help desk operations and at the same time increase customer satisfaction leading to higher adoption rates. In fact, some of the start-ups used the concept of social media to bring about the sharing economy, a new age concept where people share apartments, cars, books and multiple other things. Then there were financial technology start-ups who came up with products that could provide functions like KYC, customer onboarding and fraud prevention using social networks.

In summary, the social media ushered in an entirely different kind of world order and an economic cycle that was quite different from the traditional industries. One of the big changes that social media brought in was that now people were able to connect among themselves in a seamless manner and at the same time were able to conduct business as well. Additionally, since the digital native generation trusted digital media more than in-person sales representatives, they considered transacting using social media more trustworthy than transacting in person. During the same time, social media platforms like Facebook enabled the capability to launch applications and websites within their platforms, which was soon followed by multiple other platforms; soon this became the new mass media communication platform. If a start-up had a good proposition to offer, it could get itself live on any of these social media channels with its own website and it would be known to multiple other people using the "share" and "like" concept. The social media platforms have the information for an individual's contact stored locally. Some of these platforms also let you know if you can connect with a stranger using your contacts. This has helped people grow their contacts network exponentially by creating a chain of multilevel contacts. FinTechs and start-ups have leveraged this capability of social media to effectively connect to multiple prospects by creating a chain of references. Some FinTechs have also used social media to effectively raise funds for themselves. Other platforms have used the same for charity and donation purposes. Some of the platforms have gone ahead and even crowdsourced work from multiple people using social media.

A catalyst to people communicating over social media is the capability to transmit information at high speed to multiple people. As mentioned earlier, devices were now capable of capturing video, photos, music and multiple other forms of media through a single action like a click. The information thus captured could be transmitted using high data speed, to a device at a different location in no time. Video conferencing or chat, which earlier required an expensive infrastructure, was now available at a miniscule cost with no wires being connected to any devices. People could not only text each other, but they were able to see each other and send photos to each other in real time. Communication between a company and its prospect/customers, partners and own workforce became instant and cost-effective using these multimedia capabilities on devices. Some of the FinTechs and start-ups were able to leverage the same to provide complex business functionalities like medical care, counseling, etc. by using the video capability within the devices. The devices also made it possible for an individual to capture photos of an accident or create video surveillance of a high-rise building and transmit the same instantly. FinTechs in the insurance industry utilized these technologies to help customers raise accident claims by themselves, often referred to as "self-service or straight-through processing," and ease the surveyor's job. This enables them to respond quickly and save expensive visits by surveyors. It also enables FinTechs to offer road-side assistance to the customer and prospects and even linking up with emergency services for critical cases.

App Stores Helping FinTechs Expand Globally

The introduction of mobile applications has been one of the single largest disruptions in the manner we consume content and functionality. Every organization interacts with its customers through content or functionality. It could be a catalog of insurance products or functionality like an account summary, etc. Therefore, we can summarily say all the applications interacting with customers primarily are comprised of content mixed with business functionality. Initially, the applications were available with very simple user interface elements on the client, and most of the business logic was residing on the server. The websites were only rendering the information received from the server and the business processes were being executed at the server. This resulted in a restrictive customer experience, as the applications were downloading and rendering minimalistic user interface components on the browsers. A highly interactive customer experience would mean downloading enormous amounts of user interface components. This in turn would impact the rendering time for the application, thus offering a slow user experience. The personalization of the user experience was strictly no-no as it would mean provisioning for more performance load on the server as everything was rendered from the server and an additional logic would typically slow down the response of the application.

Another alternative was to have a dedicated client interface residing on the client's machine so that complex customer experience could be executed locally with high performance. The only challenge with this approach was to control distribution as there were multiple different OSs and devices that would be required to run the same applications. Additionally, there was always a problem of providing upgrades across multiple platforms and lastly, the governance for notifying and publishing upgrades was also very complex. The only alternative was to rely on the centralized Web-based online applications rendered through the bowsers.

Mobile applications and the introduction of the App Store changed the way applications were distributed. The mobile applications could be loaded at a centralized location and then distributed in a controlled manner through App Stores. Since now loading applications from an App Store required certification, there was a governance that ensured valid versions were available. Also, the versioning mechanism available from an App Store helped the user to download the most relevant versions. The notification to download the latest versions also helped the user to keep himself/herself updated with the latest versions. One of key aspects of the App

Store was that one could now charge the user for the content download, instead of charging a monthly, quarterly or annual subscription fee for becoming a member of the organization distributing the content. Now the application owner could make the entire application available for free and charge only when a certain content was downloaded and uploaded. This changed the entire economy from using a sub-scription model to a pay-per-use model. Additionally, through App Stores, an app owner could make some part of the application functionality usable for free and the other parts of functionality chargeable. This is called in-app purchase. FinTechs used this feature to offer basic functions/services as free and then charge for addi-tional functionality, services and content.

App Stores are offered by device manufacturers, by the companies who intro-duced the mobile operating systems, by telecom service provider and some of the cross-platform App Stores. Some of the popular App Stores are the Apple App Store, Google Play, Amazon App Store, Samsung Apps, Lenovo App Store, Verizon App Store, T-Mobile App Store, etc. The entire app world has become huge, and has already crossed a billion app downloads. A majority of apps on the App Store in public domain have business to consumer (B2C) apps. Mobile device management (MDM) vendors offer publishing and hosting enterprise mobile applications, primarily for the business to business (B2B) community. They are often referred to as enterprise App Stores. Some of the MDM vendors are BlackBerry, Mobile Iron, Symantec, Airwatch, etc. These vendors provide tools and platforms to enterprises for hosting enterprise appli-cations. These vendors, through their platforms, ensure that the enterprise data and application is accessed by the workforce in a secure manner. The platforms offer fea-tures like remote wipe, single sign-on, etc. to manage and administer enterprise appli-cations and data remotely. Both public and enterprise App Stores are available over the Internet and therefore, they are accessible anywhere and anytime. If enabled and permitted, some of the App Stores can also track the usage of mobile apps including analytics related to customer usage patterns. Enterprises can use this information to develop their user interface to offer a personalized customer experience.

The resident applications on mobile devices are referred to as native applications and they are developed using programming languages native to the OS of respec-tive phone/mobile devices. As a result, most of these applications have an appealing customer interface that responds fast to user actions and is available on-demand by clicking on the application icon on the phone. Businesses soon realized that their business applications on mobile phones need not be a replica of their online appli-cations. Instead for a better customer interaction, the mobile applications need to offer only the business critical and time critical functions on the mobile phones. Therefore, there was a rush to build apps that would offer business and time-critical functions through an out of the world user experience.

In the case of the native application that is responsible for displaying or playing content like music, video, etc., the application can itself be activated by clicking the icon on the phone device, but the bulk of the content common across the applica-tion is downloaded from the server for the first time and then the user-specific content in the form of data and information is loaded on-demand. FinTechs and start-ups are using native applications extensively to offer a compelling user experience. In case of most of the "native" financial applications, there is a one-time download of the catalog of services and offerings. The user-specific data, like an account summary, profile details, etc. is downloaded on-demand from a centralized location. The FinTech firms and even the established financial firms are using mobile to enable the customer to execute all the standard financial transactions like bill pay, fund transfers, buy/sell securities, etc. anywhere through their respective mobile applications.

Even for nonfinancial applications, the ease of making content available on mobile applications prompted the enterprises to push their product catalogs to the devices. This was much different from traditional ways of promoting the products by distributing paper brochures or handouts. Therefore with catalogs available on mobile devices, now the entire customer experience was interactive, and the information for latest products could be pushed to the devices immediately. Consequently, the salesperson could now stand at a point of maximum footfall within a store, like near the entrance, with a mobile device in his/her hand to attract and interact with the customer. This was a transformational experience for both the customer and the salesperson, since now the salesperson could sell products anywhere, anytime. An example would be, a salesperson selling a health insurance product in a shopping mall using the information available on mobile devices. Since the entire discussion was being done in a shopping mall, a customer would typically be more akin to spend time and listen to the salesperson in a shopping mall on a weekend, rather than during his/her work hours. Therefore, the salesperson had a greater chance of convincing the prospect into buying the product. This also helped the customer, since he would have enough time discuss the complete offering, get an instant quote and give his/her consent to purchase the product.

FinTechs, especially in the cards and loyalty domain, started seeing new ways of doing transactions and managing loyalty. All the e-commerce mobile applications were traditionally built to select an item from the website, adding the same to the cart, then checkout, followed by the last stage, i.e., providing payment details in the purchase cycle. The entire process from start to finish was quick and could be done with a few clicks. It was only during checkout that one had to call payment interfaces from established banks. This created a distorted customer experience, as one would have had to go to a bank application for activating the payments and then come back to the e-commerce application after success/failure of the payment. This prompted a lot of FinTechs to introduce their own wallets that would provide a quicker interface and the payment step would just be one more click rather than entering a whole lot of information. The wallets in turn would maintain and manage the payment- and delivery-related information like credit card information, shipping details, etc. This was a sea change in customer experience, since now a person could order items from an online store from anywhere, e.g., while standing at a train station to find the same delivered when he/she reaches home.

FinTechs Make Payments Seamless Using Mobile Payments

The advancement in mobile technology has enabled mobile devices to initiate and make payments. In addition to making online payments, the devices have been enabled to make payments at different POS systems as well. These technologies have turned mobile phones into a virtual replica of physical wallets, including the capability to execute payments in a secure manner. In the early days, quick response (QR) codes were considered to be a viable option for doing mobile payments. They were more commonly used where both the transacting parties were trusted parties, that is, an individual making a payment to the merchant required to be a registered and authorized customer by the merchant. Payments made by customers at Starbucks using the Starbucks app is an example of the same. Since QR codes are easy to replicate, therefore, they have been considered as a less secure solution for mobile payments.

Subsequently, mobile device manufacturers and telecom providers together introduced SIM cards to store payment instruments like credit and debit cards virtually and securely using encryption. The wallet applications on the mobile devices used this information stored on SIM cards to make the payments. Again, this was a closed group-payment mechanism since only the applications registered and authorized to make payments by the merchant could use this mechanism of payment. The mobile payment space transformed dramatically when near-field communication (NFC) was introduced into the devices. NFC, a technology evolution of communication protocols between devices, enabled devices to communicate over radio frequencies with each other in a secure manner. NFC has its own standards and encryption algorithms to transmit information between devices. This can be loosely compared with the protocols and encryption standards followed while transmitting credit card information between multiple entities initiated through a card swipe at POS.

There are other mechanisms like Bluetooth which can be used to communicate between devices, but NFC technology enabled devices to communicate with each other consuming less battery power. This was important for mobile devices since they would have limited battery capacity owing to their small size. Also with NFC technology the entire experience of making payments has also transformed radically. The payments could now be done either by bringing the device closer to POS or by tapping on the POS device. The cumbersome process of pairing and then providing payment-related information all gets done implicit to the end user. Therefore, it is prophesied that NFC and similar technologies would reshape the way we understand and do payments. Many retailers across the globe have already enabled their POS terminals to accept payments from devices equipped with NFC. Devices communicate using NFC in the following ways:

1. Two-way communication—Both the devices are active devices, i.e., they can transmit information both ways and can read/write to each other like exchanging contact information, etc.

2. One-way communication—One device is an active device and the other one is a passive device and the most common format in which this is used is by embedding a NFC chip in the customer's mobile device or in the plastic card issued by a issuer (bank/credit card company). When the active device comes in contact with the passive device, it reads and writes back to the passive device and then enables payment by just tapping the phone device or plastic card on the POSterminal.

It is the second type of NFC communication that is being used in enabling NFC payments through mobile devices. If the POS systems are enabled with NFC, the user will have to launch the NFC application on his/her mobile device. The phone is then tapped on the card reader. Some terminals may ask an individual for additional authorization like providing a PIN number, passcode or finger scanning. The payment is done after transaction validation and authorization steps are completed. Payment solutions like Samsung Pay and Apple Pay have emerged recently that enable payments using NFC. Additionally, Samsung Pay has also provided interfaces for a magnetic stripe reader, using a technology called magnetic secure transmission (MST). Magnetic stripe readers in the traditional payment world are used to swipe and read plastic credit cards which are placed inside the credit card readers at most of the existing POS terminals. The card readers work by swiping the physical credit card and transmitting the relevant information to the respective payment entity. Since Samsung Pay uses MST, it can make payments through mobile phones at these terminals as well. The individual needs to select a card from Samsung Pay (an application within the phone) and just bring his/her phone within an inch of the swipe readers and then authenticate using his/her finger print on the device. This would emulate swiping of a physical card on the magnetic stripe reader. All of this can be done without even unlocking the device. It provides a seamless payment experience to the customer and is very well poised to become the solution for future payments. There are multiple other payment solutions that have emerged like ALipay, AndroidPay, etc. due to the enhanced capabilities of mobile devices.

Loyalty Redefined by FinTechs

As stated in previous sections, mobile applications started leveraging the embedded sensors to provide an exemplary customer experience. Consequently, some of the key business functions associated with the shopping experience that got transformed by mobile applications were payments, loyalty, promotions, offers and coupons. The new age mobile applications in these business areas have impacted the way customers accumulate and redeem loyalty points, avail discount coupons and promotional offers. Customers would accumulate loyalty points when they purchase a product from a respective merchant. Traditionally, redeeming loyalty points would have meant customers accessing the respective merchant's loyalty application online at home or work. They could then redeem their loyalty points by ordering a product out of limited options available from the loyalty website. A customer would have to proactively check and validate when and how his/her loyalty points were expiring. Since most of the loyalty points were accumulated by people on the move, the entire process of managing loyalty points became a time-consuming affair for the highly mobile and loyal customers. A large portion of the loyal customers were affluent customers and were able to accumulate these points because they could afford high-value purchases. For these loyal customers, using and operating these online applications was not only time consuming but also did not offer a good customer experience as well. Thus, overall, the entire loyalty experience was indirectly impacting the brand perception and was defeating the very purpose of loyalty programs to encourage customer stickiness.

FinTechs introduced customer friendly mobile applications that would enable the customers to have all the loyalty relevant information on their phones available anywhere and anytime. An ideal example of the same would be a customer accessing his/her loyalty points at check in terminals of airlines and hotels. He/she could then decide on redeeming the points to upgrade himself/herself or get a discount right at the check in terminal. There are many such examples where the customer is now empowered to take just-in-time decisions using loyalty information available on his/her mobile device. Using these applications, the customer could immediately check if his/her loyalty points have been added, redeemed or if he/she can avail a promotional offer/discount while on the move. The applications would also send short message service (SMS) message notifications updating the user on activity regarding loyalty points including advance notification for points that are about to expire. FinTechs were also able to offer customers redemption of their points across multiple partner e-commerce sites by connecting the application seamlessly to these sites. Therefore, the customer now had many choices from which to purchase a product using his/her accumulated points.

FinTechs were also able to leverage the geolocation-related embedded sensors in mobile devices to identify the location of a specific device and accordingly push discount coupons and offers from nearby locations. This was a science fiction-type of a user experience for the customer as now using analytics, the application was able to proactively notify the customer regarding his/her next buying aspiration located nearby. The application would then go a step further to suggest how a customer could get a better deal on the same by redeeming his/her loyalty points or using discount coupons and offers for the same. Additionally, the application also pushed offers and coupons that one could avail of while inside a store. Over time many more applications started being developed on these devices capable of doing multiple other business functions.

Similar to payments and loyalty business functions, FinTechs introduced applications that would transform the lending, wealth management and insurance business functions as well.

Cloud Computing

One of the other impacts of high-speed networking is cloud computing, a concept that was similar to using computing power as utilities. Cloud computing is primarily based on the concept of virtualization of hardware resources. In cloud computing the hardware resources, typically the servers that host and run the applications can be provisioned automatically, without any manual intervention from any of the users. Though the concept is being discussed extensively in research labs and educational institutes a couple of decades back, its practical implementation started in the last decade. The three primary reasons that were responsible for making cloud computing a reality were

- Increase in network transmission speeds
- Low cost yet compact hardware
- Service-oriented architecture
- Increased automation in deployment processes

Anybody Can Start a FinTech Using Pay-per-Use Models from the Cloud

Cloud computing also made the sharing of hardware possible between different users without the end-user of the application experiencing any of such switchovers, thus providing a high degree of availability, accessibility, scalability and performance. One of the biggest advantages of cloud computing is it converts the capital expenditure to operational expenditure. Therefore, in cloud computing an organization pays for the infrastructure that it only uses and does not pay for ownership of the entire infrastructure.

The server farm or data centers required for the cloud setup is done at low-cost locations. The entire low-cost infrastructure setup can be offered at an affordable price to enterprises and individuals remotely. It is rented and can be monitored from any location using a mobile device or a browser. This in turn reduces the overall cost for an organization, especially the ones who are starting up. Cloud computing also provides elasticity of the infrastructure, an important aspect for FinTechs and start-ups to manage unanticipated peak loads. It means that during peak load time the cloud service provider can automatically add additional hardware depending on usage and load to meet the demand on the increased user base, thus providing the desired throughput, and it can scale it back when the demand tapers down. The rental cost paid by the application owner is only for the hardware that was used at different points in time and not for the entire hardware. This makes the entire proposition promising for most start-ups, and FinTechs especially, during their promotional offer/launch. Therefore, with cloud computing the scale at which FinTech products are being adopted determines what the FinTechs spend on infrastructure and can go up and down based entirely on adoption and usage patterns.

Cloud Service Models

There are different service models that cloud service providers offer including some of the key ones explained below:

- Software as a service (SaaS)—It is also referred as an on-demand software service and is usually priced on a pay-per-use basis. In this model, the application software is available on the cloud and the user can use the same through a client software provided by the cloud provider. Therefore, the user does not have to pay for the entire software and instead pays based on the usage of software on the cloud. Since the users are accessing the software using cloud client, they do not have to install the same on their own environment. This has achieved major savings for start-ups/FinTechs.
- Platform as a service (PaaS)—In this mode, the cloud provider offers a development platform to application developers. This could include providing the relevant OS, integrated development environment (IDE), compiling and execution environment, associated databases, Web servers and associated disk storage. In some cases, they can provide a complete deployment environment with test execution capability and monitoring support for application postproduction.
- Infrastructure as a Service (IaaS)—This is primarily used to refer to the infrastructure services provided by the cloud vendors to the application owners to host their application with the desired level of security, back-up provision and other deployment-related infrastructure. This service also includes providing elastic hardware/software whenever there is a scale-up and scale-down requirement for resources. All the associated networks, storage and all relevant infrastructure management is taken care by the cloud service provider. In some of the cases, raw infrastructure is provided by the cloud vendor and the application vendor can install and run software relevant to them for their respective OS.

Cloud Deployment Models

There are different cloud deployment models that are currently practiced and the most common type of deployments are:

a. Public cloud—It is used to refer to the cloud service that is provided over a network that is open to the public. Some of the public cloud service providers are Amazon Web Services (AWS), Microsoft Azure, etc.
b. Private cloud—This is a cloud infrastructure setup that is managed for a closed group of users. It can be for a department in an organization, a subsidiary of the organization, for the organization itself or for group companies for the industrial house. The main characteristic of this type of cloud setup

is that the cloud service provider manages the infrastructure, but the infrastructure is not shared with any other customer or for purposes other than what the cloud infrastructure has been set up. The same is not available on an open network and only certain elements of the same is exposed to the outside world through a very secure channel. Also, in this kind of network, most of the hardware setup is usually done on the premises. This type of the cloud has been most widely adopted by large established organizations to ensure that most of their organization setup is within their control and only some limited characteristics of the network are exposed to the outside world.

c. Hybrid model—This is a model wherein both private and public clouds coexist within the same organization/setup, with each having a secure interface to exchange information between themselves. This is the setup that most start-ups have typically adopted. They use the public cloud for doing most of the development work that does not involve sensitive data, and use of the private cloud for the production setup that usually involves storage and management of sensitive information. Start-ups and, in particular, FinTechs use the hybrid cloud model to keep all the sensitive information on premise or in a very secured cloud environment while the online application is exposed to the open public through a public cloud setup.

The Cloud Enables FinTechs to Offer Premium Products at Affordable Prices

Increased computing capability also enabled more server capacity with less hardware size. Now cloud providers could fit more servers into a small location as compared to the large space required for server farms in the early days. Thus, the increased computing capability over a lesser space enables cloud companies to provide a high-performing setup at an affordable cost. The cloud computing, in turn now makes it possible to share the computing power across applications as well as across organizations. Consequently, the cost of managing the application from an infrastructure perspective has dropped dramatically. This helped start-ups as they could now share the IT infrastructure as against setting it up dedicated for themselves, thereby reducing the setup cost considerably. Cloud computing enabled, software tools and services to be made available on pay-per-use models. This again helped the start-ups as the hardware and software tools cost is a major component of the initial setup cost. The cloud not only transformed and brought down the initial setup costs for most FinTechs, but it also dramatically reduced the running cost as well. The running cost was again proportionate to the hardware and software capacity utilized, with the capability to immediately ramp-up and ramp-down hardware capacity.

Prior to the cloud, if a start-up launched an application or a product, it was difficult to predict the number of users that would be using the application. If the estimation was on the lower side, then it would have meant a slower response to initial users, leading to a bad customer experience, which in turn would lead most of the users away from the platform and bad publicity. In case the estimation was on the higher side, the organization would end up spending more for the infra-structure. The start-ups, before cloud computing, would most likely factor in the additional spending on infrastructure to minimize losses at a later stage, and the expense of infrastructure would either reflect in their pricing or they would show it as a cost and take a cut in the overall profits. Thus, for start-ups it was always a catch-22 situation since the increase in pricing due to a high setup cost would bring in competitive pressure from their established peers and any cut in the profit would make it difficult for them to sustain beyond a certain time.

After the introduction of the cloud, this concern of start-ups was addressed by renting the infrastructure in a pay-per-use model. Now the start-ups would have to pay only for the time their application was being used. Additionally, since the pro-cessing capability was elastic, the increased number of users meant paying for the differential load only. Cloud computing came as a boon to applications that could be accessed over the Web and had variable loads, i.e., an unpredictable increase and decrease in the number of users during different time intervals.

Cloud computing brought in another question regarding the security of appli-cations that were hosted on the cloud. Enhanced encryption coupled with improve-ment in security tools made it possible for cloud providers to offer secure computing capability with breaches being monitored, tracked and resolved, thus ensuring cus-tomer confidence regarding security and the safety of their data and information in the cloud. The cloud soon became a more industrialized offering and corporations worldwide started migrating their application and data to the cloud.

FinTechs started using cloud setup coupled with social media extensively to establish connectivity with their prospects and customers. Using mobile and online applications over the cloud they were now able to reach out to customers any-where anytime. Since a public cloud can be accessed over an open network like the Internet, the ability to host applications on the cloud and the ability to down-load the same on mobile devices enabled them to reach out to customers globally. Consequently, the overhead costs of setting up branch locations and equipping the same with representatives at multiple locations were reduced radically and in some cases, eliminated entirely. FinTechs passed on this benefit to their customers and were more price-competitive as compared to their established peers since the latter was still continually spending money and effort over building physical assets and equipping them with requisite manpower.

How FinTechs Are Leveraging the Cloud Service Providers

The large cloud players have also started building capabilities that are best-suited for financial services. The main constituent of their financial services offerings are listed below:

1. A large number of cloud players have established a dedicated partner enablement program for financial services. The program includes sharing information and implementation guides for some of the established financial product platforms. The platforms could be core banking or card products.
2. Some of the cloud players have established certifications and partnership status based on the kind and complexity of the financial services implementation. Some of these implementations could include a completely cloud-hosted digital bank.
3. These cloud players are also encouraging financial services technology partners to have a dedicated practice on the cloud and should have a certain minimum experience and expertise with the well-known solutions. The partners could be system integrators, product implementation firms or could be purely a consulting firm.
4. All these cloud players also realize that the financial services industry is a highly regulated industry, therefore, they have partnered with federal regulators to ensure the platforms are compliant.

Some of the business domains that have benefited largely by adopting the cloud in their infrastructure are mentioned below.

FinTechs on cloud platforms are helping take care of health of persons living in poverty and running other community-benefit programs. These FinTechs, with their, or a third party, cloud-based healthcare API platform are able to launch new health-care products that are affordable to the poor and bring them to scale in no time without the worry of downtime. The benefit programs that help the poor are primarily driven through promotions and charity events, and the timing to launch these programs are typically dependent upon circumstances. Therefore, the speed to market and it being available when needed drives the success of such a program, therefore, the cloud platforms through their availability and ease of configuration coupled by a faster time to market are helping these segments of FinTechs.

A large number of credit scoring companies that uses alternative methods of credit scoring, need an immense amount of data to be analyzed quickly. Additionally, since the process of on-boarding the customer involves getting back with a loan/credit eligibility, which is usually done by the field agents on the field like in a shopping mall,they would need the analysis back almost in real-time. The situation becomes much more challenging when MFIs are involved. Since they are at remote locations with very little connectivity, they cannot wait longer for servers to process the information and come back. This requirement of real-time analysis and an approval/denial of a loan/mortgage has become further challenged by the diverse data formats and sources that are available. Therefore, the systems processing this information has to be able to store huge amounts of information and additionally should have a good processing capability to analyze the information stored in the data store. Building this infrastructure in-house would lead to high start-up cost, therefore, a large number of FinTechs use cloud systems to store information and data, and they themselves analyze this information and data using their proprietary engines and offer actionable insight like an approval or denial for credit/loan. Some of these alternative credit scoring FinTechs even run their analysis application, online application and business reporting applications on the cloud. FinTechs are also using the cloud to run credit risk simulations that have helped these and other lending FinTechs to reduce the average-time-to-solution from hours to few minutes.

FinTechs specializing in financial advising and wealth management platforms are using the cloud extensively to carry out their respective business functions. A large number of these firms are also using robo-advisors. Robo-advisors work by taking financial information for a financial instrument like a mutual fund from multiple online feeds and other sources in social media feeds, and then, based on the risk profile of the customer, adjust the portfolio accordingly. Therefore, to crunch and analyze such an immense volume of information and data at a fast rate, and to translate the same into actionable insights requires huge processing throughput coupled with a large data repository to build patterns and AI algorithms on them. Therefore, setting up such an infrastructure by themselves would mean high start-up cost for the FinTechs. The costs can be brought down by using a pay-per-use model of the cloud providers. The financial advising and wealth management FinTechs have been able to bring their setup costs down by implementing the cloud in the following areas:

1. Offering financial management and planning tools to all the customers by hosting the corresponding application on a cloud infrastructure.
2. Setting up wealth management applications and mobile trading apps on the cloud and using the cloud to store customer and trading data securely. They further analyze this data to drive personalized financial advice to their customers.
3. FinTech companies specializing in social trading have their platforms on the cloud wherein the traders can discuss trading strategies and can copy one another's traders' portfolio.
4. Financial advising FinTechs that help customers aggregate all their bank and investment accounts thus enabling them to save automatically for their goals, use the cloud to host their platforms as well.

FinTechs providing wallet services, clearing house services and payment providers need to perform extensive real-time services. In fact, a large part of their business is dependent on the speed of the response for their transactions. If the transactions are not done in a timely manner, then there is a very big chance that their customers would move to a different application/site. Again, a lot of these FinTechs will have to scale-up and scale-down their infrastructure demands depending on surges in volumes from a source or a destination platform. For example, in case of a sale going on for a retailer through online or retail store channels, there will be a surge in transactions from the source (retail store or an online channel). The surge would be existent until the promotion or an event is there and then the demand for services related to the wallet, payment or clearing house would come back to normalcy. Consequently, the infrastructure would have to also scale-up to address the surge and come back to the standard load during normalcy. This would translate to high-grade infrastructure that a FinTech would need during the initial setup phase. Most FinTechs have overcome the challenges by using the cloud extensively, thus bringing down the overall setup costs and are then able to scale-up and scale-down based on the surge and normal loads. The different kind of FinTechs who have benefitted largely from the cloud are:

1. Bitcoin wallet provider companies with operations worldwide use the cloud to run its Bitcoin exchange, wallets and analytical insights.
2. Payment platform companies delivering PCI-compliant payment platforms use the cloud with all the security best practices.
3. SAAS banking platforms use the cloud for managing credit and deposit products quickly, simply and affordably.
4. FinTechs and clearing services that are doing power credit value adjustments (CVA) intraday calculations have also benefited using the cloud.
5. Large B2B firms offering clearing services to businesses also use the cloud to provide their platform services.

FinTechbanks and FIs have differentiated themselves from the legacy-established banks and FIs by providing an exemplary customer experience. Offering a differentiated customer experience required that these FinTechs move away from some of the monolithic banking platforms, since these FinTech were being setup with low initial capital, therefore for them setting up traditional core banking product and then building customizations on top of it to offer the desired customer experience was an expensive proposition. This problem to some extent was resolved by the core banking and cards platform providers upgrading their products to offer their platforms on a pay-per-use model. This has helped start-ups including the FinTech banks and FIs to use these platforms available on the cloud to reduce their overall deployment costs and at the same time give a customer a personalized yet secured experience. Some of the entities who have benefited in the entire process of bringing banks on to the cloud are:

1. Core banking and cards platform providers that are using the cloud to provide banking services and cards services worldwide.
2. Some of the new age online banks have been able to push for personalization using cloud infrastructure and are able to offer the desired products to the customer, almost in real time. In fact, using the cloud they could now provide 24/7 availability of their platforms at low cost, thus enabling them to have some of their branches open almost every day. Additionally, because of the quick response of the entire platform on the cloud, they are able to provide same day account opening and quick card printing services.

A couple of years back, the insurance world used to run with a very few products and would typically introduce a new product every 6 months. FinTechs in the insurance space, also known as InsureTech, have come up with disruptive business models, thus making them capable of launching a new product frequently, which could even mean that they launch a new product every day, provided they have requisite regulatory approvals. The on-demand insurance and pay-per-use or pay-per-mile insurance is redefining the entire insurance world. Therefore, these InsureTechs would need real-time and process-intensive calculations like actuarial calculations being done in a very short time span. This would mean that either InsureTechs deploy their own infrastructure, leading to a high setup cost, or use the infrastructure from the cloud provider on a pay-per-use basis, since the cloud model augments the new way of doing insurance including pay-per-use and pay-per-mile insurance. Therefore, a large number of FinTechs and established insurance players are using the cloud extensively, and some of them are using the same to run complex actuarial simulation models.

There are other cloud services and service providers like Salesforce which has multiple solutions deployed in the insurance and banking industry.

Cloud adoption in the financial services industry is picking up as the cloud vendors ensure that they have regulatory compliance and all the necessary security requirements. Some of the benefits the FinTechs have been able to achieve by deploying their platforms on the cloud are as follows:

1. Reduced infrastructure cost
2. Reduced time to market
3. Less manpower for maintenance
4. On-demand Scaling-up and scaling-down of the infrastructure.

FinTechs Using Web2.0 and Responsive Web Design (RWD) for Rapid Launches

The introduction of the mainframe by IBM can be termed as one of the first technology disruptions in the information technology industry. The introduction of desktop computers and Macintosh in subsequent decades by Microsoft and Apple respectively, changed the computing landscape entirely. Prior to the introduction of the Internet, the applications that were being developed for desktop computers were client server applications. Almost a decade later, the Internet further transformed the computing world by letting the user access information, data and content anytime, anywhere. The applications referred to as websites were now residing on the server and once the user typed in the requisite URL they would render onto the browser. The technology was still restrictive as the content that got published was primarily driven by the owner of the website rather than by the consumer of the website. Soon enough, a new set of technologies evolved which would enable even the consumers to create and publish content. This change of consumers being able to create and publish content has been quite a big disruption in the way people shared content with their contact groups. Now organizations were able to offer customers the capability to create content and share it with their contacts, friends and family. This capability was one of the key reasons to make platforms like WhatsApp, Instagram and Facebook hugely successful. Organizations/start-ups leveraged the capability to develop P2P interaction capability between their customers as a specified group or for broadcasting messages to everybody.

With new technology platforms, it is now possible to build websites which would adjust themselves based on the screen size available on the device. The architecture and design principles for building such websites is collectively called responsive Web design (RWD). A website developed using these principles is called a responsive website. As explained earlier, in the last couple of decades smartphone proliferation globally has achieved exponential growth. In order to cater to customer needs to viewing content in different resolutions, smartphone manufacturers started offering phone models with different screen sizes. Some of the consumers wanted a bigger screen so that they could use it more like a handy computer while others wanted to use it like a gaming device. The fragmentation was much deeper in the android like OS, as it was open source and device manufacturers were free to define the screen sizes for respective mobile devices. Consequently, the browser sizes in most of the devices were different, and as a result, a website which was made specifically for desktop, would not correctly render on these devices with smaller screen sizes.

A solution was to create separate applications for each and every form factor (screen size). This was an expensive proposition, as any organization planning to reach out to these mobile consumers would have had to develop multiple versions of the same application so that it renders correctly across multiple different screen sizes. This was a very big challenge for FinTechs, as such an approach would mean a large initial investment. Investors are typically reluctant to invest heavily in a start-up that is yet to build its product and launch the same, therefore, it would have been a show stopper for start-ups. Since without the initial investments, they would not be able to launch their product, and without the product being launched, they would not get any investors. Responsive Web design came to the rescue of FinTechs as they were now able to develop and launch online application as responsive websites that could run across multiple screen sizes, leading to the reduction in the development and maintenance cost for most of the FinTechs.

RWD Making Cross-Channel Application a Reality for FinTechs

RWD, originally introduced by Ethan Marcotte, helps a website change its layout based on the size and capabilities of the browser within that device. With the adoption of mobile devices with a different size and shape, the framework has become quite popular. It has three key elements, namely media queries, fluid grid and flexible images.

Media Queries

Media queries help the screens to be designed for different layouts based on the screen sizes. Media queries are used to configure the style, font and other properties of visual elements of a single code base to specific screen sizes. The properties for visual elements, like the text box, the drop-downs, etc. is usually managed using style sheets. The media queries, as a first step, identify the screen size that the visual elements need to be adjusted into. As a second step, the elements/variables within the style sheet take the respective values of the defined screen size. Consequently, the visual elements are rendered as the resized application, fitting to the device-specific browser.

Fluid Grid

A typical HTML defines different visual elements like the text box, dropdown, etc. as fixed-width elements, and they are positioned relative to a desktop screen. In a fluid grid-based design, all the components are defined relative to the base element. The size of the elements and location parameters are not specified in absolute terms, but in percentage terms, again relative to the base element. Therefore, when the screen sizes change as per device, all the elements redefine their relative positioning to fit into the desired screen size.

Flexible Images

Images are rendered in their native size and it scales according to any change in the screen size. To ensure images do not get chopped off, the maximum image width is set to 100% of the container. If the screen size reduces, the image size is reduced accordingly through the style sheet code directly.

There are multiple technical frameworks, open-source and commercial software that help build a responsive website in a structured manner and in short time. Some of the most commonly used frameworks are:

1. Bootstrap is the most popular front-end framework created by Twitter developers to build responsive, mobile-first websites. It is an open toolkit for developing websites using HTML, CSS, and JavaScript (JS). It is equipped with 12-column grid system that helps a website adjust itself to a suitable screen resolution. It is supported by almost all the browsers such as IE, Chrome, Opera, Firefox and Safari. It has prebuilt components and powerful jQuery plug-ins.

2. Sematic UI is the latest framework which uses natural language to code and is simpler to interpret and implement.
3. Material UI implements Google's material design specifications and is built on a LESS preprocessor. It uses multiple in-built components.
4. Pure was created by the Yahoo development team and comes with a lightweight CSS module. It is extremely lightweight and therefore is preferred by developers for mobile development.
5. Foundation is a highly advanced and complex framework used on sites like Facebook, eBay and Mozilla. It also has lightweight sections for mobile devices that can be downloaded on-demand. It runs on a Sass preprocessor.
6. UIKit a front-end framework that uses both a Sass and Less preprocessor. It has navigation components, HTML forms and other components.

Besides these frameworks, there are multiple preprocessors that help make the entire CSS code maintainable. The three key preprocessors are SASS, LESS and Stylus. With the responsive websites using a plain style sheet would make the entire website complex, especially while delivering multiple complex business functions like retail banking, corporate banking, wealth management solutions, etc. Therefore, using these preprocessors as part of the website development process is becoming very common. The preprocessor allows some of the key features like:

a. Capability to declare stylesheet elements as named variables, thus enabling ease of use and readability.
b. Providing a visual hierarchy for different subelements of a complex style definition.
c. Capability to select and compile the code specific to the browser where the website is rendering.
d. Availability of different color-related functions that help to change color directly through function operations.
e. Enabling multiple operations like If/else, iterators, etc.

FinTechs Launching New Products at an Unmatched Pace Using New Age JS (Javascript) Technologies

Advancement in frameworks to manage the CSS and style sheets has been complemented by the evolution of multiple JS frameworks. These JS frameworks are making the JS code manageable and maintainable for large and complex websites. JS is now being used both for client and server sides as well. JS has changed the go-to market time for websites, which earlier used to take months to develop and now can be developed in a weeks' time. Since most JS frameworks are open-source and free, they have helped FinTechs develop websites with a low cost and faster time to market. Some of the key JS frameworks are discussed below:

1. Angular JS is referred to as a model-view-controller (MVC) framework for the JS development and is being leveraged by developers to build manageable and maintainable websites. It offers some of the best design and development capabilities including component design capability, inclusion of typescript for detecting coding errors and an automated unit test script generation capability. Therefore, Angular JS can be considered as a complete framework for faster development and deployment. It has also a high code readability and is the most widely used JS framework for single page application development.
2. React.js is often considered as a library than as a framework. It has been used extensively for the development of Facebook and Instagram. There are multiple frameworks like Redux that uses React libraries to provide a complete end-to-end framework. React also has libraries for native development and is fast becoming a popular framework to be adopted. Since it is a library rather than an elaborate framework, it is a lightweight option to other complete frameworks.
3. Ember.js is commonly used for feature-rich complex Web applications and is used by websites like LinkedIn, Netflix and others. It uses a fastboot.js module to provide a fast yet complex user interface (UI) and is also considered as a MVC framework.
4. Vue.js is a framework that is often considered as a best overlap of Ember, React and Angular. It is considered as one of the fastest JS frameworks and considered to be a better solution for cross-platform development.
5. Meteor.js is a full-stack framework that comes with features for back-end and front-end development and includes managing a database. Since it is a full-stack development platform, it enables a faster time to market. Additionally, since it is an integrated framework across the stack, the performance of the platform is also quite fast. Organizations like Ikea are using this platform.

Since most of the FinTech companies were starting from scratch, they could easily embrace this new way of developing a website with multitier architecture. It also gave them a capability to make their users owners of their content as well. Word-of-mouth spread, and soon customers started embracing these websites. It was now easy for friends and families to notice an individual registering a "like" on Facebook for an organization, an offer or a promotional website, rather than spending millions on advertisements. In contrast to the same, the large traditional peers were carrying the legacy of creating massive monolithic tightly coupled applications. Some of it was clearly segregated as presentations and business logic, but in majority of cases, different architectural layers were all mixed-up. Therefore upgrading to the new responsive design became a herculean task for most of the established financial services industries.

Majority of the websites built using these new technologies have their presentations primarily being rendered on the customer browser, depending on the browser configuration. One of the primary requirements of responsive design is that the presentation logic should be separated from the business logic.

FinTechs and established traditional firms were quick to realize the impact of the change that responsive design would cause and they soon started on building their own platforms that could make their applications responsive on multiple screen sizes. While the established firms were migrating their existing financial applications, FinTechs were building the same from scratch. Thus, FinTechs were able to build and launch their platforms quickly, whereas it would typically take years for established peers to migrate their existing platforms to the new technologies. The FinTechs were therefore able to take a lead in the market and provide exemplary customer experience than what would be provided by websites from traditional institutions. This automatically started creating a perception that traditional institutions were legacies and FinTechs were new. One thing led to another and the perception that FinTechs provided a better customer experience started making them popular and as a result, there was greater adoption.

FinTechs, by offering a new way of interacting with customers using new RWD and Web 2.0 technologies, disrupted the earlier tech-savvy business of traditional companies. Moreover, since FinTechs were more experimental in nature, they started bringing in new elements of customer experience on their websites like gamification, video chats, community discussions, etc. In contrast, the traditional companies were reluctant to experiment, fearing a negative impact on their brand if perceived negatively by their customers.

API-fication

A large number of the FinTechs started their organization with a single innovative business idea. In order to make the business idea operational, they would have had to collaborate with multiple parties. An example of the same would be a FinTech firm that aggregates account information and does personal financial management. The company has its own unique set of functionalities, but for activities like account aggregation, etc., it has to collaborate with multiple banks and payment providers. Collaborating across multiple entities would consume lot of time and energy for an already manpower-crunched FinTech. Additionally, the collaborating entities could end up spending time and energy resolving legal challenges like IP, content ownership, etc., within themselves and with the outside world as well. The extent of collaboration was often limited by the technical capability and willingness of the participating entities to share the necessary interfaces for integration. There could also be issues in terms of a handshake between the consuming app and the interface as more often than not it would end up stalling or crashing the consuming application. This was applicable to most of the online applications as well.

In the last decade and after the financial crisis of 2008, a large number of FinTechs and established financial firms started publishing their own applications and mobile apps which could do payments, lending, wealth management, etc. Initially there were very few applications, but over time, a large number of applications were delivering identical functionality. It soon became a challenge for customers to choose the right app to address his/her needs in totality as individual apps would offer necessary as well as unnecessary functionality. Some of these apps, though, were offering identical functionalities but they were also offering a set of unique functionalities or differentiators as well. An example of the same would be, a large number of wallet apps in the App Stores that are offering almost identical functionalities, yet quite a number of them have their own differentiators as well.

Additionally, there are applications from technology firms that act as enabler applications like an application providing insights into a customer purchasing pattern, or an application that helps on-board a new customer, etc. In the traditional setup, these applications would need to undertake custom integration of services from enabler applications. An example would be all the applications having payment-related transactions would be required to do custom integration of the services offered by the payment providers into their application. Therefore, a large number of applications would end up doing custom integration with a payment interface from a specific payment provider into their application. Consequently, this necessitated the dependence on interface provider for every integration and subsequent upgrades. Additionally, the interface provider could charge different license/royalty fees for each of the integrations. This soon started becoming a huge integration and maintenance activity for both the collaborating entities. This also resulted into a disconnected customer experience as the same was dependent on the level of support for integration services provided by the interface owner.

Moreover, in the last decade, FinTechs with their innovative ideas were disrupting the conventional ways of doing business. Large monolithic firms, because of their large IT footprint, chose to collaborate with FinTechs for a faster go-to-market. This was much easier said than done as there were multiple differences in their ways of working, their infrastructure setup and their liability/branding concerns. Therefore, even though large FIs decided to collaborate with FinTechs, both the entities soon discovered that the actual integration was much more challenging, and in most cases, the same was not even feasible.

Consequently, one of the most viable options that would work for all the collaborating parties would be to share functionality, data, and even the business logic as well as using a single common interface. The sharing was possible either by embedding the code inside the consuming application or by sharing the functionality through web services. The emergence of the cloud as a technology acted as a catalyst to the entire services-sharing capability. The companies could now expose their functionalities using web services over a cloud. Though the solution of exposing functionality using web services existing prior to the introduction of cloud technology, it was more usually achieved through point-to-point integration, and in most cases, the web services were built specific for a particular integration and were not reusable. Using cloud technology and associated infrastructure, a company could now make their functionality available as a common and reusable interface in the public domain using a specific set of protocols. This exposing of business functionality over the cloud was termed as API-fication of the application/business. Therefore, now all the applications intending to consume the services available as standard APIs could do so by calling the same set of interfaces available in public domain, and be charged on a pay-per-use basis.

FinTechs Monetizing Their Platforms through API-fication

The FinTechs and established financial firms latched onto the potential of monetizing such a technology possibility, though a large number of them were initially apprehensive regarding the security of the information and data moving through APIs. A combination of https and tokenization helped most of the organizations to tackle the security concerns. Consequently, a large number of the companies started exposing their core business functions as micro-services and APIs. Since the sharing was now being done on the basis of an online contract between the interfacing parties, viz., a provider of API and consumer of API, it was possible to charge the consumer on a pay-per-use basis rather than on a subscription model. Additionally, API providers were able to track the usage of the respective APIs, leading to a further evolution of the pay-per-use model to offer premium/discount based on usage trends. Amazon Web Services, Facebook, Google, Twitter and many other companies now have their functionality available as APIs in the cloud. As of today, there are more than 10,000+ APIs available from various providers. Some of the ways in which APIs have helped FinTechs disrupt the financial world include:

1. Access to data and information from multiple sources facilitating real-time integration to data, information and business logic from multiple sources including social media, news feeds, curated content in public domain, etc., thus enabling FinTechs to aggregate, assimilate and analyze this data to provide an all-informed customer assistance. Using this capability of getting the information and data from multiple data sources in real time using APIs has enabled FinTechs to do customer onboarding faster than traditional firms, as well as provide a personalized customer experience based on the analysis of information received from different data and information sources including social media.

   FinTechs are now able to offer personalized customer experience using API-fication since applications can now share data and information about a customer after complying with regulations and getting consent from the customer. Having an entirely personalized and context-aware solution has resulted in customer delight leading to promotion through word-of-mouth. An example of the same would be that an individual would be more loyal to a restaurant chain and an airline that he/she is a member of, if his/her mobile application prompts him/her to use airline miles to pay the bill at the member restaurant chain. This is possible only if both the restaurant chain and the airline shares data and services for the customer through API-fication.

2. Enabling selling across multiple channels—FinTechs, because of their limited funding, are able to spend a small amount on the traditional channels for promoting their offering as compared to their established peers, therefore limiting their reach to a wider group of customers. Exposing their functionality as APIs and partnerships with established businesses have enabled them to reach out to a larger audience and also explore channels other than being available online only. An example would be FinTech platforms being made available through kiosks and touch panels at retail stores, train stations, etc. In this case, FinTechs would have partnered with kiosk and touch panel media companies and as well exposed the APIs of their functionality like onboarding to the media company owning the kiosks.

3. Transforming customer journeys—Initially the customer journeys were more reflective of the services that the organization was able to offer. All the other services from partners and third parties were usually offered through a portlet, a separate widget or through a link to an entirely different website. Since it was not contained within the parent organization's technology setup there was no guarantee that the same would work always. All these additional services were referred to as value-added services.

The ability to consume and share information, data and functionality through APIs in real-time enabled most of the FinTechs to provide transformational user journeys to their customers. An example of the same would be enabling customers to redeem loyalty points on partner e-commerce websites seamlessly using APIs made available by the e-commerce website.

Powered by PSD2, FinTechs Have an Exciting Future

PSD2, a payment service directive designed by the European Union countries is expected to revolutionize the payment industry. The compliance for the same would mean that all the financial enterprises would have to make the requisite payment-related functionality and data available as APIs, to be used by third party. The FIs could charge a reasonable fee for providing access to the relevant data and functionality. An example of how this could manifest itself is an individual making a purchase online can ask the merchant to use his/her bank information to make the payments directly instead of going through a specified payment provider or using a wallet service. This could mean an end to the monopolistic kind of control that most of the traditional FIs would have commanded over their customer data. The fees in the entire process are expected to be transparent once PSD2 comes into effect. As part of PSD2 specifications, it introduces two new players into the financial landscape, account information service providers (AISP) and payment information service providers (PISP).

AISP

The account information service providers have access to balance and transaction data for a customer from banks, card companies and payment providers. Thus, AISPs can aggregate information from multiple accounts that the customer may be holding with different banks to provide a global view of the balances and transactions across all the accounts. The AISPs using this information can also provide value-added analysis of the information aggregated like spending patterns, need analysis, promotional offers, etc.

PISP

Payment information service providers are the service providers initiating a payment on behalf of the user. Services like bill payments, fund transfer, etc. could be offered by such service providers.

It is expected that traditional FIs like banks and credit card companies would not only have to incur expenses and spend effort and time providing these interfaces, but they would also lose revenues in terms of fees charged to retailers for transactions. As of now, the retailers can directly complete a transaction with the help of API services. PSD2 is being brought into implementation with an aim to unify the European Union markets and once successful, it is perceived that the same can expand globally. It is expected that the unified approach would enable the customers to transact cross-border easily, thus increasing sales and profits for the most efficient organizations. This would also help organizations to operate cross-country with similar financial regulations.

One of the biggest barriers for most of the nonbank FinTech companies to start in financing business, especially the functionality linked to banking and investment, was the requirement to have a license from the government, central banks or regulatory authorities for conducting banking/investment business. Therefore these firms would be eligible to ask for a license from authorities only when they had adequate capital available and when they were in a position to comply with regulatory and financial requirements. Thus, any start-up firm will need to have a large seed capital to start a bank and would require large investments in infrastructure and compliance. The established banks and FIs have been using this as a barrier to restrict entry of start-ups and thus monopolizing the customer information and data. Despite this, some of the start-ups were still able to strike tie-ups and partnerships with banks to get customer information and data, but the same was made available by these banks and FIs for exorbitant fees, resulting in making the overall offering from the start-ups expensive.

The PSD2 regulation is now making it mandatory for banks in Europe to comply with the regulations and therefore is helping start-ups in breaking these barriers,, thus fueling innovation in providing alternative business models for banking, investing and insurance. With banking information regarding a customer now available on-demand, the customers would now be able to switch banks or financing companies that have the best differentiator, the differentiating factor could be the best interest rates being charged on loans or an extended credit period, etc. This, therefore, could result in a greater competition among FIs like leading to a possible interest rate war between them in order to get a larger market share. This could further lead to making the FIs offer the most optimum competitive pricing. Consequently, it is expected that PSD2 will increase competition between FIs as well as nonbank institutions. Also, consequent to PSD2 implementations the FIs, be it a FinTech or an established bank/FI, that will be able to do more value-added partnerships with other FinTechs will start becoming a preferred choice for the customer. This could further lead to the trend of large banks lining up for multiple successful start-ups/FinTechs to get them to use their APIs rather than FinTechs and start-ups lining up in front of banks to get their partnerships.

PSD2 or no PSD2, FIs worldwide are realizing the importance of API and the associated economy. It is predicted that APIs would lead to elimination of a lot of duplication of services that exists currently, and the organizations providing the best services would have integration requirements and automatically become the most used service or API platform. One of the critical factors that would determine API success for an organization would be the response speed and the data integrity from API. These would probably be the most critical factors in determining the overall customer experience. As explained in earlier sections even the nonfinance companies are already offering their services through API-fication and there are FinTechs dealing with financial products have also opened their APIs. APIs are expected to provide tech savvy consumers with financial service offerings that are faster, less formal, more personalized, easily accessible and cheap.

FinTechs Enabling Payment Integration Leveraging API-fication

Some of the large payment providers and wallet services have exposed their payment APIs for their partners and customers to use them. These APIs would be typically used after a user has completed his/her shopping on an e-commerce site and wants to pay using these payment providers or wallet services. These APIs are a great example of how API-fication can ease integration between collaborating partners. Using these APIs, any e-commerce or any financial transaction site could easily integrate payments or wallet-related functionalities. One of the key features of these APIs is that they work in the background while retaining the user interface/user experience (UI/UX) of the parent application. The entire transaction is authorized in real-time. These APIs have a complete toolkit that helps the integration of the APIs to the corresponding underlying core processing application. They are secured because all the API transactions use API-specific certificates and are transmitted using Secure Sockets Layer (SSL), a standard for all secure Internet-based transactions. A merchant, when making a payment API call, typically provides a user ID, password, API certificate, and the following information: (1) billing information, (2) item information, (3) transaction information, (4) credit card information and (5) security-related information. The payment provider processes the transaction in real-time and sends back the following: (1) transaction status (success/failure), (2) error logs and (3) AVS and CVV2 response. The same has to be used in conjunction with a checkout. These payment providers are also enabling P2P transactions and some of the payment providers have integrated "Siri," thus enabling users to send money using a voice command. These APIs by some of the platform providers, have been extended to providing mass payments, invoicing, etc.

Some of the FinTech firms that enable P2P payments have provided Automated Clearing House (ACH) payment capability as APIs from their platform for any start-up/established firm to integrate ACH payment functionality into their app/application. ACH is an electronic network that allows banks and their customers to send funds to each other. It represents all the payments made through banking accounts and does not include credit card payments. There are separate clearing houses for credit card payments. A transaction once initiated remains in a pending ACH transfer state until both the originating and receiving FIs have confirmed the availability of funds and transaction confirmation respectively. Typically, automated salary deposits, bill payments, etc. are handled through ACH payments.

The infrastructure required to manage the data and multiple business scenarios for a clearing house require very heavy and high-performance infrastructure, supported by a very capable team, ready to work 24/7. Additionally, issues with regulatory and security compliance also has to be dealt with. A FinTech firm planning to build ACH services on their own, as part of their retail banking offering would need huge seed investments. The same as explained in an earlier section is fraught with high risk and has very little possibility of being a success. It is also a herculean task to convince investors for funding a start-up that acts as a clearing house. Therefore, a start-up planning to offer ACH capability as part of offering banking-related functions like payments to businesses, moving funds or providing bill payments will have to either connect to a large FI or a third party ACH payment provider. In the traditional world before API-fication, the integration would have meant development and testing of desired interfaces and time-consuming legal activities around multiple arrangements and agreements.

Thus, these APIs make integrating ACH payments into the application/app owner platform easy and seamless while managing fraud and compliance considerations. Some of the key business areas where other FinTechs and established enterprises are integrating ACH payments APIs are as follows:

1. A large number of enterprises and FinTechs are employing ACH payments to make automated payments to their suppliers, partners and franchisees.
2. Almost all the FinTechs are employing ACH payment APIs to offer instant payments through bank transfers.
3. Brick and mortar establishments like colleges, gymnasiums and sports club and using ACH Payment APIs to help students and members pay fees through bank transfers.

4. Multiple investment platforms are integrating ACH Payment APIs to help investors transfer funds for investing activities.

A large number of these platforms offer an out-of-box dashboard that helps track customer transactions by tracking the API transactions. The same could be further analyzed using analytical tools to provide key business insights, thus offering personalization for most of the customers.

There are other FinTechs that provide the technical, fraud prevention and banking infrastructure required to operate online payments. These platforms have software development kits (SDKs) for iOS and android devices that can be directly integrated with any firm's application that wishes to use these functionalities. Most successful mobile commerce and e-commerce companies use these APIs. These platforms also offer APIs that help marketplaces and other online platforms to accept money and payouts to third parties. They have building blocks to support on-demand businesses, e-commerce, crowdfunding and multiple other businesses. They have prebuilt UI components and the right set of APIs for onboarding, complex money movements, integrated financial reporting and multiple other complex functionalities including international financial transactions. These APIs can facilitate credit card processing capabilities globally, accepting payments and payouts in multiple currencies.

There are multiple other payment processing companies that have exposed payments and credit card payment processing functionalities through APIs. Some of the payment processing companies have also exposed APIs that support Bitcoin-related payments.

There are FinTech companies that specialize in accounting software, and platforms that aggregate different bank accounts of a customer and offer financial planning using the same. These software help manage finances, business and taxes for small businesses, freelancers and financial planners. They also have products that help professional accountants prepare taxes. They have extended their platforms through APIs that can be integrated into individual applications.

As mentioned in earlier sections, PSD2 will usher in an era of open banking. The regulation specifies that consumers have the right to use any third-party provider for their online banking services. Consequently, the entity hosting customer's balance and transaction-related information will have to share the same with third-party providers. This has resulted in the emergence of multiple third-party entities like:

1. AISPs that provide consumers with visibility across all their banking accounts with a single app.
2. PISPs that offer direct fund transfers for online transactions.

All the payment- and banking-related API integrations would need to secure all the information exchange using fraud-free authentication and a secure access management. According to a leading authentication API provider, about one-third of the individuals surveyed would leave their bank, if another provider was offering a more secure service. Therefore, these security platforms have multiple security, identity and access management functionality exposed as API, that could help entities in the open banking space to ensure secure access and protect the digital interaction of employees, partners and customers, thus enabling FinTech firms to provide a more secure and better service.

There are FinTechs that have launched their platforms with an intent to facilitate group payments by making it easier for groups of friends and small organizations to make payments between themselves. Some of these platforms are now going a step ahead and creating a new international payments network to rival credit and debit card companies. These platforms have created APIs that has been optimized so that the same could be integrated with less time and effort. Some of these APIs have:

1. Automatic direct debit logic that helps the automatic calculation of the next charge date and can be reused directly. An example of their implementation would be for doing trip payments between friends on an automatic calculated date every month.
2. Avoids duplicate payments through unique keys and automatic validation, resulting in lower failure rates.
3. Ensuring compliance through (a) ready-to-use emails for notifications and (b) PDF mandates prefilled with customer information.

These APIs allow a complete customizable integration and are developer friendly.

There are credit card-processing FinTechs that have multiple API solutions available for integration. They have also launched platforms for developers that help developers create next generation commerce solutions. It enables developers to have access to a diverse range of APIs for digital payments, data and security. The partners can access more than a million APIs. These platforms provide a clear, transparent and developer-friendly documentation along with their SDKs. These APIs typically perform the following applications:

- Enabling payment with any card, anywhere and with any device.
- Provide increased security to card numbers through tokenization.
- Deliver all kinds of payments to a debit account including P2P payments and remittances.
- Access trends and sales data.
- Insights to commercial real estate.
- Measure the impact of digital media campaigns.
- Allows a merchant to obtain a transaction score to detect frauds. The higher the score, the higher the likelihood is for fraud.
- Identify potential high-risk merchants.
- Identify the confidence level of user identity and can be leveraged for any further authentication if required.

- Provides bot integration with e-commerce platforms.
- Helps connect an individual's mobile app directly to a vending machine.

There are multiple other APIs that help do multiple functions like adding cash to cards, etc. In summary, these APIs cover all the functions that a credit card service integration would need. One of the most interesting things about these platforms are that they have also released APIs that help humanitarian efforts being carried out by their partners' worldwide. Some of the key functionalities these APIs address are listed below:

- Returns detail for the core business like transactions, products, programs, etc.
- Provides access to reports relating to programs.

There are other lending and banking FinTechs that have exposed APIs that allow customers to access the platform. The typical services exposed include:

- Account-related APIs that provide information like account summaries and profile-related information.
- Investment and portfolio-related services that provide the details of a customer's portfolio and enabling buy/sell transactions. Some of the FinTechs have the complete personal financial management (PFM) functionality exposed through APIs.
- Payment and transaction-related services are one of the most often used services and provide details regarding a payment or a transaction. The services also enable third-party application providers to get value-added information from these services to make further analysis for the same.
- Mortgage and loan-related services are some of the services that provide details about a customer with regards to his/her eligibility, previous loan defaults, etc. Some of the FinTechs even provide a score for creditworthiness derived through alternate credit scoring mechanisms as an API
- Credit card and card transaction-related services.

FinTechs Extending Their Wealth Management Platforms

Xignite, a company that started as a wealth management platform, soon created their own sets of APIs to access market data and they currently have 50 Web services, offer more than 1,000 APIs, serve more than 1 trillion API calls annually and count 1,000 innovative companies as their clients. They have a large number of leading FinTech disruptors as their clients namely Betterment, FutureAdvisor, Motif Investing, Personal Capital, Robinhood, SoFi, StockTwits, Wealthfront and Yodlee. They use AWS native cloud and have more than 1.5 trillion API requests served in 2016 with about 250 billion requests per month. They have been rated as one of the coolest brands in the banking industry. Some of the APIs provided as part of the API catalog are:

- CloudAlerts—It provides exception-based alerting for market events.
- CloudStreaming—Provides real-time financial market data to real-time applications.
- XigniteFactSetEstimates—Earnings, estimates and recommendation APIs for global companies
- XigniteGlobalCurrencies—Real-time and historical foreign currency exchange rates API.
- CloudWidgets—Stock market and forex widgets, financial charts and tickers available as plug and play.

There are many more APIs on the list that help get the desired market data and wealth management functionality integrated into the parent application (Source: http://www.xignite.com).

There are other firms that provide trading capabilities on their platform with transparent pricing and low fees and have exposed the platform capabilities as APIs for other partners to integrate. With these platforms available as APIs, advisors and developers can launch their trading platforms and offer - trading, market data and brokerage instantly, without spending time and effort to build a new trading and brokerage platform. There are multiple FinTechs and established organizations who have already joined these platforms. Some of the functionalities addressed by these APIs are:

1. Fetch balances, positions, activity and orders using a user or account number.
2. Watchlists help users keep track of their interests.
3. Get live updates to market and order data in real-time.
4. Execute simple and complex trading orders.
5. Get real-time equities and option quotes, chains, expirations, strikes and tick-based time and sales.
6. Historical tick data for multiple days and long-term historical data spanning as far back as possible.

There are yet other FinTech firms that have enabled trading APIs to developers and advisors alike for integration, which was earlier restricted to only established financial firms. The main goal of APIs is to let the partners focus on providing the experience and these firms can provide the ability to view brokerage accounts, portfolio information, see real-time tradable quotes and execute orders across multiple brokerages in several asset classes. These platforms take care of regulatory due diligence, system infrastructure maintenance and other integration aspects while helping partners integrate their APIs. A large number of these APIs use OAuth2 for authentication users. All API-enabled communication is carried out using https and typically the servers are located at top secured data centers. Some of these platforms have multiple brokerages added to their platforms from across the globe, therefore these platforms are now offering a one global multi-asset trading platform for foreign exchange, stock commodities and indices. Some of the APIs offered by these platforms include, authentication and authorization APIs, real-time bid/ask quotes APIs, account summary and portfolio management APIs, buy/sell and position management APIs, market, limit and stop orders APIs, etc.

Some of the other FinTechs, though do not have APIs available as a public API, but they have extended their platform to other third parties and the same can be easily integrated into other trading platforms. They have integrated their platforms with other trading firms. These partners can have the FinTech firms' accounts directly trade in their respective products and provide a free or chargeable stock trading platform to the customers from the trading partners. Also, some of these platforms use their APIs or third-party APIs to make the overall onboarding process easy.

FinTechs Leveraging API-fication to Offer Proprietary Platforms

There are currency exchange FinTechs that have exposed their exchange rate API for businesses to build their applications upon. Some of these platforms leverage their proprietary trading platforms and algorithms to calculate the most accurate exchange rates based on the actual forex transactions. Through their multilevel security and load-balancing servers, these platforms make the data available real-time in a secure manner. The API provides the forex data and related information and the same could be used in individual apps for currency conversion which in turn would be required for accounting and financial reporting purposes, product pricing in different geographical regions, payroll calculations, etc. These platforms offer forex data as daily averages, real-time forex rates, and granular tick-by-tick exchange rates data.

P2P micro-lending platforms have also exposed APIs to help application creators integrate P2P functionality in their application/apps. The same is typically done through some of the key functionalities exposed as APIs to developers, including:

■ The API that provides information regarding the different investment groups a lender belongs to as part of his/her portfolios.
■ Get detailed information about a lending group or different lending groups available.
■ Details of all the different funds that are actively raising loans on the platform.

A cryptocurrency-based currency exchange platform conducting transactions for multiple currencies including Bitcoin have also exposed their functionalities using APIs to integrate Bitcoin, Litecoin and Etherium payments into applications. These platforms offer APIs, client libraries and mobile SDKs that help third-party application providers to integrate cryptocurrency-related functionalities.

FinTechs using cloud communications have exposed their API for messaging, voice, video and authentication. The functionality, data and information exposed as APIs by these platforms can be summarized as (1) Voice and video capability which makes, receives and control calls from any app, and allows advance call control, (2) Send and receive global SMSs, MMSs and chat messages from any app and (3) Strengthen website log ins with two-factor authentication.

The API platforms are often named backend as a service (BaaS) or mobile backend as a service (MBaaS) and would have either the API management or API gateway solutions, and in some cases both coexist.

The API management solution in the API platform typically comprises features that enable an API provider organization to manage its API users. It would provide a dashboard and listing of all the APIs, their documentation, library repositories and an administrative portal to manage aspects like access, security permissions and policies for individuals or groups of API users. They would also enable the API provider to create a portal for the sign in of API users and manage their security credentials. Some of the key vendors providing API management services are Microsoft's Azure API Management, IBM API Connect, Adobe Coldfusion API Management Platform and Axway API Management Plus.

The API Gateway Solutions provide a wide gamut of features for REST/SOAP APIs, messaging, file transfer, security integration and mobile support. Gateways Solutions provide typical infrastructure for authentication, authorization and other identity and security services and policies. API Gateway Solutions also provide for protection services like protection from malformed request attacks, etc. Some of the key vendors providing API Gateway Solutions are Amazon API Gateway, Axway API Gateway, Google Cloud Endpoints, IBM API Connect, Oracle API Gateway and SAP Gateway.

IOT

It was in the late 1980s when the manufacturing process which were manual started getting automated. It was an inflection point for most of the manufacturing companies, since sensors and robotics started determining and controlling the manufacturing process. Therefore, the processes which were earlier done by the human workforce like bottling, packaging, etc. with the help of sensors, robotics and automation, was now being done entirely by machines. The initial sensors were bulky, had limited accuracy and would have had to be replaced often.

With a large amount of investment for research and development of sensors, the accuracy and reliability of most of the sensors increased over time. Sensors, which were restricted to manufacturing sites and heavy duty equipment, were now available in smaller sizes and affordable rates. As the sensor size reduced and its capability incremented, they started getting embedded in everyday-use appliances like washing machines, irons, etc. Some of these sensors also found their use in automobiles and moving devices. There were sensors that were also helping solve challenging issues in the medical field. Sensors were now capable of detecting blood pressure, diabetes, etc. The development of sensors in the areas of household items, medicine and mobile devices together started transforming the way business was done. The possibilities of multiple new ways of conducting business created a host of opportunities for FinTechs and start-ups. They were quick to jump on the opportunity and started becoming either the consumer of the sensors or started providing services on top of the sensors that could be used by the end-customer.

Before we delve further into this, let us try to understand what sensors mean. Sensors in this context are devices that could be electronic or manual equipment that can detect environmental changes and provide relevant signals to the host systems. In the last decade, sensors have become an omnipresent element in our daily life, like the use of sensors in starting or stopping a washing machine or detecting rain and activating the windshield wipers in a car and many other everyday activities.

During the late 20th century, sensors were mostly used in the manufacturing and engineering industry. The systems that were built using these sensors interpreted the data and information received from sensors to convert the same into action immediately. These systems would control machine responses based on the feedback received from the multiple sensors embedded in the machine. Since these systems would react to the feedback immediately, they were not capable of storing or analyzing data/information received from the sensors and to use the same to further determine patterns and behaviors. These early sensor-based systems were only acting on the interrupts provided by the underlying mechanical parts being monitored. In the early 21st century, the systems were more enhanced to store and send large amounts of information recorded from the sensors at certain defined-time frequencies. The accompanying hardware and software was also capable to store this vast amount of data and analyze the corresponding information derived from the data sets. The systems were again used mainly in the manufacturing sector and were known as supervisory control and data acquisition (SCADA) systems or manufacturing execution systems (MES). In the due course of time, the entire concept evolved, and the biggest transformation has been the capability of sensors to communicate over Wi-Fi. Additionally, owing to the sensor size, it is now possible to embed these sensors in almost every device from watches to electrical switches. Since all of these devices can communicate over Wi-Fi, a network can be formed with one Wi-Fi-enabled sensor communicating with another Wi-Fi-enabled sensor. This entire technology setup of having intelligent sensors connected over the Internet is called an Internet of things (IOT).

FinTechs Employing Intelligent Devices to Disrupt Financial Services

IOT can be defined as a network of sensors embedded in vehicles, physical devices, electronic appliances, buildings, lighting equipment, etc. that can communicate with each other in a meaningful fashion. IOT enables objects to be sensed or controlled remotely over a network, thereby extending computing capabilities to all these devices like washing machines, etc. Most of these devices would have a processor and a sensor embedded within them. Devices that only have sensors embedded in them can still communicate over the network, therefore all such devices, often referred to as dumb devices, can communicate with a parent processor. The parent processor in turn can interpret the information transmitted by these devices over the network and can control associated devices. Things in the IOT paradigm are devices that collect useful data and information from their environment which can then be analyzed further to trigger actions from the devices they are connected to.

IOT, when coupled with AI can derive patterns that can lead to predictive behavior, thus help building smart systems. An example of the same in home automation would be the capability of a bot to understand when an individual typically wants the lights to be on, and based on a derived pattern, the next time the individual enters the house, it can set the lights on for respective rooms. There is almost an infinite range of possible smart and automated solutions that can emerge out of a combination of all of these devices, high-speed data transmission capability and use of mobile devices. This new technology disruption has unleashed multiple opportunities for many technology companies.

FinTechs have been able to employ IOT to provide the next-generation customer experience. Some of the FinTech insurance companies have been able to analyze, understand and predict driver behavior using a telematics device installed in an individual's vehicle and provide recommendations for the same. Others have used smart devices to offer personalized insurance based on an individual's driving usage. There have also been FinTechs which are using drones and other devices with sensors to provide field survey options to multiple insurance companies.

Health insurance FinTech companies have also tapped into the capability of IOT devices to provide an individual's health information like blood pressure, blood glucose level, heart rate, etc. The same has been used by Telemedico companies to connect with patients remotely and providing a diagnosis based on the reports received from these devices. The devices embedded in utility/luxury accessories like watches, etc. have enabled some of the health insurance companies to monitor the fitness programs for their customers and in turn offer them discounts on their insurance policies. In some cases, these devices have been helpful in identifying chronic symptoms ahead of time before they become critical, resulting in a timely diagnosis and remediation.

In the banking and payments industry as well, IOT devices are transforming the customer experience in a big way. For instance, a large automobile manufacturer is planning to launch payment services directly from the sensors embedded in the vehicle. The vehicle will pay by itself when passing through a tollbooth using the information stored in the embedded sensors. All of this will be managed through communication between embedded sensors in the vehicle and the toll-booth and the payment gateways, thus transforming the payment experience completely.

IOT can also be used to reorder items when the stock of a particular item has gone down. There are devices that connects to replacement services that will prompt a user to reorder materials from an e-commerce store required for these devices when they are running low.

There are also smart refrigerators that can look inside and indicate the spoilage as well as help user make a shopping list based on the items that are going to expire, etc. The refrigerator is connected to a mobile and an iPad app and has multiple utilities like a calendar, etc., thus giving a holistic customer experience with help of smart sensors.

The biggest use of sensors and devices in the financial industry has also been to prevent fraud and money laundering using biometrics and geolocation capabilities of devices. The biometrics solutions include voice-based, fingerprinting and facial recognition. Geolocation capabilities help a bank identify if there are any location mismatches for a transaction being done by the customers. An example of the same would be two transactions being done at different locations across the globe in short time intervals.

Amazon Go is where an individual can walk into the store and the purchases are recorded through sensors and the customer is billed automatically on the mobile device.

IOT devices coupled with AI can define the person completely in terms of his/her behavior and even the likes and dislikes of an individual. FIs can leverage this information to provide the right set of solutions that will not only satisfy the financial requirement of the customer, but will also appeal to the emotional needs and aspirations of the individual. Though IOT is at a nascent stage, it is envisaged to be the technology of the future when used along with analytics and AI. IOT devices can also help in detecting and anticipating risks in the insurance, regulatory, banking, cards and investment industry.

Data has always been important for any industry, as it provides insights into what has happened in the past. If patterns could be derived on the same, it could be predicted with a fair degree of accuracy as to what will happen in the future. Collecting data either from the entire population or from a sample and then analyzing the same for trends has been a practice that has been followed for many centuries until now. Most of the data gathering until the start of the decade was done manually and usually through data collecting agencies. But this was a slow process and also the analysis was done on a snapshot of information at a particular time. The applicability of the same was always questionable because it represented information collected at a specific moment and was not real-time. Additionally, since the data was not real-time, future predictability of data in most cases used to be doubtful. It was more important in industrial applications because they were operating on systems that required real-time information. Soon the mechanism of collecting information and predicting manually was rendered ineffective as it was taking too much time and effort.

The emergence of digital technologies in the early 21st century started transforming the way data was being collected and analyzed. With IOT sensors available and mobile devices capturing the information through embedded sensors within, it was possible that the data be streamed over a network. Thus, data gathering to a great extent started becoming real-time. An increase in the computing capability of processors, the reduction in their size and the increase in the transmission speed of telecom networks made it possible that the data be collected in real-time from multiple locations. The same could then be analyzed by computers/devices with high-processing capabilities, thereby deriving patterns that would help validate the existing transaction and predict the future of an expected set of transactions in real-time. With the data collection and analysis becoming real-time almost every application/device was enabled to transmit data and information over the network. This resulted in a vast amount of data being collected and the existing databases were not able to manage the data size.

IOT Disrupting the Way Banking, Payments and Insurance Is Done

FinTechs have built IOT platforms that are a part of banking platforms that enable people to log into their bank accounts and securely connect to a range of smart devices. These platforms have already integrated wearable devices, that based on an individual's spending limit defined in their banking account gives electric shocks (minor). An example of how the same would work is that the user logs into the banking app and then connects to the wearable device like a watch and thermostat. The user would then decide the spending limit for the month. Let us assume it is set to $1,000. Presuming it is nearing the end of the month and the user visits to a shop and his overall spending crosses $1,000 by $10. The first step the banking app would do is send a notification on the user's mobile device and wearable device stating that "you have overspent, please stop. If you will spend more, you could get an electric shock." If the user ignores the notification and say spends $100 more than the spending limit he/she would get an electric shock. The purpose of the same is to correct the overspending habit of the user.

Personal finance FinTechs have brought in mobile apps that use gamification and IOT to trigger saving habits among its users. Based on certain rules, it moves money from the user's saving account to a special account. The application can also integrate with different IOT devices to trigger saving habits based on certain health habits. For example, connecting to a wearable device that tracks the number of steps taken over a time period allows the user to set a rule to transfer a predefined amount based on the steps (physical movement) he/she is taking in a day.

There are other FinTechs who are building platforms that would ensure device-to-device payments processed by them meet the desired regulatory and security compliance requirements. The platform would enable payments being made by one device to the other with minimalistic human intervention. This would be applicable in the case of connecting to cars, wearables, smart home and cities wherein there would be checks and balances, and replenishment could happen based directly on behavioral analysis or preset rules, and payments could be made directly by the devices. A simple example would be an individual traveling by a train would get the cost of the ticket deducted automatically from his/her account based on the embedded sensors within the train and phone/wearable devices with the users talking to each other. These platforms take the account number from a debit/credit card and converts the same into a digital credential that can be provisioned into any type of Internet-connected device. This would therefore result in fueling at a gas station, paying at tollbooths, paying for parking, etc., automatically without any human intervention. This would change the payment experience dramatically. Biometrics would be a key element in authenticating the users before making payments from one device to another.

Big Data, Analytics and AI

In late 1990, John Mahey came up with the term "Big Data" which was representative of the complex popular data format. Big Data represents a large amount of data and information that cannot be processed by conventional database system in an acceptable time frame. The data which could be collectively called as Big Data could be in structured/unstructured data format. Big Data has also been defined through the following characteristics:

1. Volume—The volume of data usually determines if the data can be considered as Big Data. Most of the organizations are collecting data from multiple sources like social media, machine-to-machine data, etc. Since most of this data is collected at high frequency, therefore within a short time-frame a large volume of data will be collected.
2. Velocity—The speed with which the data is collected. The IOT devices, mobile devices and multiple other sensors are generating multiple terabytes of data in hours.
3. Variety—The data being generated by most of the devices, sensors, etc. would come in multiple formats like text documents, videos, etc.
4. Variability—The datasets that come in are of different types and from multiple sources. It would be difficult for conventional data systems to handle the multiple data formats at the same time.
5. Veracity—The data that comes in would be of different qualities. Some of the data received could be meaningful and other data could be noise.

The data having the above-mentioned characteristics is complex enough, therefore, the same will need to be processed with advance tools to analyze the patterns and delivering conclusions in real-time. There are multiple systems that have been developed to handle the scale, speed, variety, etc. of Big Data. Some of the widely known systems are provided by the Teradata Corporation, Google, LexisNexis and names of respective systems such as DBC 1012 Systems, HPCC and MapReduce.

Big Data has helped multiple initiatives worldwide to analyze data and associated information that was not possible earlier. It has helped governments, scientists and medical professionals to collect data from multiple complex data sources. Some of the initiatives where Big Data has been used include:

- To understand the common man's reaction to government initiatives.
- Analyze data for weather variations and predictions.
- Decoding the human genome.
- Analyze celestial object behaviors.

The vast amount of data that is generated can be analyzed in totality or in samples depending on the goal and objective of the analysis. Based on the objective of the analysis required, only relevant datasets could be observed instead of the entire data, e.g., to analyze which product is popular in the market, a sample could suffice. But to understand a person's behavior, a large dataset may be required.

FinTechs Redefining Credit Scoring Using Big Data, AI and Analytics

This capability of capturing large amounts of data from multiple sources and then analyzing them to understand patterns and predict or derive conclusions is being used by FinTechs to provide innovative and personalized solutions to the end-consumers. One of the most successful implementations of Big Data and predictive analytics has been in the P2P lending domain institutions. The established financial firms before lending would determine the creditworthiness of an individual based on his/her credit score calculated by a credit bureau. The credit score would be derived after applying certain rules and weightages to the limited information being shared and/or collected from various other FIs, where the customer would have done credit transactions in the past. Established FIs, to ensure compliance to regulatory requirements, rely on the credit scores provided by credit bureaus to classify their loan portfolios into different risk levels. The concept of determining the creditworthiness of an individual based on his/her credit scores resulted in lending to only those people who were repaying their debt/credit in time, who were financially literate and managed their finances well in the formal banking and cards system. This methodology, though structured, was eliminating a large population of first-time borrowers, individuals who had the capability to repay but were not registered in the financial system because of multiple other issues like having immigrated recently or they were unbanked.

FinTechs, in order to grab the opportunity of lending to this vast majority of credit-worthy people with not a good credit score, started using Big Data, analytics and AI to ascertain creditworthiness of borrowers using data collected from various sources like social media, bill payment providers, etc. FinTechs are using the data/information from various sources using Big Data and analytics to understand the patterns of defaults and then predict if the next borrower has the repaying capability. Another use of FinTechs using Big Data and analytics has been to identify driver behaviors using telematics information, photos and videos collected while driving. Big Data has also been used by technology firms in the insurance industry to collect and analyze video streams of an accident or natural disaster to assess the extent of damage to property, auto and human life.

The same is also useful in predicting the next possible purchase of a customer by analyzing their buying patterns and pushing offers and coupons accordingly. Some of the FinTech firms have been able to use Big Data and analytics to determine spending patterns and then to assist the customer in financial planning, thereby reducing financial liability, improving their credit score and assisting the customers in making prudent investment decisions. Some of the other uses where Big Data, analytics and AI has been used by FinTechs are in the field of wealth management, to provide personalized investment recommendations to the customers based on the analysis of past trading patterns and, accordingly, building an actual and recommended risk profile for the customer. Big Data and analytics have also been used by FinTechs and investors alike to understand the acceptability of an innovative idea and chances of it becoming a success. FinTechs and established firms are using these technologies to identify possible fraud transactions in banking systems, thereby flashing a timely alert to the customer and the bank. One of key areas where FinTechs are using Big Data is to meet regulatory compliance-related requirements by providing audit information from both structured and unstructured data sources, thus avoiding penalties and litigations.

Big Data and analytics are now being extensively used along with AI and machine learning to understand the patterns and then predict different conclusions using the same. Traditional business intelligence (BI) tools are primarily used for presenting dashboards and reports. These tools help business users understand performance and trends in detail. BI reports provide a snapshot of past performance across multiple measures. AI and machine learning is applied on the past data collected to forecast behavior and results, thereby driving future actions. The accuracy and reliability of an AI engine is dependent upon the sample size used to arrive at trends and conclusions. After the introduction of Big Data, the sample size and the variety of data has become extensive. Using high-computing capability available with new age systems, it is now possible to arrive at a trend quickly and then execute an action based on the same. In some cases, the entire process can be executed in real-time. This analysis leading to future forecasts and actions is also referred to as predictive analytics. The same is also used to make multiple simulation to understand how a certain change in action will impact the future trends. There are different mathematical models used to understand and analyze the existing data and then forecast the future trend based on the same. Some of the models are:

1. Predictive models—These are the models that predict how likely a customer is expected to exhibit a specific behavior. A typical example is customers with high credit scores are less likely to default on a loan than customers with a lower credit score. These models derive isolated patterns from a large dataset to arrive at different conclusions such as what a fraudulent customer behavior would be.
2. Descriptive models—These models identify multiple relationships between different entities to come out with different trends for different sets of input parameters, e.g., likelihood of banking mobile app adoption across different age groups of customers.
3. Decision models—Mostly used in simulation scenarios, takes input from multiple models and variables to predict possible outcomes based on a combination of input parameters.

The predictive analytics is done either using regression techniques or through machine-learning techniques. A regression technique involves creating a mathematical equation or a statistical series to create a model that represents the interaction between the variables identified. Some of the models that can be applied while performing predictive analytics are:

1. Linear regression model—It can be simplistically said to be predicting the response as a function of dependent variables, which when plotted on a graph appear in a straight line. The effort is to minimize residual value, i.e., the values outside the straight line function of dependent variables arrived at. The predictive power of the same is indicated by how large or less is the deviation of residual values from the model.
2. Discrete choice model—It is applied to cases where the responses are discrete and not continuous as in the case of a linear regression model. There is a specific type of these models used when the dependent variable is binary and then there is another type that is used when there are binary outcomes expected for a set of conditions. A trend is identified by considering all the outcomes which typically translates into a complex mathematical equation comprising of variables and coefficient, then by applying these outcomes the significance of each coefficient in the model is identified. The equation thus derived provides a fair predictability of a binary outcome of an event like whether a customer would purchase a product or not. In cases where there is more than one outcome, other regression models could be used.
3. Time series model—This technique is used for data collected over time that is understood to have an internal structure, such as autocorrelation, trend or

seasonal variation, that needs to be accounted for while building the predictive analytics.

4. Survival or duration analysis—It is primarily used in medical science and is a statistical model used for analyzing the expected duration of time until one or more events happen. This type of analysis only focuses on information for a time duration and includes data points that have shown a change during the duration under consideration.

In cases where there is insufficient data or wherein the data sample size is too complex to be interpreted, machine-learning techniques are applied for predicting the future state of certain input conditions. Machine-learning techniques emulate human cognition and learn from training examples to predict future outcomes. Some of the common modeling techniques used in machine learning are:

1. Neural networks—It is used when the exact nature of relationships between output and input is not known and neural networks learn the relationship between inputs and outputs through training and experience.
2. Multilayer perceptron—It consists of a layer between input and output variables whose weight is adjusted through learning to ensure desired values are being retrieved for a set of input variables.

There are multiple other models that help in predictive modeling with some of them being support vector machines, Naïve Bayes and others. All of the above models are being used by financial organizations and specifically start-ups to predict an outcome by identifying patterns of input behaviors to predict a future outcome/action for the same. These patterns are then further used to predict outcomes and accordingly drive actions on the new data/information received. Some of the examples include identifying a fraudulent customer or using machine-learning techniques to train a chabot. Some of the start-ups/FinTechs, as mentioned below, are using Big Data, analytics, AI and predictive modeling to create disruptions in traditional business models like providing an alternative credit scoring model.

FinTechs Enabling Just-in-Time Information and Analysis for Investors

AI and machine-learning FinTechs are applying analytics and machine-learning techniques to social media feeds in real-time, to identify high-impact events happening globally. The analysis is then used to provide their customers, wealth advisors and traders alerts across channels like mobile devices and online in a convenient and detailed format. The entire intent is to provide timely advice for users to initiate action on his/her portfolio immediately. They are in many cases able to push the events to their consumer before the same is published through the traditional news channels. They deliver alerts based on product launches, conferences, policy announcements, currency movements, geopolitical incidents and more such events. Most of these FinTechs use a proprietary classification system to build connections among thousands of companies, tickers, brands and subsidiaries. The customer gets only the alerts that are tailored to his/her interests.

There are other FinTechs that have built a platform that index massive amounts of alternative data including nonfinancial payment reporting data-like bills, annual reports, etc., off the Internet for professional investors. Usually investors evaluate the performance and potential of an organization before investing in it on the basis of market data and information provided by the organization in their annual reports. These FinTechs unlike traditional investors aggregate the data trails that multiple companies leave behind when they go to the Internet. They then further provide unique insights based on the aggregated data for various organizations to their customers. These customers can then use this information to make their investment decisions. They additionally aggregate multiple data inputs like the unemployment rate, household income, etc. and then correlate the potential impact of the same on individual businesses, and in some cases on their competitors business as well. The data they find through the Internet is all publicly available data. They have APIs available that corporations can subscribe to for using them in their respective applications. They offer dataset libraries from various industries which can be leveraged to analyze and correlate information.

AlphaSense, a technology company based out of New York and founded in 2008, has created a specialized search engine for financial services professionals, The search engine product applies advanced linguistic search technology to search millions of documents of primarily corporate information to provide data points of interest for an advisor/investor, thus reducing research time dramatically. While searching, legacy search tools search for exact keyword phrases one at a time. AlphaSense uses a sophisticated algorithm to expand the search while filtering out false positives. It captures synonyms for over 10,000 financial and business terms. AlphaSense aggregates all the critical content like SEC and global filings, broker research, conference call transcripts, news, press releases, trade journals, etc. Advisors/investors can upload their own content and any in-house research content they have. The entire data is uploaded after encryption into the AlphaSense data infrastructure. It has also received the best analytics product award from Waters Technology. The product can send relevant search snippets and documents through email alerts. It offers advanced tagging and relevance filtering to find the right content in no time. The product also has a tool that helps extract tables or broker reports directly to Excel, and a Web clipper that helps clip Web pages to be searched alongside other content. Some of the companies that are using AlphaSense are Microsoft, CreditSuisse, Pfizer, JP Morgan Asset Management, Parnassus Investment, Oracle and multiple other financial advisor and investment firms (Source: https://www.alpha-sense.com/).

Some FinTechs have developed platforms that use cognitive computing and machine-learning analytics capability to automate the analysis of multiple data sources. These platforms even assimilate information generated through human communication and uses the same to provide relevant alerts. The FinTechs and established financial firms use this information to ensure better customer service, derive competitive advantage, understand the underlying product requirements, etc. Law enforcement agencies and governments are also using these platforms to anticipate threats and risks to establishments, people, countries, etc. These platforms monitor all forms of cognitive communications, such as email, chat, phone calls, etc. to intelligently provide an entity-centric view. The same could be used to analyze customer demographics behavior and in some cases, can even be used to understand employee behavior as well. These platforms also automatically and semantically analyze information from any customer data source like website communications, social media, business content and multiple other sources, thus providing a new and innovative way of building KYC solutions, thus allowing organizations to build and continually update risk profiles of their customers, and consequently addressing the main goal of KYC to reveal risks associated with the customers. The platforms also help provide critical insights into an organization's customers by analyzing email, chats, phone calls and other customer data sources. These platforms also have an AI-built engine that learns how customers communicate and what they are communicating about and can then highlight opportunities to cross-sell and up-sell products as customers are transacting and communicating. Therefore, the platform grows smarter over time and learns when customers are dissatisfied or frustrated, which can be early signs of customer attrition. With the power of cognitive computing, businesses can now improve the way they service their customers, sell their products and equip their salesforce with the information that identify the needs of their clients. This in the end helps improve revenues significantly for companies and reduces the customer attrition.

FinTechs Encouraging Transparent Lending and Customer-Friendly Ways of Debt Recovery

2008 was a year when quality and performance of multiple financial derivatives took a dip and soon FinTechs sprang up in the lending business, who were taking the entire mortgage market by storm. The bull run in the mortgage market led most of these start-ups to create complex derivative products for the lenders on their platforms. These FinTechs have most of their loan portfolios emanating from P2P lending bundled into tradable securities. As a result, there emerged a need to track performance of underlying loan portfolios across multiple measures. There is also a need to ensure transparency and financial discipline in recordkeeping and reporting and providing analytics on the underlying information that can be trusted.

There are companies that offer a reporting and analytics platform that brings transparency and insight to lending markets, making them more efficient for institutional investors. They provide one source of transparent data for bonds and loans.

Their reporting and analytics platform has offered institutional investors insights into multibillion dollars of consumer, small business, real estate, auto and student loans from online lenders. These platforms integrate into customer onboarding and origination platforms, thus ensuring all data received is direct from the source. The information received is then analyzed using custom rules at both ends of the data processing and all the intermediate layers. They further conduct specific checks to ensure that all the loans on the lending platform meet the desired compliance and guideline requirements. The platforms go a step further to investigate if the loans generated are being serviced/collected in accordance with the corresponding policies.

These platforms can be used by investors and lenders for analyzing and generating reports for a particular online lender. The offerings from these platforms include:

1. Research reports that help gain an in-depth understanding into the quality of debt with online lenders.
2. Benchmarking the loan portfolio to the overall loan portfolio.
3. AI algorithms to detect anomalies and under/over performers.
4. Predict future returns and associated risks based on prepay and default conditions.
5. Analyze how adverse economic scenarios can impact marketplace-asset performance.

Since these platforms have access to extensive historical data for all major lenders, they would have more elaborate analytics-based solutions covering the desired length and breadth of services.

There are FinTech firms that are working with leading investors and loan originators to create a secondary marketplace for P2P lending. As mentioned above, P2P lending has leapfrogged into being one of the biggest disruptors in the mortgage industry. The companies that are involved in P2P lending are actively seeking investors for their capital-related requirements and also to back the secondary products created out of the lending activities. These FinTechs either by themselves or partnering with other FinTechs provide solutions for both the originators and investors to provide a consistent and transparent view of the loan books and other relevant information of the lending firms being studied/watched. Some of the features offered as part of these solutions include:

1. Multilevel quality checks on data received from originators to ensure quality and consistency.
2. Automated processes and rules-based processing to provide comparative benchmarking.
3. Continuously updating the rules with new data and information received, thus enriching the existing data.

4. Track and report performance based on data gathered for payments, recoveries and delinquencies.
5. Helping investors with the comparison to peer group data to assist with underwriting, marketing and raising new capital.
6. Capability to run stress tests and pricing analysis.
7. Reporting capabilities for analyzing, monitoring, reporting or distribution of the accumulated data.
8. Portfolio monitoring including a view of the investor's profile, credit facilities and products.

Debt recovery has been at its harshest in recent years, all the more so after the financial crisis. The debt recovery agents and companies have been harsh with anybody having payments dues, irrespective if the debtor all the while has been making regular loan repayments, but have missed on some recent payments. The experience with debt recovery continues to be scary. This in turn takes away the brand and reputation with which companies lend to consumers. In most cases, the treatment may not convert bad payers to start paying, but definitely it makes the good lenders with paying capacity to refrain from taking on debt again.

There are FinTechs that are transforming the customer experience with a debt recovery process. Based on data, analytics and machine-learning they have created products that make debt recovery a better customer experience and at the same time delivering better results than conventional debt recovery mechanisms. These platforms have a behavioral-based engine that ensures that communication with the borrower is made with a certain relevance and is customized based on the borrower's reaction. Therefore, the communication is done in such a manner that the corresponding debt is at the forefront of the borrower's mind, thereby having a greater likelihood of getting paid the first as soon as borrower has some money. Over time, the information of these data points help provide insights into the entire collection process resulting in identifying what works and what does not. This further feeds into the AI algorithm to eliminate fraud and ascertain distressed borrower situations more accurately. The focus from these platforms is debt recovery from high-yield defaulted customers through automation instead of employing a stressed collector for harassing the borrower. These FinTechs therefore employ a data-driven strategy aimed at maximizing returns in a short period of time.

Using these platforms, debt recovery organizations can enable its collection team for a better throughput equipped with machine-learning techniques. Debt collection functions have traditionally been a very unpleasant experience both for the recovery agent and the borrower. It starts with the agents following up consistently and sometimes irritatingly with the borrower and then sometimes pushing an offer the next time to help get the recovery done faster. With these platforms, a debt recovery organization can improve the overall experience using a combination of machine-learning and behavioral science, thus resulting in a better debt recovery process.

Blockchain

In 2008, when financial trust was at its lowest with the financial crisis on the horizon, Satoshi Nakamoto evolved a concept of chaining transaction blocks in a distributed manner. The same was implemented in creating the first digital currency, the Bitcoin. Since then, the concept has evolved into every possible use that can potentially be implemented using blockchain. Some of the blockchain concepts that have been implemented or being experimented with include building a nonmutable ledger for government records, creating other digital currencies besides Bitcoin and using it as a distributed ledger for cross-border transactions.

Blockchain Explained

The way blockchain works is when an individual requests a transaction and the same is broadcast to a network, the network nodes validate the transaction using predefined logic and rules. The verified transaction is then combined with other transactions to create a block. This block is then added to the existing chains of block, thus making it unique and nonmodifiable. The transaction then is deemed complete. The blockchain concept has been employed in building digital currencies because it is secure, cannot be duplicated and at the same time is distributed globally without intervention from government agencies. Though there have been multiple debates of the same being regularized by central banks and governments, nonetheless it is being adopted by some industry players as a valid currency. Some of the key aspects of blockchain are:

1. It works as a distributed ledger—The transaction in a blockchain is shared across multiple nodes and all the entities can edit the same single copy of the transaction. This feature of blockchain allows it to be used like a distributed ledger and is therefore useful in all the multiparty transactions. In most of the multiparty transactions, a lot of time is spent because only one entity edits the record, and while the entity is editing the record it locks the record for editing by any other party. Once the record is edited, the entity submits it for viewing and reviewing to all the parties and unlocks it for editing. Any party that has any issues or changes goes through the same processes. In financial transactions, this could take multiple iterations and days to arrive at a consensus between the different parties involved. This also involves keeping multiple copies of the database at individual nodes, versioning every transaction and encrypting every transaction. Thus, besides being a time-consuming process, the entire multiparty transaction also involves replicating the infrastructure and software at each of the nodes. This could also lead to a large amount of interactions between these systems for a single document or system of records.

    A solution to such scenarios was to introduce a third-party clearing house that would identify the protocols of information exchange and authorities with individual entities in the nodes, that could alter only a certain set of information in the document. Additionally, such an intermediary agency also defined rules or workflows to ensure how document flow is governed across multiple entities. Therefore, multiple entities with replicated infrastructure, system of records and software evolved over time.

In contrast, the distributed ledger is a concept which postulates that the database is shared, replicated and synchronized among the members of the network. The distributed ledger records a transaction by an entity in the network and then the same true copy is visible to all the participants for viewing and editing. The distributed ledger can also impose rules on the sections within that record that is available for individual participants to edit, and since all the entities within the network are updating the same record, any changes made are available in real-time to all the available entities.

All the participants in the distributed ledger agree on a mechanism or logic to update and approve changes on the document through a consensus mechanism. Since the record is managed by all the entities involved, the distributed ledger eliminates the requirement of having a third party or an intermediary define rules and workflow for consensus and authorization of the record in question. Also in a distributed ledger, every record has a timestamp and unique cryptographic signature, thus enabling audited trails and logging through the entire transaction history. In the financial world, multiple entities come together to execute a transaction often called a contract.

Blockchain is a concept that closely relates to the distributed ledger concept as:

- It records a transaction in public or private networks.
- All the history relating to the transaction is permanently recorded in a sequential chain of blocks.
- All the blocks are protected through cryptography and linked to each other through a hash code using the cryptography.
- All the blocks are linked in a chain from the start of the transaction to the current state.
- Each individual entity can only view/edit the blocks in the chain it is authorized to.
- Last, the entities would be accessing the single true copy of the transaction all the time until it is posted.

2. Consensus—Members in a blockchain need to agree on the validity of the transaction before it is posted on the chain. Once a transaction is posted, it cannot be modified but can be appended only. It is necessary that all the participants executing the transaction in the network need to agree to the transaction before the same is posted. The mechanism by which all these entities agree to the validity of a transaction is called consensus. There are multiple algorithms that make it possible for entities to agree on a transaction. Some of the common algorithms used are the practical Byzantine

fault tolerance algorithm (PBFT), the proof-of-work algorithm (PoW) and the proof-of-stake algorithm (PoS). This mechanism ensures that the shared ledger have the exact same copies, as any tampering to the same will have to occur across the board at the same time.

3. Cryptographic hashes—It ensures that any changes to a transaction in the chain results into a different hash being computed than the original hash. The value gets changed even if there is a minuscule change in the hash. If the origin and current hashes for the same transactions are different, then the entities can confirm that the transaction has been tampered with. A hash function is an encryption algorithm applied to input data in such a manner that the transformed output cannot be duplicated. The various algorithms that are applied in the blockchain world are SHA256 and RIPEMD.

4. Digital signatures—All transactions in a blockchain are stored digitally and the identity of the transaction is available in digital format to all the entities within the system. A transaction in a blockchain is available to all the participants of the network, and consensus ensures the valid users have made valid changes to the same before it is posted into the chain. This system, though, encourages transparency among the members of the network, but it could also lead to exposure of information that is selective in nature. One of the solutions is to encrypt the transaction using cryptographic hashes and then provide public keys to decipher the same. The solution still does not address the privacy requirement associated with a transaction. One of the mechanism's transaction owners could employ is digital signing of the document and providing a private key to individual stakeholders in the network. This will ensure that the document is opened by the right entity and the right individual in the organizations, and is viewed/edited and approved by only the responsible people authorized to do the same respectively. Thus, digital signatures ensure the prevention of fraudulent entities altering the document before it is submitted to the chain.

5. Smart contracts could be executed in a blockchain—Blockchain works as an online repository of all the transactions and takes care of the version management of transaction on its own. By the very nature of blockchain, everything in it is executed in a digital mode. The way blockchain is supposed to work is that if the relevant parties in a network agree through a consensus, then the transaction is considered as valid and is stored in a chain of transactions; but for their execution, human intervention is needed. An example would be a contract that would have a penalty clause could be entered in the blockchain database as a valid transaction, but will need human intervention time and again to get the same executed. In a smart contract, there would be conditions applied to the transaction, and as soon as the conditions are met the next set of transactions would be automatically initiated. In the example, if an individual is not able to provide deliverables in time as per the contract condition, the blockchain

would deduct the penalty automatically from owner's account. In a traditional financial transaction of a similar nature that does not involve blockchain, it would be handled through an escrow account that individuals can withdraw from only if certain conditions are met, or else the amount gets refunded to the owner. All of this would be managed through multiple human intervention steps.

Besides the above-mentioned features, there are multiple other features like auditability, exception handling, etc. that are built into a blockchain system inherently by the way it is developed. Additionally, there could be extended implementations that ensure different aspects of a unique, nonrefutable transaction is maintained and delivered through a blockchain.

FinTechs Adopting Blockchains to Bring in Security and Transparency

R3CEV is a New York City firm that leads a consortium of large number of the world's largest FIs in research and development of blockchain database usage in financial systems. The consortium's joint efforts have created an open-source distributed ledger platform called Corda that is more tuned toward the financial world as it handles complex transactions and restricts access to transaction data. Corda is now being called more of a distributed ledger, than a blockchain. Corda participants can transact without the need for central authorities creating a world of frictionless commerce.

The core concepts in the Corda model are:

- State objects, representing an agreement between two or more parties, is governed by machine-readable contract code. This code references, and is intended to implement, portions of human-readable legal prose.
- Transactions, which transition state objects through a lifecycle.
- Transaction protocols or business flow, enabling parties to coordinate actions without a central controller.

A combination of all of the above along with relevant APIs, plugins and an customer experience can be thought of as a shared ledger application. This is the core set of components a contract developer on the platform should expect to build.

Though Corda has been declared as a distributed ledger and not a blockchain platform, it still has similarities to blockchain platforms like Bitcoin and Ethereum. Some of the similar properties are immutable states, multiple input and output, the contract is a function and not a storage and code runs in a powerful virtual machine.

Source code for Corda is available for download and a complete developer portal with documents, training, source code and support information is available on their website (Source: https://www.corda.net/).

A large number of FinTechs based out of Africa are transforming the remittance industry in Africa like never before. A large pool of people from the sub-Saharan region and other African countries are living abroad and typically use the services of companies like Western Union, etc. to send money back to their country. This is also true for businesses that want to transact money from any country outside and the African/SSA countries. Besides using money transfer services, they can also transfer money using agents, who take the cash at one end and then send a message to a corresponding party at another end. The recipient would be authorized to receive the payments, and accordingly he would be paid in the local currency. The banks in these countries are scaling up their platforms to handle money transfers, but with the complexity of the platforms and the setup requirements along with the regulatory support to be built into the proposed platforms would take years, and then the same has to be adopted by locals as well. These platforms have tried to resolve this by using a Bitcoin paradigm built on blockchain. These platforms allow people to buy Bitcoin in the local currency and then it transfers the Bitcoin thus purchased to the country it has to be transferred to. In African countries, these platforms either themselves have Bitcoin exchanges or are tied up with Bitcoin exchanges that would convert them into relevant local currencies like the Kenyan shilling in Kenya. Since the entire Bitcoin concept is built independently outside of any government or FIs, the platforms are free to send and receive Bitcoin, and the same can be done faster as well. It could take from minutes to a maximum an hour to transfer money using Bitcoin, thus by employing digital currency, these exchanges aim to reduce the fees and time for money transfers against their competitors who would do the regular remittance services. These platforms also transfer money to wallets across Africa, thus enabling B2B payments across Africa.

Some of these platforms are being used by businesses as well to make payments to employees, distributors, or suppliers, and also to collect payments from African customers. This includes payment from popular mobile money services as well as delivery to an organization's national or international bank account on the same day. These platforms have become the fastest and most cost-effective mechanism to send and receive payments in Africa. Some of these platforms have been leveraged by exporters, logistics and shipping companies to make and receive cross-border payments. Owing to transparency and trust these platforms have earned in Africa, they are being widely used for doing bulk transfers and cross-border lending in African countries like Kenya, Nigeria, Uganda and Tanzania.

Diamonds are said to be the most valued gemstones, and different mythologies across the globe have attributed different levels of importance to possessing/wearing diamonds. The Western world, influenced by the Italian belief that a diamond maintained harmony between a husband and wife, typically has a diamond as the stone to be set in wedding rings. The same is considered as sacrosanct and people usually spend an enormous amount of money buying the wedding ring. Besides wedding rings, the diamond has also been used by influential families to indicate status and privileges. The diamond, being precious and important beyond the financial aspect is preserved the most by owners, but if lost, it has the biggest financial and emotional impact for the owner. According to a study almost two-thirds of fraudulent claims go undetected.

Additionally, from a thief's perspective it, is the easiest commodity to sell in the market, as there is no track record of a diamond maintained either by a government or any of the private agencies. There is no unique identification number and the ownership record is only a bill. There is also a very big possibility that the bill may either get damaged over time or the bill issuing entity may not exist anymore. Therefore, there is a need to make the entire process of buying and transacting diamonds more secure, auditable and traceable over time. There are limitations to the extent, the entire security setup can help including personnel like the police and the infrastructure like closed-circuit television (CCTV), etc. to prevent theft and fraud in the diamond industry.

Therefore, it is necessary to digitize the diamond, so that a single registry of the diamond can be maintained. The registry would help trace back all the valid and invalid transactions in the overall lifecycle of a diamond. Diamonds are usually traded cross-border and across multiple parties. Therefore, the requirement for a diamond registry was to have a single digitized version of the diamonds across multiple parties involved, and any transactions on the registry is done through a consensus of all the stakeholders, including government agencies.

Since some of these characteristics are in-built features provided by a blockchain implementation, consequently, there are platforms that are attempting to digitize the diamond and track all the transactions thereof using blockchain technology. In turn, ensuring the fraud and theft problems associated by diamond is tackled faster using a traceable system of records.

There are about 1,000,000+ diamonds digitized and uploaded on their platform, each diamond in the repository is identified uniquely using 40 data points related to each stone, along with the information about cut, color, carat and clarity of the diamond. Any diamond over 0.16 carats will also have a serial number inscribed on its girdle using the grading process. There is a possibility that a thief might want to cut or reshape the diamond, but diamond is valued because of the way it is cut and presented in particular, therefore any further cutting would result in the loss of value, and in many cases the appeal, attractiveness, dazzle, etc. Consequently, we can say if a diamond is digitized, it is fairly more secure and the transactions are traceable resulting in low theft and fraud in the industry.

Everledger is a global emerging technology enterprise focused on tracking the provenance of high-value assets including diamonds on a digital global ledger, enabling transparency along the supply chain for the mitigation of risk and fraud. It has partnerships with key industry stakeholders along the supply chain in various markets. Everledger builds this digitized repository on both public and private blockchain to achieve a hybrid technical model. This allows the best use of both the worlds, high security of public blockchain combined with permissioned controls in private blockchains. A unique set of data points is extracted from an asset to create a digital thumbprint which is then encrypted onto the blockchain permanently, with each movement along the supply chain subsequently encrypted onto the same blockchain throughout its lifetime journey. From there, a clear audit trail is provided to be used by multiple parties throughout the supply chain to verify authenticity and identify the chain of custody. This way of digitizing physical assets has proven to be immutable as well as secure and can be applied to multiple other asset types. (Source: https://www.everledger.io/).

Every year millions of people are dying and are getting displaced because of natural disasters, with children becoming orphaned. There are people in war-ravaged countries that need help. Medical aid to the needy is also required, and there is a large section of rich and middle-income people who understand the importance of donating and giving back to society. In fact, a large number of them would volunteer to do social service. The problem that stops most of the donors from giving donations is how exactly their donations are being utilized to help the cause they have donated for, since in most cases, the organizations collecting donations are not the same that are executing the welfare programs using the donations collected. Therefore, it is difficult for all the entities to track down how the funds from a donor is being exactly put to use. Some of the other parameters that usually are the cause of anxiety for donors are listed below:

1. Transparency of the funds collected—Most of the charities collect funds highlighting the cause that they would serve. The person donating never gets a statement of the audit, highlighting how his/her fund was used for which event and on what day. Also, the segregation between how much different intermediaries are charging and how much is reaching the intended person from the amount donated is neither indicated in any reports nor the donor is informed about the same.

2. Inefficiencies in operations—There are no reports provided to the user indicating if there has been efficient deployment of the funds for the intentions of which the donations are collected. Since these funds are typically deployed in difficult areas and regions, especially in the third world countries, where law and governance is not quite supportive, it requires the right management skills and governance to deploy and utilize funds in these geographies. Often the donations may end up going into the wrong hands like terrorists or corrupt public officers.

3. Fraud—There have been many instances of fraud and money laundering being conducted by nonprofit organizations wherein they have swindled large amounts of money for self-interest, usually in collusion with the authorities. Such instances also take away the faith from the agencies responsible for collecting and managing donations agencies and also the nonprofit institutions.

All the above have caused immense distrust among the donors and they would prefer a donation platform that is transparent, can be audited and gives them the freedom to choose the manner in which their money is intended to be used.

There are FinTech platforms that use blockchain to provide a fast and transparent P2P donation system. These platforms are used to connect the donors directly to those needing the donation, thus eliminating the middleman in the form of the donation-collecting agencies, nongovernmental welfare agencies, etc. These platforms manage donations through a public ledger in blockchain. The platforms are available to all the users worldwide, so natural disasters happening worldwide would be made available by the network participants, and the best information regarding the same would get updated because of the consensus mechanism within the blockchain. This in turn would ensure that the system would be transparent about the disaster, who are getting impacted by the disaster and in the end, who is receiving the money. This view will be available to all the signed-in users of the platform. The user will have an option to donate to the event he/she is viewing using a preset and an agreed algorithm for the amount to be donated, or for any other event that would have a different algorithm. These platforms are also useful for organizations managing these charities as they can show transparently on how their funds are being used. Some of these platforms offer an opportunity for donors to send donations in less than an hour all around the world. These platforms typically do not charge the donor anything if the payment mode is free. Thus, there is no commission or intermediary charges for the donor. Donors can also make payments using debit cards and the donation-accepting individual or organization has the choice to accept Bitcoin or the local currency. Some of these platforms have also incorporated a multisignature wallet for all the users or a digital signature scheme that allows a group of users to sign a single document and be used as an additional security measure in Bitcoin transactions. It drastically reduces the risk of theft and misuse of donations. All the members on the platform can donate and receive the donations as well.

Cashaa, founded in 2016, is creating a better bank, challenging legacy banking by building an app and products with input from its community of users. Their blockchain-based platform enables their community to store, save, spend, receive, borrow and get insured, with a simplified user experience in a legally compliant way. Ultimately, Cashaa aims to become a one-stop-shop for financial needs. Together with Mastercard service provider, they have built the world's first wallet that enables their users to store or transfer money to any card in the world. The sender and receiver transact in the local currency and need no awareness of cryptocurrencies or blockchain technology. Money in the Cashaa wallet will move faster and easier than cryptocurrencies, receivers will be able to get the money within 30 minutes in their local currency to any card, bank account or wallet in the world in the network.

Cashaa wallet users can store USD, GBP, EUR, INR, etc. or cryptocurrencies* (depending upon the regulation), just like a bank account. Using a Cashaa card, users can spend at shopping malls, buy things online and transfer money to anywhere in the world in a matter of minutes. Some of the features of the Cashaa wallet are instant updates, send, receive or pay with their exemplary user interfaces. Now users can have one account where they can deposit fiat or crypto* and use it as they want.

1. National currencies in the Cashaa wallet will move cheaper, faster and easier than cryptocurrencies and can be transferred to any card, bank account or wallet in the world, including cards issued by traditional banks or FinTech start-ups.
2. Payments will be settled in less than 30 minutes, across the world in 200+ countries.
3. Cashaa cards can be tokenized to store on a smartwatch, smartphone, etc. to make payments without physical cards. The receiver in the Cashaa network does not need to have a Cashaa account or a presence of Cashaa in their jurisdiction.
4. Writing all their transactions on a blockchain will make Cashaa the first FI in the world which will leverage the transparency and auditability features of blockchain technology for the masses.

Summarily, Cashaa empowers the banked and unbanked population, facilitates low-cost currency exchanges, enables participation in the global economy and develops a new outlook for this community by using open architecture. Instead of rebuilding or riding on the rails of archaic banking infrastructure, Cashaa is built to allow consumer adoption of cryptocurrencies, which let people move money as they wish at low cost and high speed, without having to understand the technical details of crypto and blockchain technology, thereby making it user-friendly, secure and affordable.

The initial version of Cashaa attracted 12,770 beta users across 141 countries transacting 2108.23486 Bitcoins. In the upcoming version, Cashaa is using the blockchain capabilities together with liquidity from the existing FIs. Due to its huge potential and capability to solve the huge existing financial problems, it became a top 20 most influential blockchain company in the world.

The following were the key learnings from the beta tests:

1. Cross-border payments can be made instant and cheaper.
2. Their system can work between countries and within the cities/states of the same country.
3. Advanced escrow features increase the protection of stakeholders from any manipulation, thus mitigating counterparty risk so that customers can use the platform with confidence.
4. The platform is upgraded with strong KYC, AML policies and compliance to make it fully compliant with regulations.
5. Their open API is used to build world-class payment solutions with higher security and compliance.

6. Operational processes optimize their user experience by involving their community in the bug bounty program through their social media and helpdesk.
7. Their unique technology always provides better forex than market with complete transparency and clarity to consumers.
8. Their platform went through several iterations to be robust, and is now capable of handling large transaction volumes.
9. All participants are making and saving money, and justified the need for a community-based company built on blockchain technology.

(Source: https://cashaa.com/)

There are other FinTechs that are providing an end-to-end open-account trade finance platform powered by distributed ledger technology. These platforms are a trade asset marketplace that helps connect lenders, bankers and now even retailers to trade assets using a distributed ledger. Since it is using a distributed ledger, it can provide security and efficiency in the origination, distribution, tracking, settlement and reconciliation of the trade assets. These platforms facilitate a supply chain network directly with the owners or other supply chains to optimize working capital for businesses and streamline the supply chain operations. These platforms are also able to extend a corporation's enterprise resource planning (ERP) and e-invoicing platform through their trade asset marketplace to provide a supply chain finance and receivables finance solutions directly to the customers.

Fintechs are using blockchain and IOT for developing innovative platforms for the sharing economy. These platforms would use blockchain to enable P2P renting, sharing and selling almost any entity or objects. Once an object has been onboarded to the platforms by the manufacturer, the owner or anybody having possession of the same, then the same would be available to be rented or on a pay-per-use basis for all the other users on the blockchain. The access will be controlled and monitored by the blockchain network and the owner/manufacturer will be able to provide/revoke access to the user by unlocking/locking the object through the network. The platforms are using the smart contract and IOT technology to bring the implementation to reality. Through these networks and objects mounted with IOT, an owner would be able to control the access and usage time for the device using simple mobile devices. The same could also be extended to a level where the devices are talking to each other automatically. Using these networks and IOT, a door to a particular facility rented only for an hour could open itself as soon as the user with access to the facility enters for the said duration. The user will open the app, find the object, will pay the rent for it and would then get the access to use the device for that particular duration. Mobile phones now become the key to all the objects. There is no need to register or log in for the service. Therefore, these FinTechs are building the next-generation platform for the sharing economy. The network is therefore envisaged to form a financial market where machines cannot only sell or rent themselves but also pay for each other's service. For example, a refrigerator could order its own repairs and pay for the same as well.

These platforms aim to address security, identity, coordination and privacy across millions of devices by making them autonomous. These platforms give connected objects an identity, the ability to receive payments, enter into complex agreements and transact without an intermediary.

Some of the FinTechs are helping financial organizations build and deploy identity management solutions using blockchain. As mentioned above, a blockchain consists of a node and any transaction comprises a chain of blocks that have been accepted by the participating node through a consensus mechanism. One of the most important elements in the blockchain is the identity of a node, and once the node has been identified flawlessly, the entire transaction becomes trustworthy. This also has become one of the key regulatory requirements for most of the FIs in the form of:

- The KYC and AML requirement mandates that financial firms should have all the relevant and necessary data of their customers.
- For most of the identity-related frauds, the onus of liability is usually put upon the bank.

These FinTechs create an identity management and verification cryptograph based on AML and KYC requirements that are based on the country-specific regulation. The same is stored virtually and a part of this information is released to the counterparty at the time of transaction to suffice the counterparty's requirement. The entire solution is built on the distributed ledger where an enterprise is a node and the platforms developed by FinTechs provide a cryptographic code for each node based on KYC and AML requirements.

Chapter 4

The State of FinTechs Globally

The start of the FinTech revolution can in some ways be attributed to the initial start-ups in North America that saw an opportunity in the financial crisis of 2008 and the subsequent collapse of big banks globally. In the following decade, the start-ups globally seized the opportunity to disrupt the conventional financial industry, that has now transformed itself into a revolution. The emergence of start-ups have not followed any particular path or trend across geographies. FinTechs have emerged in the sub-Saharan countries which do not have a very evolved financial systems as well as it is flourishing in the countries with the most developed financial systems like in Europe and the United States. Also, there is no specific correlation one can deduce with either the population or the complexity of business/technology barriers or any other issues that the FinTechs are offering as a solution. Despite there being no commonality or correlation between the reasons for emergence of FinTech, all the FinTechs have exhibited certain common characteristics like almost all the start-ups began by solving a customer experience problem and soon extended themselves to solving issues for all the other entities within the value chain by transforming the business process.

Since the financial crisis started in the United States, resulting in the emergence of the FinTech start-ups, the United States has a large share of the global FinTechs. A large number of all FinTech globally are from the United States. It is ironic that most of the financial firms in North America are centered in and around the East coast, while a large number of FinTechs have emerged from Silicon Valley, which is on the West coast. It is a wonder that the industry which once was considered to be "too big to fall" has been shaken by smaller start-ups thousands of miles apart. The primary reasons why Silicon Valley has been able to incubate the FinTechs is the availability of the venture capitalist (VC) ecosystem and availability of a technical pool. As elaborated in the previous chapters, technology disruptors like digital, artificial intelligence (AI), blockchain and the Internet of things (IOT) have been the key drivers for the FinTech revolution. These technologies have also led FinTechs to provide alternative business models to customers and businesses alike. Since most of the thought leadership for these technology disruptors originated from Silicon Valley, therefore, the ability to harness the potential of this new-found technology was ably placed with the technocrats there. Since they were not rooted in age-old processes of the financial industry, they could think afresh and bring about the desired disruption. Silicon Valley also has been the hub for most of the other technology start-ups like Microsoft, Apple, etc., and in almost all of the cases, the start-ups were funded by VCs at some stage. Therefore, there was already an ecosystem existing for start-ups in Silicon Valley who immediately saw the opportunity to start a financial revolution that was equipped with the most advanced technology. A large number of FinTechs are from Silicon Valley followed by the financial centers in New York, Atlanta and Chicago. Though most of these FinTechs have originated in Silicon Valley, they were fast enough to explore/exploit the financial services ecosystem in New York and some of the start-ups have already shifted their base to New York.

The United States has also been a very progressive country in terms of adopting new regulations and also has one of the best Internet protocol (IP) and patent protection mechanisms in the world. Consequently, FinTechs, or financial technology start-ups, are legally protected from any IP/regulation violations, therefore the team can focus on building the techno-functional disruptor and IP/regulatory-related activities could be taken up by the management teams of the VC firms. The IP/regulatory-related activities would include patent filing, legal issues, promotions, tie-ups and other such activities.

An existent framework for IP protection in addition to liberal workforce laws has enabled a small group of talented people to get in an arrangement quickly to form a financial services start-up. Additionally, the United States is one of the very few countries that fosters one of the best incubation platforms for start-ups, starting with incubation being done in:

1. Undergraduate and postgraduate institutions through research funding.
2. Accelerator programs being launched by corporates from financial and non-financial institutions (FIs).
3. Government-funded initiatives.
4. Incubation programs by VCs.

The UK and Ireland has long been the financial centers for most of the world. Most of the big institutions originated from the UK and then they spread themselves globally. As was discussed in most of the earlier section, most of the insurance companies also started from the UK. Since the UK was one of the leading countries in terms of trade and commerce, it was also impacted by the 2008 crisis, and some of the leading banks in the UK also went under. Consequently, there were layoffs from these banks resulting in some of the best technical and functional experts in the country looking for jobs. As in the case of the United States, some of these experts got together to build the next FinTech, disrupting the financial industry. Additionally, since the UK is mostly an English-speaking country with a fast rate of technology adoption,, it was possible for most of the entrepreneurs to utilize the technology disruptions to bring in innovative concepts and ways of doing business for the UK financial services industry as well.

Incidentally, some of the best technology and business schools are from the UK and Ireland. Consequently, similar to the United States, the start-ups from the UK and Ireland have also used the set-ups available in prominent educational institutions for incubating themselves. The UK's financial sector typically accounts for more than a tenth of GDP. The financial firms with headquarters in the UK have been the most active in large parts of Europe and Asia as well and employs a large number of financial and technical talent. The UK's financial system has a greater presence in Africa, Southeast Asia and the Middle East as compared to the United States. Southeast Asia has also been at the forefront of mobile technology disruption and a large part of the finance for FinTechs in these regions have also been funded by the wealthy Middle East financial industry. A large number of the talented workforce and/or funds for most of the banks in Africa, Southeast Asia and the Middle East, excluding China and India, are from the UK. They all have largely influenced the UK, and in particular London, becoming the hub of the FinTech revolution in the UK, Africa and regions of Asia. The UK being a large trading hub, has one of the largest number of cross-border transactions. Consequently, there are enough opportunities for multiple start-ups to transform the age-old cross-border transactions. Blockchain technology has helped ease out distributed transactions with cross-border transactions being one of them, therefore, a large number of blockchain start-ups specializing in cross-border transactions have emerged in the UK.

Europe, which is a hub to a large number of non-English speaking countries, is also seeing a major growth across the board for FinTech companies, and the reasons are much similar to that of the UK. Some of the reasons enabling the FinTech revolution in Europe include:

1. The presence of large global FIs providing enough market share for FinTechs to disrupt.
2. Access to a large talent pool from good educational institutions that are also acting as incubators for these start-ups.
3. Existence of complex cross-border financial services within European countries that are part of the eurozone.
4. A pool of talented technology and financial experts, some of them coming from erstwhile established banks and technology companies.
5. Easing up of regulations by governments and government support to FinTechs.

Europe traditionally has been a host to a large number of manufacturing companies building niche products and IP/innovations has been the mainstay for these companies. This has also led to a large number of European companies becoming market leaders in their field of expertise. Most of these innovations until the late 1990s were concentrated in the areas of industrial engineering innovations. Beginning in the 2000s, a large number of innovators started disrupting the financial services industry as well using information technology. The difference in FinTechs emerging out of Europe is that they have brought in the disruption in financial industries using a combination of multiple technologies linked to the industrial engineering industry like IOT, Robotics, Process Automation, etc. Additionally, the complex cross-border financial transactions across the European Union has ushered in FinTechs specializing in disruptions for cross-border transactions. The regulatory and labor laws are also different across Europe, therefore a large number of legal and regulatory-related start-ups, often referred to as regtechs, have also emerged in Europe. Europe is also bringing up regulations regarding data sharing and API-fication resulting in the emergence of FinTechs around blockchain and API-fication to address these changes.

Another continent besides the Americas and Europe that is undergoing a FinTech revolution is Africa, in particular the sub-Saharan region. There are multiple reasons why Africa has also become the testing ground for most of the FinTechs. African countries have diverse interests across different regions and their demographic segments. The wide diversification of interests is even visible within a single country in Africa. Additionally, African cities are geographical distant apart from each other and they are separated by difficult natural conditions. One of the key important events that is fueling this revolution is the adoption of mobile services throughout the continent, which is in the range of 70%–90%. Mobile services are helping connect disparate parts of the countries through digital, and since a majority of Africa is unbanked, it has further improved financial inclusion in the continent. Additionally, a large part of the population is above the age of 20, leading to a greater adoption of the new age technology and increased usage of payment and lending alternatives available through FinTechs. A large pool of young Africans have immigrated abroad and are working in most of the European and U.S. economies for a while now. Some of these young professionals are trying to bring about a significant change in their home country/town/city, leveraging FinTechs or even starting a start-up themselves. Additionally, these people have also been sending money back home through the remittance route, resulting in a large number of cross-border transactions in the form of remittances, donations targeted to help people in their home country and for multiple other reasons. Consequently, a large number of FinTechs in Africa are focused around payments, lending and cross-border transactions.

Asia, from a FinTech perspective, has been active in this decade. There are different reasons and areas of success for FinTechs specific to every country in Asia. In China, it is the rapid adoption of digital technology and an innovative customer experience from shopping to banking. In India, it has been more to drive inclusion of the unbanked and tapping the high-income baby boomers. In Southeast Asian countries, the ease of conducting business has been driving FinTechs. In the Middle East, which has been impacted by regional issues and dropping oil prices, the driving factor has been providing an enhanced experience to business and tourists, offering them an ease of doing business and an appealing customer experience. The mobile penetration and the large population of youth has been the main reason for the adoption of new age technologies driving the FinTech revolution in these countries. In most of the Asian countries, the information technology (IT) infrastructure has leapfrogged in the last decade, and governments in these countries are actively supporting and encouraging innovative start-ups. In the last couple of decades most of the Asian countries have improved their educational systems, and a large number of top engineering and management institutes are churning the talent needed for building the requisite technological and management disruption.

Australia and New Zealand has also been at the forefront of the FinTech revolution, fueled by the real estate boom and digital transformation in the banking and retail industry. The adoption of mobile technologies and availability of a large functional pool in the financial services industry has also been a key catalyst for bringing in the disruptions in a predominantly conventional financial services industry. The major innovations have been centered around the origination, lending and trading industry. Disruption through innovation is happening in other parts of world, but it is more driven by established financial firms or large legacy corporations. Therefore, the agility and sustenance of the innovations is questionable, but there is a large and concentrated focus around harnessing the new technology disruptions to provide alternative business models.

The United States: The Revolution Started from Here

The United States accounts for more than half of the world's FinTechs. The United States has about half of the world's millionaires and has the most funding being raised by FinTech companies. Since Silicon Valley was where the green shoots of the FinTech revolution started, it is worth mentioning that 7 out of 10 of the best start-up accelerators in the United States are in California. Another city on the East coast that is the next hub for the FinTech revolution is New York City where you will find technocrats and business people all suited up while working in big FIs. New York City was one of the first cities to accept Bitcoin for parking ticket payments. Most of the leading FinTech accelerator programs are all based in New York City. The United States is also a country that has the highest ratings in "ease of doing business." The country is also host to a number of the most reputed engineering and management colleges in the world.

The most important thing that triggered the FinTech revolution in the United States is the availability of a pool of talent that was equipped with domain knowledge and easy availability of finance through VCs. A large number of FinTechs have a particular combination of a domain of subject matter experts (SME) teaming with a group of technology experts, thus delivering innovative solutions in the financial domain through disruptive technologies. After the 2008 financial crisis, a large number of wealth advisors, bankers and technology experts in the financial domain lost their jobs. Some of these people were enterprising enough to start up their own businesses aided by VC funding resulting in creating a potentially disruptive business environment. Additionally, the infrastructure requirement was easily met as most of the transformative technologies for infrastructure like the cloud, Big Data, customer relationship management (CRM), etc. were built in the United States itself, and were now offering their services in a pay-per-use model at affordable prices.

A start-up in the United States would start with an entrepreneur or group of entrepreneurs getting together, possibly in a rented low-cost accommodation, to develop a product around an idea. The only expense they would have is paying for the food for everybody. This would continue for some time, ranging from 6 months to 2 years until the team launches a product that manifests the underlying idea. The entire setup could be self-funded if the promoters have adequate capital, or they could seek initial seed funding after their idea or product has reached a logical step. After this stage, the promoters can decide to keep funding themselves for the subsequent stages of growth. In most of the other cases, funding would be done by VCs until either the company goes public or it is acquired by another company. The funding in the later stages increase due to expenses including promotion, selling, partnerships, etc.

A start-up would go through similar stages elsewhere in the world, but the advantage in the United States is that they have been doing the same thing for decades. Therefore, a start-up would not spend much time getting access to capital, but instead would build upon the idea and see how technology could be best used to deliver the idea in question. Thus, summarily it can be said the United States is more equipped to handle the entire lifecycle management for innovation. FinTechs were able to leverage the same setup to ideate, develop and launch themselves, thus causing a disruption in the financial services domain. The disruptions caused by these FinTechs in the United States and worldwide have taken away up to a one-fourth share of the total revenue made by the traditional financial services industry.

The average American was the one most affected by the 2008 financial crisis as they invested a large part of their savings either in insurance, wealth instruments or in real estate, and these were the exact three investment avenues that lost their market value in the financial crisis. Therefore, unlike in other parts of the world, erosion of trust in the FIs was the worst in the United States. This led to an increased adoption of FinTechs since they came up with new business models that were transparent and offered products that would ensure there was little or no loss of the base capital. Consequently, start-ups on both ends of spectrum emerged, one that was safeguarding individual's interest while making profits or offering benefit for the individual, and on the other end of the spectrum, offering high-risk assets like participating in individual unsecured debt was made available to the customer through P2P lending. Since most of these opportunities were offered in a transparent manner, a large number of customers adopted the same.

It was the United States which was also spearheading the technology revolution with multiple innovations like the Apple iPhone, cloud services through Amazon Web Services (AWS), etc. Americans who in the past have been witness to multiple technology revolutions like IBM mainframes, desktops, servers, etc. were quick enough to adopt these new technology disruptions as well. Therefore, for FinTechs in the United States, the tech savvy and financial literate customers were the early adopters of the alternative, yet transparent, business model offered by them.

All the above-mentioned factors, an innovation ecosystem and a customer who was ready to embrace a new way of doing business, facilitated the emergence of FinTechs in the United States. Therefore, the largest number of successful FinTechs are from the United States with more than a dozen FinTechs having valuations greater than $1 billion. Money transfers, payments, savings and investments are the most used FinTech services. The FinTech outlook in the United States looks promising with the focus shifting from customer experience to back-office and automation start-ups. Cloud and software as a service (SaaS) adoption would increase in the United States, with more people understanding the capabilities and limitations of the same. A large number of FinTech businesses in the United States are centered around:

1. Lending—The P2P and online lending market is expected to cross a trillion dollar mark in the next decade, therefore this space is revolutionized by FinTechs providing alternative lending solutions like P2P lending, lending to a first-time borrower, lending to creditworthy customers with less or no formal credit scores, etc. Prosper, Lending Club and OnDeck are some of the FinTech companies that are doing good business and are having steep valuations.

2. Payments—Mobile payments in the United States are poised to hit half a billion dollars by 2020 and there are clear signs that the payments industry is transforming with FinTech offerings like P2P payment, digital wallets, loyalty, Bitcoin payments, payment banks and eliminating the payment interface itself. Coinbase, PayPal, ApplePay, Square and Stripe are some of payment FinTechs that are disrupting the payments and cards industry.

3. Personal financial management and robo-advising—A large number of FinTechs are focusing on giving financial advice, personal financial management and robo-advising affordable to the common man. This results into tapping hundreds of prospects, who have small corpus to be invested, but are not aware of the avenues for the same. Additionally, since they are not financially aware, providing them an automated mechanism to invest with prefixed

criteria helps them invest their money safely through robo-advising. Some of the companies making news in this space are Betterment, Wealthfront, Motif and Folio.

4. Insurance—Insurance is more than a trillion dollar industry globally, and there are multiple start-ups in the United States in this space, that are disrupting traditional insurance by providing insurance based on customer behavior, pay-per-use insurance, P2P insurance, donating while insuring, quick claim processing and using data and analytics to detect fraud. Lemonade, Cyence, Bright Health, Metromile and Clover Health are some of the insurance companies disrupting the insurance market.

Besides the above domains, there are other FinTech companies that are providing cybersecurity, analytics and AI-related solutions to FIs.

Europe and the UK

Although a large number of FinTechs are from the United States, Europe and the UK are also picking up in terms of the FinTech industry. There are significant deals happening in the insurance sector in Europe witnessed by the steep valuations for some of the insurance firms and wealth management firms. Additionally, the second payment services directive (PSD2) compliance rush is also resulting in multiple FinTechs who have built application program interface (API)-related products/platforms thus helping organizations to build, publish and consume APIs. There are also FinTechs emerging that provide alternative ways of doing the banking, lending, trading and payment processing using the data that will be exposed by banks. Fintech activity on the solutions that are transforming the legacy back end is also an uptick in the Europe. Recent successes of the platforms that help connecting legacy applications to the customer-facing and external-facing applications are clear signs of rise of the noncustomer-facing FinTechs. FinTechs in Europe are also pursuing banking licenses, similar to the rush in the United States for taking brokerage licenses. There are consolidations across Europe in the areas that are already crowded like P2P lending and payments space, yet new entrants are making news for steep valuations. The rise of digital banks, regulations to support innovation through start-ups and the popularity of online payments are all driving the FinTech revolution in Europe. A large number of European FinTechs are profitable and have already become an unicorn or are anticipated to become one very soon. Blockchain, cybersecurity and AI are some of the emerging areas for FinTechs in Europe.

UK: The FinTech Hub

The UK is one of the market leaders in banking, cross-border transactions, insurance and trading. P2P lending and aggregator FinTechs have been a real success in the UK. The UK also has the highest Internet and mobile phone penetration. London has one of the world's most active accelerator programs, that not only provides office space and infrastructure to FinTechs, but also helps them collaborate with the industry to test out ideas and corresponding implementations. There are meet up groups based in London, which have a network of thousands of professionals involved in financial innovation. A large number of regulatory authorities are also based in London. Other cities in the UK like Edinburgh, Belfast, Manchester, Birmingham and Leeds are the center to most of the large insurance and banking organizations. The UK's government has not accepted Bitcoin as a formal currency, but has also not banned or levied taxes on it like many other countries. A large chunk of the investments for FinTechs in 2017 was primarily centered around the cities of London, Berlin, Stockholm, Paris, Barcelona and Amsterdam. One-third of the investments in FinTechs are companies from London. Since the United States, the UK, Australia and New Zealand are English-speaking countries, it is more likely that an application developed in the United States and the UK is easily replicated across in the UK, the United States, Australia and New Zealand, respectively. The FinTech industry employs about a million people directly or indirectly in the UK and is generating multibillion dollar revenue. One of the key differences between the UK and other emerging markets is the support they are getting from the central bank and the regulator. The Bank of England leads the effort in promoting FinTechs in the UK. Additionally, FinTechs are able to participate in the regulatory sandbox, which means FinTech can test their business models for 3–6 months in the market, free from many of the regulatory demands they might be subject to otherwise.

FinTechGermany: Playing the Catch-Up Game

After the UK, Germany is the second largest FinTech destination in Europe. A large group of FinTechs are payments, lending and crowdfunding platforms, and most of them work closely with established banks to create a collaborative financial services environment. The highest growth sector in the FinTech market in Germany has been the robo-advising market, which has grown tenfold between 2017 and 2015. The social trading and crowd investment platforms have growth rates in triple digits during the same time. Germany appeals to start-ups because the cost of living is still low. The other drivers for FinTech growth this year and in the future could be the Brexit vote, when Britain decided to leave the EU. Since Brexit, a lot of UK FinTechs would not have direct access to EU assets and markets, which would therefore help Germany participate more aggressively in the entire EU market. The changing rules in regard to PSD2 and the flexibility to adopt digital measures for identification and legitimation of customers is further fueling the emergence of new FinTechs in Europe and specifically in Germany.

Sweden: The Place Where Skype and Spotify Were Born

Sweden is the EU's third largest country and the FinTech industry there is all set to become one of the most influential in Europe. Sweden is also one of the leading countries to pursue becoming an entirely cashless economy. Stockholm is second in the world in terms of the number of unicorns per capita. The engineering culture is evident in Sweden with many inventions like pacemakers, refrigerators and ultrasound originating from Sweden and large engineering companies being based in Sweden. Sweden also has a large financial industry that is one-third of the overall Swedish economy. It is also the highest-funded city in Europe after the UK and has been mentioned as "Europe's No 2 FinTech City." Some of the reasons that can be enumerated for success of Sweden in the FinTech space are:

1. An abundance of wealth and capital-rich economy leading to heavy investment in R&D and technological infrastructure.
2. The state and nonstate is more supportive for entrepreneurship from a funding and knowledge perspective.
3. The corporate tax rate is also less than the EU average tax rate.
4. Swiss FSA is playing a proactive role in delivering changes and information about regulations.
5. Encouragement to e-identity tools and becoming cashless.
6. Setting up a new public fund for a fund investment company by the government to invest in private VC funds.

Sweden's FinTechs are primarily centered around payments, trading, lending and solutions using cryptocurrencies.

France: Gearing Up for the Next Revolution, the FinTech Revolution

France has over 150 FinTechs, over 200 public and private incubation centers and multi billion euros worth of investments. It is the sixth largest economy in the world and is one of the leading global financial centers. In 2015, the France FinTech Association was formed due to the collaboration of 36 companies. Some of the other criteria that is helping FinTech growth in France are:

1. A favorable tax regime for capital gains from investments.
2. High networth individuals (HNIs) get a 50% discount on investments in small and medium enterprises (SMEs).
3. A start-up immigration program that includes a free co-working space and unconditional government grants to promote entrepreneurship by immigrants in France.

4. France's fund of funds contributed multimillion euros to a private VC fund for innovation through the French Public Investment Bank (bpiFrance).
5. Regulators like ACPR created initiatives to help FinTechs with the regulatory requirements and overcome barriers.
6. Introduced an agility program offering a 2WeekTicket for UK start-ups to get them started with all the regulatory approvals and an English-speaking assistance program.

China: The FinTech Dragon Awakens

Silicon Valley has been a leader in hosting the FinTechs until recently. In the last year, China has overtaken Silicon Valley in terms of the number of FinTechs and the overall investment in the FinTechs. The Chinese Internet giants are currently the ones who are dominating the FinTech revolution globally.

China, which is the most populous country and is also the second largest economy in the world with a multitrillion dollar GDP, is quickly catching up with London, New York and Silicon Valley to become a leading center for FinTech innovation. Shanghai and Hong Kong have been recognized as one of the leading FinTech hubs globally. The growth of China in FinTech space is evident as it is home to now almost a third of the unicorns valued at $100+ billion. The world's four biggest unicorns are all from China. The FinTech growth in China has been primarily centered around payments, wealth management and P2P lending.

The drivers for the FinTech growth in China can be enumerated as follows:

1. Chinese economic growth has been exceptional in the last decade and especially the growth of the middle class population in China and their growing income levels. While the income levels have grown over time, unfortunately the lack of the diversification of products and the customization of financial products to an individual's need has made the high income middle class to look for alternatives. This in turn has fueled FinTechs to fill in the gaps unaddressed by established banks. Retail customers are usually offered/pushed products that are low on financial returns like real estate, etc. as compared to any other market-linked products. It has resulted in a large number of FinTechs coming up with innovative products to manage their customer's wealth.
2. High Internet and mobile penetration in the hands of the educated and rising middle class has given rise to high Internet-based shopping. The Internet economy in China is expected to be a significant proportion of China's GDP in next 5 years. This resulted in the highest e-commerce and digital transactions being reported from China. The majority of e-commerce transactions would mean that payments would be done online and therefore a large chunk

of FinTechs are from payment space. It is estimated that half of Chinese consumers are using the new payment methods.

3. Financial inclusion has been low in China, even though Chinese banks have become one of the largest banks in the world. One in five of China's adult population is unbanked. The SMEs are also underserved and make up for a quarter of all the disbursed loans while accounting for over half of GDP. Consequently, a large number of P2P lending solutions emerged.

4. Inadequate regulatory structure has led to multiple FinTechs emerging as there was little or no requirements for any government regulatory approval for opening a start-up in areas of lending and wealth management.

5. The government has launched an "Internet plus" initiative that has various development targets, help for local Internet companies, financial funding and tax relief for key projects. It has also created a multibillion dollar emerging industries innovation investment fund to promote digital industries in China. It also operates multiple funds to raise money for start-ups and has been able to raise about a quarter of trillion dollars to fund them. They are also taxed at lower corporate tax rates than established industries. In 2016, the first angel fund from a private company was launched to fund FinTechs with the intent to invest a large part of their corpus in FinTechs.

6. The technical and functional talent is also available in abundance in China, with companies like IBM, Microsoft, JD.com existing in Beijing and local tech giants like Huawei and ZTE in Shenzen. China is also host to some of the leading universities that rank among the top universities in the world, namely Peking University and Tsingua University.

7. China has a large population of tech savvy millennials and GenY who are giving preference to customer experience and the flexibility offered by the FinTechs as compared to the rigid and state-oriented outlook of established banks. Additionally, the Chinese are less anxious to share their personal data, therefore, a large number of FinTechs have been able to create customer-centric personalized offerings.

Some of the FinTech areas that are leading China's growth into the FinTech space are:

1. Some of the leading payment-provider FinTechs are from China. These FinTechs are offering a facial recognition-based payment service. They also provide an escrow service for e-commerce shopping as a protection from low-quality products being made available to consumers. Some of these payment services have integrated a social media chat application as part of their payment application, thus helping customers to pay using the chat applications. Besides facilitating payments for individuals using chat platforms, a large number of FinTechs are also facilitating businesses to make B2B and B2C payments using chat platforms. A large number of these FinTechs have also

been instrumental in transacting for gifts that include billions of red enve-lopes being sent over a holiday period using these FinTechs during the year-end holidays.

2. P2P lending platforms have been a rage in China as a large population is unbanked and underserved, but in absence of regulatory controls, a huge number of these platforms went out of business. Since then, regulations have been tightened around the same. Some of the players who established their reputation in the market have collaborated with established FIs in China. There are couple of large P2P lending platforms who have a major share of the overall P2P lending.

3. Wealth management and personal finance management—Wealth manage-ment is a thriving industry in China, and by 2015 had expanded to about one-third of the country's GDP. There are major digital wealth manage-ment platforms that by mid-2016, had more than a quarter billion customers offering funds from as little as RMB1. A large number of wealth manage-ment firms are also launching mobile apps to lure young professionals who are interested in managing their wealth themselves. FinTech companies in wealth management have their mobile apps for investing in stocks. Some of the digital wealth management firms are also offering robo-advising plat-forms. There are now multiple platforms offering robo-advising services to B2B and B2C customers.

India: The FinTech Tiger Is Roaring

The Indian economy is the sixth largest in the world on a nominal GDP basis and third largest by purchasing power parity. The country also became the world's fastest growing economy since the last quarter of 2014. India is the third largest start-up hub in the world, with an investment of about a half billion dollars in 2015. The Indian FinTech is primarily divided into the following categories: insurance, banking and securities and public and private banks. The Indian FinTech market is dominated by financial service integration companies that have a large share in the overall FinTech market segment. A large number of FinTech companies in India are focused around payment processing, banking and trading solutions. India is the second most populous nation in the world with a population of over a billion people with a majority of them being young and under the age of 35. This coupled with a large percentage of this population equipped with technical and functional combi-nations has become the ideal destination for FinTechs and start-ups to launch green field operations. Some of the drivers that are catalyzing this FinTech growth are:

1. Almost half of the Indian population is unbanked, thus leading to a majority of insurance and the banking functions, primarily savings and lending, han-dled through community banking, which at times is informal and may not

provide the best returns. Secondly, most of these institutions are very small with no regulatory approvals and localized to one or a few villages/townships. Some of the government majority-owned, yet publicly traded financial and insurance companies have tried to drive financial inclusions in the villages through service agents. The service agents are typically from the same community or within the close group of investor himself/herself and are responsible for managing savings and lending for their contacts, who are customers as well. But the cost of the operation for these large institutions, owing to their infrastructure and processes, often ends up eroding profits and therefore, such initiatives ended up being more of a corporate social responsibility (CSR) initiative rather than tapping the underlying opportunity. A large part of the microfinancing FinTechs are now trying to build their business model to tap this greenfield opportunity. Therefore, start-ups in India are innovating to bring financing to the masses.

2. A large portion of payments, about four-fifth of the total payments, in India is made in cash. This trend has been worrisome for the government as well, since it leads to cash hoarding, corruption and the lack of a money trail. Internet penetration and mobile usage in India is assumed to be touching two-thirds of the entire population in next couple of years, thereby laying a huge potential for technology start-ups to bring in alternate payment solutions. The government of India has also taken multiple positive steps recently by issuing payment banking licenses and opening up regulations in regard to the payment industry overall. Some of the key steps that the government has taken up to promote digital economy through events like demonetization, ceiling on cash transactions and incentivizing digital payments have all helped the traditional banks to launch an entirely new payment offering and/ or have FinTech start-ups tap into the opportunity. One of the key initiatives in this area from the government of India has been to provide the unique payment interface (UPI) and the launching of a centralized bill payment interface, Bharat bill payment system (BBPS). All of this is coupled with the relaxation from the central bank of India–Reserve Bank of India (RBI) on KYC norms for transactions up to 10,000 per month have all helped FinTechs launch greenfield operations in this space. Paytm, Mobikwik and Oxigen are some of the leading FinTechs in this space.

3. The retail industry in India is projected to be over a trillion dollars by the end of this decade and is one of the high-growth industries in India. Most of Indian retail is dominated by small pop and mom shops and is also driven by a very long supply chain. Past multiple studies had pointed out that though these small retail shops offer employment to the less educated, from a perspective of economies of scale, the customer is at a disadvantage by paying more and the shopkeeper also not getting the desired benefit. The industry has been revolutionized by the entry of e-commerce firms like Flipkart and Amazon. The rising income levels of the Indian middle class

increased working hours and infrastructure impediments, together have created the next perfect storm for e-commerce to rise. Increasing mobile penetration in the industry has also been a catalyst in the exponential growth of e-commerce in India. This in turn has given an uplift to the wallet economy and a large number of brick and mortar retail chains also have partnered with a wallet or launched their own wallets. Reliance Jio and Freecharge are some examples of these wallets.

4. The IT sector in India contributes to about one-tenth of India's GDP and it is one of the high-growth industries with high-paying jobs. Consequently, all the dependent economies like real estate, automobile industry, etc. have a high-growth rate as well. A consequence of this has been that there are now about eight cities considered as Tier-1 cities as compared to four Tier-1 cities in 2007. Additionally, because of liberalization, there are now a host of opportunities available for a common man to invest his/her money with. Consequently, a large number of equity, commodity and multiple other financial institutions have emerged, besides real estate and gold that were considered to be a safe investment alternatives. Some of the successful FinTechs identified the opportunity and are offering wealth management and personal financial management (PFM) solutions. Goalwise and Upstox are some of these FinTechs. Central banks controlling the interest rates and limited equity options have made it difficult for an average investor to earn more profits from traditional options. On the other end, the SMEs in the country are underserved, owing to stricter regulations from the public and private banks. Consequently, P2P FinTechs have emerged that are helping connect SME businesses to retail and small investors. Faircent and i-lend are two prominent players in this industry.

5. India is one of the largest English speaking nation in the world and have about a million graduates entering the organized/disorganized sector annually, and India being host to one of the world's e top institutions and universities in the world, there is a vast amount of technology talent available in India for the FinTech industry. A large pool of financial-domain specialists available with knowledge of global risk and compliance requirements has helped FinTechs to innovate with the most advanced concepts in India. Though a major portion of technology star-tups are currently in the telecom, retail and food segment, they all have hooks into the FinTech segment. Some of the technology providers like TCS and Infosys have brought in their own core banking products and there are others like Appzillion who have brought in their own mobile platform-based banking solutions. Most of the innovation in the financial space has been done with products that enable banks and FIs to achieve digital transformation.

6. Multiple other factors besides mentioned above have also aided the start-ups in the financial industry. Creating a central database for biometric identification through Aadhaar has helped in cutting down KYC time. Therefore,

onboarding and payment interfaces has been cut down to minutes as against days. Additionally, opening up of industries through flexible regulations have helped companies get brokerage and insurance licenses, thus facilitating the growth of FinTechs. Active participation of the Securities and Exchange Board of India (SEBI), the stock exchange regulator, has ensured the trust in the system is ever-increasing and the same is evident from an increasing number of people choosing to invest into mutual funds as against investing in real estate and gold. The launching of Jan Dhan Yojna by the government has helped bring in a large portion of unbanked individuals into the banking economy. Last but not the least, bringing in a centralized goods and services tax (GST) across the country, the ease of doing business has dramatically increased within the country. With all these initiatives, it would be not exaggerating to say the government of India is acting as a financial start-up itself.

Some of the key FinTechs reshaping the industry are:

1. Mobile wallets are some of the most talked about FinTechs in this space. These wallets are primarily used for mobile recharges, bill payments and online commerce. These wallets also have tied up with cab services, retail stores, educational institutes and gas stations to increase the reach and usage of their wallet services.
2. Prepaid cards provide solutions with agent-assisted offerings to people who are not digitally well-equipped. The primary usage of these cards is for expense management, remittances and railway bookings.
3. There are P2P lenders, that use digital proprietary models to do credit-risk evaluation, so that loans could be processed in 48 hours. The P2P lenders provide investors an opportunity to lend to individuals and SMEs alike to gain better interest rates across the board. Some of the emerging FinTechs are an invoice discounting start-up that helps the micro, small and medium enterprises by taking over their invoices that are tied up for 30–90 days payment, thereby helping these enterprises in unlocking the working capital required for operations. This in turn reduces the working capital debt requirement for these organizations.
4. There are other wealth investment FinTechs who have brought a zero-brokerage concept to India. They charge a fixed fee for transactions as opposed to a percentage of the transaction being charged by lending banks and investment firms. They have their platforms available in multiple different regional languages. High-volume traders are benefitting largely from this platform as they are being charged with a fixed fee as opposed to a percentage of the transaction. There are also online investment platforms providing access to investing in mutual funds, equities and other securities.
5. Insuretech in India is mainly comprised of smart aggregators where each one has a different customer experience to offer. Some of these aggregators are Coverfox, PolicyBazaar and BankBazaar. Almost all of the aggregators

are spending majorly in customer acquisition and assist the customer either through a back-office support or through a facilitator.

6. There are FinTech platforms that provide market data. These platforms provide analytical capabilities along with predictive analytics on the data, from an investor perspective.

Africa: A Young FinTech Continent

The FinTech revolution is as big in Africa as in most of the other continents like the Americas and Europe. There are a large number of FinTechs in Africa spread across the South, Western and Eastern Africa. South Africa has the highest FinTech activity amounting to about one-third of continent's FinTech start-ups. Nigeria and Kenya take up the second and third position respectively for the same. FinTechs in Africa have been able to get multibillion dollars in FinTech investments. The payments and remittance space is one of the areas that have seen the highest consumer demand as well as FinTech investment, closely followed by lending and personal finance management FinTechs. A recent trend has shown, increasing investments in blockchain-related start-ups. Africa is also one of the youngest continents on earth with the average age being 18 years old, though a large proportion of this population is unbanked. In a country that is severely unbanked, it is ironical that it has the highest mobile penetration in the world. There are currently about a billion mobile subscriptions across Africa. Only about half the total number of children in Africa are enrolled in schools, and in most of the schools, English and French are taught as either the secondary or primary language. Due to age-old systems followed by the banks in Africa, it was difficult for an entrepreneur to setup a business, but with the digital enablement of the continent, multiple FinTech start-ups have grown in a very short time to provide for, where the large banks/insurance companies cannot reach out to. Some of the key drivers that have propelled the growth of FinTechs in Africa are:

1. A large number of young educated people are starting up their own ventures, and the easy funding available through VCs outside and within the country has made these entrepreneurs innovate and bring in solutions and applications that are not only making money, but also improving the lives of the people in Africa. There are FinTechs that are helping people invest and trade even in livestock.

2. Africa is host to about 54 countries having 2,000 languages and it is not easy for most people to communicate across regions and countries due to dialect and language differences. This was challenging for large banks and FinTechs to launch a single product that can serve the entire continent, therefore, it has encouraged local FinTechs to start operations in one country and leveraging their agility to build products for other countries by employing the local

language expertise within each country. There are multiple FinTechs that have been easily able to expand themselves into multiple countries.

3. Remittances are one of the biggest sources of foreign investments for the African countries. Having so many countries with a high amount of cross-border trade and having trade connections across the globe, means a lot of money moves in and out of Africa. Because there are multiple currencies within the continent and very few banks offering foreign exchange conversions, multiple FinTechs have emerged in the payments and remittance business. There are FinTechs providing remittance services along with the standard wallet services.

4. Africa is rich in natural resources and a lot of natural/agriculture produce like spices, coffee, etc. are traded globally. This becomes a challenge in a country that has a majority of its transactions done in cash. Some of the payment challenges faced by businesses include paying employees, partners and for any cross-border transactions being done to the entities in advanced economies like the United States and Europe. A large number of FinTechs who are in the payment business have built their business that facilitates cross-border currency exchange as well as payments to their employees through digital currency. Some of the other start-ups have made cross-border transactions a convenience by facilitating instant money transfer to a mobile wallet of recipient in local/desired currency. Thus, only a mobile phone number is needed to facilitate a money transfer.

5. Financial inclusion in Africa is also a challenge, as more than 80% of the population is unbanked and a bigger challenge is the lack of last mile access for financial agencies. The absence of enough ATMs and bank branches coupled with limited road connectivity is also an issue for most of the people residing in these places. Therefore, trade in most of the remote villages and towns are usually done through mutual understanding or through community payment mechanisms. The introduction of mobile money through multiple telecom providers in partnership with FinTechs has therefore revolutionized the entire payment industry in Africa. Since mobile money can be delivered and exchanged through a mobile, and Africa having a near complete mobile penetration, it is easy and available for most of the people with phone devices to do transactions using mobile money. This has also helped telecom companies and FinTech start-ups to work together to ensure credibility of the respective mobile money is maintained. Fetswallet and M-Naira are some of the mobile money wallets existing in Africa.

6. A large part of Africa's SME is also underserved primarily because of a highly regulated industry in terms of loan disbursal and usage of evaluating credit worthiness, based on the collaterals deposited. This has opened up a new area of financing and credit scoring through FinTechs that do financing based on their own evaluation of credit scores and also enable P2P lending. A range of credit scoring companies have also emerged that do credit scores much differently form the standard algorithms used by the credit scoring companies' worldwide.

There are digital finance FinTechs offering financial services to the unbanked with a focus on micro industries and SMEs. There are other FinTechs in Africa that use an individual's data on the phone to simplify the loan processing.

7. There is a fast-growing segment of high-income groups, mostly centered in and around urban areas, that need help in terms of understanding the wealth management options they have and managing their personal wealth as well. There are platforms that enable users to invest in equities as fractional and whole shares.

8. Africa has also emerged as one of the key travel destinations in the last decade. A group of partner organizations evolved as part of the entire travel ecosystem, and again one of the biggest challenge was to enable payments to these merchants in a consistent way across countries and continents. Consequently, FinTechs have emerged that are facilitating merchant services including cross-border transactions to thousands of travel-related and other businesses.

Some of the key sectors FinTechs are transforming in Africa are:

1. Payment, remittance and mobile money—Owing to less financial inclusion and high mobile penetration, multiple FinTechs have emerged in the space of:
   a. Payment—There are FinTechs that allow businesses to accept payments from mobile money wallets. There are other FinTechs that help businesses accept payments online across the world.
   b. Remittance—Provides remittance services to Africans living abroad.
   c. Forex—There are forex FinTech companies that use Bitcoin as an intermediate currency. There are other FinTechs that help move money around Africa.
   d. Mobile money—There are mobile wallet services and mobile money wallets provided by a large number of FinTechs in the region.
2. Digital currency—The entire African continent has large number of countries with multiple FIs, and therefore, some FinTechs have come up with using digital currencies as intermediate currency for doing cross-border currency exchange. There are FinTechs that use Bitcoin for forex and provide a mobile wallet. There are other FinTechs that have introduced blockchain-based P2P payment services in Africa.
3. Wealth management and personal finance—These apps help manage money for an individual as well as enable them in investing across equities and other financial instruments like mutual funds, usecured debts, etc. for earning better than normal returns, earned through traditional banking and financing channels. There are FinTechs that help in personal financial management, and enable users to invest in fractional or whole equities.
4. Lending—As noted above, lending through traditional channels is time-consuming and has regulatory requirements like collaterals, credit scores, etc.

FinTechs have emerged in this space that are providing alternative lending. There are FinTechs offering alternative lending platforms, credit bureaus for microfinance in Africa, issuing loans on the basis of the user's mobile data, offering loans to farmers and managing the lifecycle of the loan, offering personalized credit based on the user's behavior, a loan marketplace, offering financial services to micro industries and SMEs and working as P2P lending platforms.

Australia, New Zealand and Brazil: The Emerging FinTech Countries

Australia, New Zealand and Brazil are some of the leading countries in the FinTech revolution. Almost all of the advanced economies have start-ups that are transforming the financial business by changing:

a. The business processes
b. The customer experience
c. Optimizing by workforce enablement

The two largest sectors by the number of FinTech companies and capital investments are payments and lending followed by wealthtech. FinTechs in New Zealand is just picking up, though the local tech sector is on the rise in New Zealand.

There are multiple reasons across the region that is driving this revolution. In Brazil and Latin America, it is the unavailability of banking services to a large percentage of the population. In Australia and New Zealand, it is the rigidity of the formal banking system that is driving the FinTech revolution. All three countries are growing in the technology sector and therefore there are many technology start-ups that are trying to revolutionize the financial space. One of the common drivers for FinTech proliferation across most of the countries are difficulties involved in getting capital for the SME segment. Banks in almost all these countries are highly regulated and therefore, they can offer loans only to the SMEs with good credit scores. This has left a large number of SMEs and entrepreneurs underserved, and FinTechs have targeted these SMEs by offering them fast credits/loans, using alternative credit evaluation mechanisms to evaluate their credit worthiness.

Therefore, the common areas in these three regions where FinTechs have been growing fast is in the lending and alternate finance-related areas. Additionally, there is a large group of high-income professionals who are in search of different avenues to grow their investments. Because of low interest rates offered by banks on term deposits and with limited avenues remaining to get high returns with moderate risks, these individuals are investing through FinTechs that offer greater returns through P2P lending.

Millennials have also been one of the reasons across these countries to bring about the transformation, as they would prefer a better customer experience and a more socially connected application than using something that is standard. Consequently, a large number of start-ups are focused on providing a more socially connected, differentiated customer experience. Lastly, as mentioned in previous sections, the payment sector has technologically evolved drastically in the last decade with the emergence of wallets, mobile money, etc. This has prompted a large number of FinTechs to provide an appealing payment experience which the large banks, owing to their legacy infrastructure, are not able to emulate. Some of the FinTechareas that FinTechs are redefining the financial services in these countries are:

1. Australia–There are technology-centric FinTechs, that are specialized in offering banking solutions to Australia's SMEs. There are P2P lending platforms, personal finance management (PFM) FinTechs, that allows people to spend in Bitcoin and all other currencies, There are other FinTechs that provide small loans to their customers, There are robo-advisory FinTech platforms and P2P investor platforms which also help investors investing in unpaid invoices. Besides this, there are multiple FinTechs in the space of wealth management, lending, insurance, crowdfunding, personal financial management and technologies like blockchain, data and analytics.
2. In New Zealand, the FinTechs are limited, but they are doing some of the critical functions that large banks seem to have ignored or find too difficult to achieve. Some of the FInTechs are imparting financial literacy to individuals using innovative methods like providing real-life business scenarios, using real business data to practice, etc. Other FinTechs are helping SMEs bring clarity to insurance policies and help managing them as well. There are wealth management platforms that help an individual investor manage their finances to achieve their goals. There are other FinTechs that are offering innovative health savings program that promotes healthy living and timely access to right professional. Some FinTechs are also offering an on-demand platform for landlords to manage their properties.
3. Brazil is a fast-growing economy and some of the FinTechs that are addressing the needs of consumers and businesses, by offering a personal financial management (PFM) platform, that helps individuals manage money by automating the entire financial management process. Other FinTechs have developed a platinum credit card service that an individual can manage using only their mobile phone. There are other lending platforms that focus on secure lending. There are insurance search and aggregator platforms and online P2P lending platforms offered by FinTechs as well.

There are multiple other platforms that have become quite successful and drawing attention from investors, though in these countries the established financial firms themselves have been quite active in funding or acquiring some of these FinTechs to improve their overall positioning in the market. The governments in these countries are also supporting FinTechs by relaxing compliance on regulations and at the same time creating platforms to incubate and nurture these organizations.

Chapter 5

Incubating the FinTechs and Early Stage Funding

In the second quarter of 2017, FinTech investments globally was about $8+ billion, 250+ deals, averaging about $2–3 billion across all the quarters since 2010 and especially peaking at the end of 2015 and the second quarter of 2016. More than $50 billion has been invested across 2,500 companies since 2010. In May 2016, London was ranked as the largest FinTech hub. In 2015, multiple successful FinTech initial public offerings (IPOs) like PayPal, Square, WorldPay and First Data achieved multibillion dollar market capitalization, ensuring investor confidence in FinTechs. FinTech investments quadrupled in 2015 with China accounting for one-half of the shares and India accounting for a bit over one-third of the shares. In 2015, there were just about 100 FinTech deals larger than $50 million and the megadeals greater than $1 billion have been coming across every quarter since 2015. FinTech funding is typically done through the following sources: (1) a venture capitalist, (2) corporate and private investors, (3) mergers and acquisitions and (4) public IPOs. A start-up typically goes from the bootstrapping stage, wherein the primary source of funding is friends and families to seed funding, and the series A, B and C funding leading to the company becoming public or being acquired by somebody. In most cases, the initial stage (from seed to C) funding investors typically exit the start-up. The different funding stages for a start-up can be explained as below.

Seed funding: This is usually the first stage of funding and the extent of funding varies from a few thousand dollars to a million dollars depending on the organization being funded. This fund is used by most of the founders to do the following:

1. Moving to a better place where they could attract talent. This would typically mean moving away from a garage space to a better location.

2. Augmenting the team by attracting top talent by paying high salaries and other perks.
3. Take help from third-party services like market research, media promotions, etc.

It is also during the seed-funding stage that most of the founders fine-tune their product strategy and identify the go-to market strategy.

Series A funding: After a business has developed the product completely and generated some traction in the market, Series A funding is typically done. Through Series A funding, the start-ups would aim to increase the development teams further and plan for a wider market outreach. The funding round indicates the start-up has reached a certain level of being financially viable and needs more money to monetize the product and idea. This round of funding typically is from a couple million dollars to $25 million. Depending on the promise the company is able to project, they may even get more than this in this round of funding. The major activities that start-ups typically take after getting this funding is to establish sales offices and build avenues for a better customer connection.

Series B funding: This funding comes into the picture once the company has set-up its product and wants to be a business-led set-up rather than being a development-centric set-up. After getting the funds for this round, the start-ups spend it on business development, sales, technical support teams, advertising and promotions, and acquiring top talent in all of the above areas. The series B round thus ends up building departments within the start-up. It is at this stage that lot of start-ups venture into partnerships and cobranding opportunities. Usually during this stage the fund investing teams want a greater participation in strategic decisions made by the start-up. The typical amount that is invested during this round of funding is from $10–$25 million. "Later stage" funding investing firms start participating in investments from this round onwards.

Series C funding: This round of funding typically takes place once the business has established itself into a leadership or challenger position and is commanding a noticeable market share. Large venture capital (VC) firms, investment banks, hedge funds, equity fund managers and corporates start participating in this round of funding. The funding round could range from few million dollars to hundreds of millions of dollars. The funding round is often used by the founders to acquire a stake in a competitor or a complementing start-up. The amount generated through this round of funding also helps start-ups build a presence globally and spin-off their products into a larger offering. The investors in this round typically look at two to three multiple returns of the money invested. In some of the cases, post this round of funding, a more professional organization is brought into managing the organization that until now is being a founder-led company.

All the funding done after this stage is called late stage funding and the number of rounds of late stage funding before the funding companies decide to exit depends upon the condition of the start-up and the buyers agreement with the start-ups. The figures below indicate the different FinTech investment activities courtesy of https://www.venturescanner.com/ (Figures 5.1–5.3). Venture scanners can be contacted at info@venturescanner.com for a detailed report on FinTechs.

In the initial days of FinTechs, the primary investing community was VCs and though they continue to be one of the biggest investors, trends indicate that the other three categories, i.e., corporate and private investors, mergers and acquisitions and public IPOs, of investment have also picked up in last 10 years. Initially most of the FinTechs were localized with a couple of niche offerings, but over the course of time, these FinTechs are expanding, some horizontally to cover the breadth of activities and others vertically by acquiring other start-ups in their supply/value chain.

Financing a start-up typically comes at a later stage, but what is most important for a start-up is when they are just starting. They need multiple things besides having the technology and functional talent on their team. The additional help they typically need is office space, legal counsel, seed money, access to different markets and a team that helps with regulators. An entire ecosystem is required that facilitates the start-up industry including the coworking space providers, incubator, accelerator programs, marketers, mergers and acquisitions consultants and deal brokers.

Almost all start-ups start from their garage or a one room apartment and then they need a place where their expanding team needs to sit together. Usually, it is expensive for start-ups to rent the place on their own as they are not sure, how fast/slow they would grow and how long would their funds last. Secondly, getting the

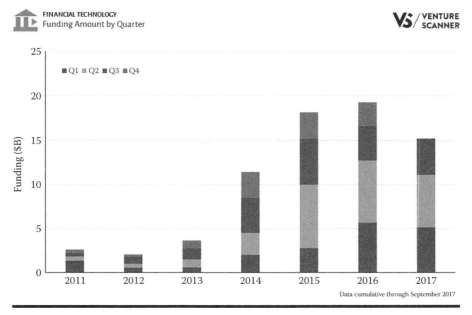

Figure 5.1   FinTech investments from 2011–2017 (From https:// www.venturescanner.com/).

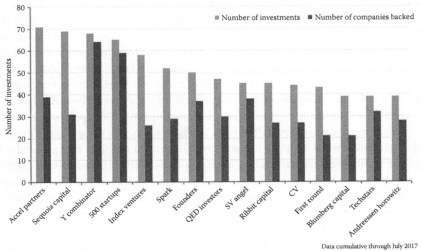

Figure 5.2 Investor activity in FinTechs (From https:// www.venturescanner. com/).

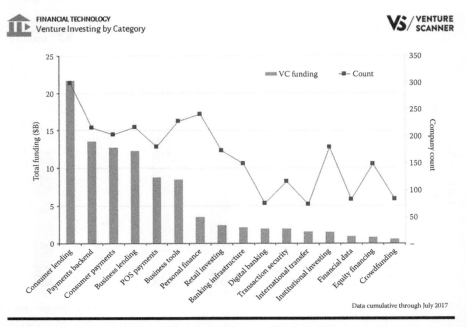

Figure 5.3 Investment activity in different FinTech domains (From https:// www.venturescanner.com/).

entire infra setup done from scratch like network connectivity, desktops, devices, etc. becomes a challenge for most of the start-ups. Therefore, the first entity in the ecosystem a start-up most likely reaches out to is a co-working space provider. A co-working space is a collaborative working space with the basic office-like infrastructure available in a shared pool and available on pay-per-use basis. Co-working spaces come in different sizes and there are multiple options and configurations available. The idea behind providing a co-working space goes beyond providing infrastructure; this in fact gives an opportunity for like-minded entrepreneurs to be at the same location. The convenience and cost savings offered by a coworking space is encouraging most of the start-ups/entrepreneurs to use the same to take their start-up to next level. Coworking space requirement in the United States is growing every year with more than half of the owners of coworking spaces, looking at expanding their space. Besides providing space, coworking spaces also typically facilitate networking events, physical space to promote brands, outsourcing administrative tasks, knowledge-sharing sessions and some of the spaces even promote business partnerships as well. We will be discussing some of the co-working spaces and their features in subsequent sections within this chapter.

Once a start-up has build upon an idea, it can opt for becoming a part of an incubator program to take it to the next level. They offer office space, legal counsel and seed funding in exchange for a small share of the ownership. Incubators take in start-ups with the most promising of ideas and train the entrepreneurs on how to take the start-up from ideation stage to becoming a successful business. The experts available in an incubator can act as a sounding board for most of the entrepreneurs with good ideas, and they can validate the multiple aspects of running a start-up like:

- Whether their ideas are really promising?
- Do they have enough potential to generate business revenue or would they be just cool ideas?
- How can they potentially protect their intellectual property (IP) and at the same time package it into an offering?

Incubators can take the entrepreneurs from being just a technology and functionally focused individuals to becoming a business person or an entrepreneur in the true sense. Incubators are usually specific to a technology or a business area. The range of services they offer could vary from just providing an office space and an expert advice. Additionally, they could include business mentoring, administrative, human resources (HR), accounting and financial help, legal advice, networking opportunities and even access to angel investors.

Accelerators also known as seed accelerators are fixed term (time-bound) programs that help start-ups bring their ideas to a business conclusion. The accelerator programs end with a demo day wherein the business implementation of proposed ideas is demoed. The programs typically run from 3–6 months and are usually privately run. The organization or the people running the accelerator program make money themselves either by taking a percentage of the overall profit or small equity of the start-up being admitted to the accelerator program. The stage at which a start-up enters into an accelerator program usually varies from accelerator to accelerator, but the start-ups who have built some initial traction, have a talented team and have a prototype to bring the ideas to the forefront are the ones who have a greater chance of getting admitted to the accelerator program. Once a start-up is admitted to the accelerator program, then the set-up provides tremendous support and access to a network of mentors, investors and workspace, including a test bed to try out the corresponding ideas.

One of the key performance indicators for an accelerator is to get the start-up ready for investors in order to bring in the desired investment to take the start-up to next level. In an accelerator, entrepreneurs get an opportunity to discuss their ideas and reshape or fine-tune them to the market/business needs through the guidance of mentors and experience from other start-ups who have completed the accelerator program. It is often said that incubators are like middle schools for start-ups and accelerators are like college. The selection criterion in accelerators is usually tough and some of the very well-known accelerator programs have application acceptance rates between 1% and 3%. The accelerator is not on-demand and in fact, the programs are conducted in batches. There are multiple accelerator-ranking websites and programs that rank different accelerators available based on the data provided by accelerator programs themselves and a survey of founders who graduated from these accelerator programs. Some of the parameters deciding these ratings are valuations, fundraising, exits and start-up satisfaction. One of the key characteristics of an accelerator program is they invest in teams as against individuals and bet only on those start-ups that can lead to valuation, financing and exits in the near term.

Coworking Space: A Place for FinTechs to Enrich and Rediscover Themselves

In 2016 there were about 1,000 coworking spaces around the globe. We will be discussing the salient features of some of the coworking spaces below which are indicative of the entire industry. The thought process behind coworking spaces is you spend about the same amount as your coffee and yet get a space equipped with Wi-Fi and other features available for you to work, which is much better than a coffee shop. Some of the key differentiating aspects of coworking spaces are found below.

The firms in the business of providing coworking spaces, besides providing coworking space, also conduct events where participants can foster collaborative learning and thought leadership. They have multiple events that bring people together that gives them an opportunity to understand the business from an overall perspective. They also offer programs that provide learning opportunities, meeting talent across multiple other start-ups and sponsors and connect with new collaborators. They have a social network platform where genuine connections are present and is not used for self-branding or promotion. They have creative and collaborative spaces as part of their workspace. These coworking spaces are there in almost every continent, with some in Africa, Malaysia, Thailand and South America as well. The offerings and rentals vary from location to location. They also have offers running at some locations, like a free coworking day on a particular day to explore and experience the area.

Some of the other coworking space providers provide private offices with glass walls to maintain privacy without sacrificing transparency or natural light. As part of the amenities, they provide the following:

1. Network connection points within the coworking space and across location with Internet connectivity. A complete Wi-Fi connectivity within all the different areas in the coworking space is available.
2. All the standard infrastructure items like desks, chairs, drawers, printers, scanners, etc. are provided as well.
3. The other value-added benefits that users may get in some of the coworking space may include soda, coffee, tea, light snacks, etc., either chargeable or for free.
4. There would also be meeting rooms, videoconference room and in some coworking space even a private area for private calls may also be made available.

They have different pricing plans available. The one starting with small membership fees and daily charges for usage usually is good for freelancers and business professionals on the move. Some of the plans allow access to a hot desk area where one can grab the next available seat. The plan also will typically have access to conference rooms within the package. Coworking spaces that are globally spread out have different plans wherein an individual can choose a primary area and then book workspace at any other location depending on the mobility options the individual has. An individual gets 24/7 access and there is also a greater chance to collaborate and interact with new individuals every day. You can get a dedicated desk space or a complete office to yourself depending upon the plans that you choose.

These coworking spaces usually host events wherein individuals get to enjoy a catered lunch while members share expertise, knowledge and valuable tips, one-on-one sessions with investors and industry leaders, multiple networking events and also wellness sessions like meditation or kickboxing. All members get access to the member network online or through the mobile app on their iOS or android phones. The app also keeps individual updates about events, allows booking space, conference rooms, finding and replying to events at corresponding locations and post job listings within the network. Some of the coworking space providers also have partnered with multiple organizations to offer negotiated rates with services like healthcare and HR solutions, benefits on payment/money processing and shipping discounts. With global access, individual companies can look at creating satellite offices using these coworking spaces. Some of these coworking space providers also offer a flexible space solution that offers companies with an intermediate workplace while they are shifting between locations or setting up a new infrastructure.

Some very niche coworking spaces not only offer an office space but also provides an opportunity for members to learn, use equipment, develop and test prototypes besides working alongside with students, entrepreneurs and professionals. They have combined the concept of education and entrepreneurship, which typically exists in university laboratories. Therefore, this could very well be the first place where entrepreneurs build and try out their ideas from scratch without spending too much on the infrastructure.

The members at these coworking spaces can also innovate, do rapid prototyping, network with like-minded people, learning and even launch their start-up. Like all other coworking spaces, these niche coworking spaces also offer multiple office space options including but not limited to hot-desking, private rooms, offices, etc. The usual services like Internet connection, free-coffee, private lockers, laser printers and other equipment are also made available. These coworking spaces have a unique offering as part of their membership wherein an individual/entrepreneur gets access to advanced prototyping and equipment. These spaces help members who are individuals/entrepreneurs to get trained on the tools and then they can decide on how to use them on their project/company. They also have help available in the form of on-site helpers who can help get the individual/entrepreneur get acquainted with the tools and get it up and running. The labs are loaded with the latest hardware and software, wherein an individual could design, create and develop their own prototypes. They also conduct multiple events that are chargeable or available for free for all the members.

Some of the coworking spaces also help incubating and accelerating the start-ups. These coworking spaces either run the space as a community for tech innovators or have very focused mentoring and guidance programs as part of their offerings. With such coworking spaces. the individual can become a member only after an individual goes through the rigorous application and selection process laid out by the management teams at these co-working space. The management in such coworking spaces typically are comprised of existing members and they screen an application and select only those applicants that can enrich the community or the group undergoing the program. The management decides based on the business idea, the industry and ultimately if as a person, the individual fits in with the coworking space. After the screening, if the person fits in to the requirements, he/she is invited for an interview or is declined. After the interview, again the candidate can be accepted or declined. Anybody can apply for membership in the club, he/she can be a first time or serial entrepreneur, a student, a freelancer or a professional. The selection criteria is primarily based on the attitude and the area of work. Therefore, individuals that are innovative, driven and interested as well as contributing actively usually becomes a member of such a coworking space.

Since the spaces are comprised of a community set-up or a group of entrepreneurs sharing the same ethos, after a rigorous selection process, these coworking spaces do not strictly monitor the usage of the facilities by a member very closely and instead rely on members being truthful and declaring their excess usage themselves. To elaborate the same, these clubs do not charge the members for every single additional usage they incur, like charging them for every minute they use the conference rooms, every page they print or every cup of coffee they drink. All of this would be included in their membership, but at the same time they expect that members do not occupy meeting rooms when they do not need it for a meeting, to leave a desk as they found it and to not direct unsolicited offers to their members or poach them. A member can bring in guests if they want to. Membership runs indefinitely unless they are cancelled, and they have a complex process to offer membership back again to individuals who have cancelled their memberships. Some of the benefit members get for being a part of the community are:

■ Introduction to investors, VCs and meeting potential cofounders.
■ Getting feedback and advice from mentors and industry experts.
■ Access to educational classes and workshops provided by experts in their field.
■ Access to exclusive member events like fireside chats, meet and pitch sessions, coffee talks and get preferred access to public events.
■ Perks and discounts from partners.
■ Community space that includes flexible desks, meeting rooms, printing and scanning, coffee, tea and water, a nap room and multiple other features.
■ Become a part of their online community and have access to the members 24/7.

Surf Office

Surf Office is a European-based facilitator for remote working retreats for companies with a combination of living and working together. It offers companies an off-beat location like a beach to conduct their next offsite meeting or is available for freelancers or business professionals who would like to work while they are travelling. They also encourage the concept of work and play by providing these offices at fun locations. They have offices at Barcelona and multiple other locations in Spain, Lisbon in Portugal and other similar locations worldwide. Multiple start-ups and established organizations like Stripe and Shopify have been their customers.

Some of the reasons corporates would want to opt for such a location is besides providing a well-equipped office set-up at an off-beat location, people get to enjoy their stay while they are working together to brainstorm, ideate or strategize on the future. Additionally, this helps companies attract young talent who are not only interested in working but also want to enjoy while doing work, as it is said "work hard and play hard." They offer a wide range of services from facilitation for the desired events to only organizing the requisite infrastructure and location. All their locations have accommodation and concierge services. They organize multiple team-building activities like surfing, hiking, coffee trips, restaurant bookings and even group cooking sessions. They offer meeting rooms and can facilitate brainstorming and strategizing sessions. They can create a personalized calendar to ensure a work-leisure balance. They have created an international community of travelers, working on the go, to network and exchange ideas. Organizations or formal/informal groups can organize meet-ups, hackathons or multiple such events to attract talent to combine work and leisure together. The costs vary from event to event and is dependent on the services demanded by the event.

Incubators

Incubators are a step above coworking spaces and a step below the accelerator programs. Coworking spaces, garages and studio apartments are some of the few places where a start-up idea is usually born. But to take it to the next level, entrepreneurs need legal advice, funding and multiple other aspects of a start-up. Most of the incubators, depending on their stage of involvement, provide a certain breadth of these activities. The distinction between an accelerator program and an incubator is bleak as usually an incubator also has an accelerator program built as part of its offering. We will be elaborating on some of the key aspects of incubators/accelerators and how they help start-ups/FinTechs launch.

A large number of incubators are early-stage incubators who have a curriculum-led program to provide early stage and aspiring entrepreneurs with the structure, training, mentor support and global networks needed to start an enterprise/start-up. Start-ups can use these incubators to test their start-up idea, build a team, get their first customer, raising funds and a multiple of other things. The curriculum is typically a 3–4-month program where an individual has to present his/her ideas and strategies to the top start-up mentors in leading start-ups. They will provide feedback, ratings and evaluations. In addition to the above, the participants will also get office hours with top entrepreneurs, and weekly real-world assignments and milestones to push their business to the next level. Participants who are not able to get the minimum score or are not able to complete the assignment may be asked to leave and join a future program. An aspiring founder with a full-time job, solo founders, teams and founders of established companies (prefunding) can apply for membership.

Since incubators are like middle schools for start-ups, most of them have a mentorship program associated with them. Therefore the participants have to go through multiple tests including a written test sometimes followed by more complex predictive admission assessment tests comprised of aptitude and personality tests. The tests are designed to identify people with the highest potential. In each program a group of start-up founders are associated with a mentor. Mentors are people who have built, led or invested in high-growth technology businesses themselves in the past. These mentors are often compensated through a very small share of the equity pooled in by the founders. Consultants, academics and service providers usually are not selected as mentors in most of the incubation programs.

Therefore, when one graduate succeeds through the program, everybody involved benefits from the same. On completing the program, graduates have access to a mentor network of corresponding incubator programs. The program curriculum typically has three stages:

1. Review and finalization of ideas being proposed.
2. Helping founders with commercial, legal and IP-related challenges.
3. A product development stage followed by a mentor review of the same.

Graduating from a top incubation program is hard and less than one-third of the accepted founders generally make it through the program to graduation. The program mentors play a crucial role in getting the right assessment done for their teams. Once the teams are finished building their product and go-to-market strategy, the incubation programs more often than not necessitate that the start-up be incorporated as a company. One of the key aspects of program completion is usually that the teams need to have completed all their assignments and cleared the requisite evaluation exams. By the end of the program, a large proportion of the entrepreneurs graduating from these programs are able to secure funding for their next phase of growth. The graduates usually also get access to the mentor network of the incubator, investment support, invitation to events and several postgraduate programs.

Typically, the incubator programs can be divided primarily into two types, basic and advanced. The basic program is a multifaceted program that helps a business in refining and validating their idea on the business. Besides providing a coworking space, this plan provides entry-level mentoring and professional services. In addition, members have access to educational lectures and networking. Members are offered entry-level business development and support.

The advanced program is designed specifically for businesses looking to grow to next level. The purpose of the advanced program is to propel the start-up from an ideation and prototype stage to building a business around the same. As part of the program, the participants get metrics-based reviews from experts, mentors, advisors and the management of the incubator program regarding skills and qualities to build a sustainable business. The main aim of these programs is to facilitate a commercial scale product launch, an effective rapid growth strategy and attraction of VCs needed for such an extension. These programs typically offer an office space, dedicated advisors in core knowledge areas, professional training programs, tailored mentor programs, introduction to funding networks and pitching programs.

The application process with most of the incubator programs is usually a two-step process, a written application and a pitch. As part of the program, a participant will learn about sales and marketing, public relations and communication, IP, legal/governance, accounting and funding requirements. The incubators typically shortlist start-ups with teams having high energy and open to accepting new ideas, challenges and ways of working. Some of the incubators programs, besides being a place where start-ups learn to start a business, also provide facilities like trips to beaches, parklands, access to bicycle trails, have on-site gyms, cafes, restaurants and childcare facilities. Some of the incubators also partner with universities to facilitate access to expensive equipment and research for start-ups within their programs. There are also incubator programs that provide full-time or short-time residency options for participants.

Most of the incubators primarily focus on putting an exceptional team and great idea together, but what usually is missing in most of these incubation programs is the ecosystem fit. Therefore, some of the incubators are focusing on building the right ecosystem while helping start-ups build their business. The essential component of building an ecosystem is the team, the eventual market opportunity and the approach of the FinTech. Therefore, these incubators put a special emphasis on the importance of the ecosystem in the success/failure of a business as opposed to having a great idea alone. The focus for such incubators is to create an ecosystem of modern, digitally native, financial services start-ups and consumers. These incubators, instead of seeking start-ups who have reached some level of success, actually believe in creating them by realizing the opportunities. The main objective behind the same is to create/design high-quality, innovative companies on-demand. The program from these incubators is a 4–6-month innovation program and incorporates multiple frameworks like design thinking, systems thinking and a lean start-up methodology to design new and disruptive businesses.

The program is comprised of different stages like passion identification, problem definition, market research, target customer identification, business design, ecosystem fit, go-to market strategy, team formation, investment strategy and venture brief development. Almost all of the incubators would have their application process and curriculum schedule that is pre-announced and published on their website. The following people can apply for being a part of the same:

a. Past entrepreneurs planning for a new start-up in the financial industry itself.
b. Recent graduates and other young professionals who have the entrepreneurial streak, an idea, a demonstrated proof of mastery in respective zones like design, coding, etc., but do not have a venture.
c. Driven entrepreneurial executives currently operating deep in the financial services sector.

These incubators also have continuous research being done to investigate the critical themes and structural changes that have, and will, impact in the way financial services industries operate. Some of these incubators also have an academy that provides learning about financial services.

Some of the well-known financial services companies around the world, have gone through different incubation programs. Some of the success stories for incubator programs include the challenger banks as well. There are multiple other incubators from product companies, system integrators, etc. that are also working toward building the next big FinTech with mixed success. There are incubators from technology integration companies that facilitate innovators and entrepreneurs to build ideas and businesses on their technology stack. They are in particular encouraging building FinTechs using their cognitive, blockchain and design capabilities.

Accelerator Programs

Accelerator programs are short time cohorts that focus on launching a start-up to market, which is already in the advanced stages of bringing the business to the market. Accelerators provide seed funding for start-ups. Seed funding is the earliest stage of venture funding. It pays for the expenses while a company is getting started. Though accelerator programs provide seed funding, it has a greater focus on building upon the idea. These accelerator programs owing to the vast experience of incubating a large number of start-ups, and they themselves had been one at some point in time, can assess the potential impact of an idea. These programs also help the entrepreneurs in defining the direction to shape the idea into a compelling business. Once this is achieved, they also introduce the entrepreneurs to the subsequent stages of funding and possible acquisition as well. There are accelerator programs that help start-ups from any discipline and then there are other start-ups that are more focused on ideas centered around financial domain or a particular technology like blockchain. Owing to the reputation that some of these accelerators have built, the fund investors are more likely to be interested in a company that has graduated from a well-known and a reputed accelerator program. The application process for these accelerator program begins with an application form and then the most promising groups are invited for discussions. Thereafter, the decision of funding is made in a very short time frame. All of the accelerator programs fund start-ups in batches and there are usually 2–3 batches each year from most of the well-known accelerator programs. The application forms are usually available online for a few months before the submission deadline.

The seed fund they invest is a few hundred thousand dollars in return for a small percentage of the company's equity. The accelerator programs make their decisions to invest based on interviews and the application form and some others may want to see demos, a business plan and a past investment history. A large number of accelerator programs want their founders to be a resident for the entire duration of the accelerator program. The founders could be international or local founders, but they all have to be a resident as colocation helps communication, and communication is very essential for all of these programs. A large number of accelerator programs host events including dinners wherein they invite an expert in some aspect of start-ups to speak. Typically, speakers include start-up founders,

VCs, journalists and executives from well-known technology companies. It is during dinners and dessert that most of these experts have informal conversations with the founders, and the conversations are quite open. Since the conversations are not recorded and not curated, a more heart-to-heart conversation happens. Therefore, founders benefit the most when they hear it straight from these experts.

Besides the events, the founders can book their time with accelerator program teams for individual conversations with the experts, mentors and founders from some of the successful start-ups. These kinds of discussions can be anything from figuring out what would be the most urgent questions to a less immediate problem like a big vision for the company. The founders more often than not change their ideas arising out of these individual conversations, and by demo day a certain few of them could be working on new ideas. The subsequent problem that takes priority is what to build first, and depending on a case, the conversation helps to prioritize the next set of actions. In about 10–12 weeks' time, the accelerator programs host a demo day where all start-ups can present their products and services to a specially selected audience.

Demo day has become a big deal in an accelerator program which usually has participation from the media, VCs and other founders. After demo day, the start-up usually has a bunch of great investor contracts. These accelerator programs will have other events besides the demo of the prototype, like a day for rehearsal before the demo days. Toward the end of the cycle, the accelerator programs also bring in the best fund raisers from among the alumni to give advice to start-ups.

Since these accelerators have funded so many start-ups, they usually have a huge alumni network, and therefore there is a great possibility that some of them might be able to help other founders with any personal, technical or functional issues they might face while at these accelerator programs. Though they provide the seed fund, they prefer not to interfere in the company's way of working by being a part of the board, etc. and also are fine with the founders' decision to quit early by getting acquired.

In some of the accelerator programs the fees can also be adjusted against the initial investment provided. Some of the accelerator programs even take a certain percentage of the investments the start-ups get in subsequent funding rounds. As part of the program, the founders get the following:

1. Access to a host of successful start-up founders, subject matter experts (SMEs) and seasoned investors provide feedback for the idea/product and guide the team to translate the same into a feasible and successful business. They also host multiple talks and fireside chats.
2. Mentoring and coaching sessions focusing on the different aspects of a business like how to do marketing, how to manage finance and handle accounting, what should be the design of the product to be launched, etc.
3. The accelerator program network comprising of a large number of company founders and mentors across the globe.

4. Help with distribution experts, who help start-ups with things like trigger emails, event-based analytics, search engine optimizations (SEOs), paid ads or/and multiple other growth techniques.
5. Since these accelerators are recognized as one of the top accelerator programs globally, they draw a set of impressive groups of people ranging from investors, strategic corporates, platform partners, peers and even the occasional celebrity. They also run events and conferences throughout the year, thus giving an immense exposure and visibility to the company.
6. A large number of these accelerator programs have coworking spaces where different start-ups work together. This helps founders as they can share and get help, advice, encouragement and support from their peers, which are more contextual as compared to get the same from an external expert.
7. Though the timelines are pressing and the objective to achieve is difficult, but fun is a part of most of the programs and there are dance sessions, games and multiple other fun activities that keep the teams bonded and yielding all the time.

The accelerator programs are focused programs helping start-ups with mentors, partners and investors to scale them up. Some of these accelerator programs are running globally that are focused on FinTechs. The key focus area for a FinTech program are blockchain, advanced analytics, mobile security, investment and personal finance, payments, financial inclusion, identity and authentication, P2P lending, wealth management, InsureTech and compliance. Some of the accelerator programs, after reviewing the application submitted, organize for Skype/personal interview with founders after shortlisting. After Skype/personal interview, if a good match between what the start-up does and their program is found, then they are invited to join a 3-day event at the program location. During this event, the founders receive pitch coaching, mentor preparation and business model training in addition to meeting mentors, investors and partners. The process concludes by inviting the finalists to the 3–4 month program. During the program, the start-ups try to scale their business by collaborating with mentors, partners and investors. Besides this, the each team gets money to cover living expenses, free office space and exclusive partner deals from leading technology providers. Each program culminates with "demo day," with a large number of guests joining to support the start-ups. Once completing the program, the founders can take part in exclusive networking events, get access to deals and receive tailored introductions as part of the alumni programs.

Impact Hub

Impact Hub, founded in 2005, is a leading global network for creative collaborative action to realize enterprising ideas for a better world. It is part innovation lab, part business incubator, part social enterprise community center. Impact Hub offers a unique ecosystem of resources, inspiration and collaboration opportunities to increase a positive impact on the world. The network continues to rapidly expand worldwide with a global community of more than 16,000 members in 100+ locations on 5 continents from Accra to São Paulo, Phnom Penh to Zurich, they provide access to connections, knowledge, talent, spaces and investments to turn ideas into action. They believe a better world evolves through the combined accomplishments of compassionate, creative and committed individuals focused on a common purpose.

Established Financial Institutions Incubating Start-Ups

Taking a cue from the success of some of these accelerators and with an intent to convert the FinTech threat to an opportunity, most of the large banks and financial service providers as well as systems integrators worldwide have opened their own FinTech accelerators through partnerships or independently. The purpose of some of these accelerator programs is as follows:

a. The FinTech accelerator program was launched by a large bank in England with an intent to harness FinTech innovation for the bank and partner firms engaged in short proof-of-concepts (POCs), relevant to the bank's mission with all commercial considerations taken into account.
b. Another bank in the UK has a 13-week accelerator program in partnership with an American accelerator program. The program is being run out of multiple locations globally.
c. There are accelerator programs launched by banks in partnership with their own investment division and some leading investors with an aim to encourage innovative new business.
d. A U.S. investment bank has launched an in-residence accelerator program that gives the selected start-ups a chance to join the bank for the duration of the program with access to the bank's facilities, systems and expertise (subject to security and nondisclosure conditions). Residents retain control of their innovations and may receive continued support from the bank even after the residency period in an effort to bring their solutions to the market.
e. There are banks that have multiple accelerator programs globally across all the leading FinTech sectors. They also conduct virtual hackathons and incubator programs focused in a specific region. The participants are provided mentorship and a virtual on-site boot camp curriculum as in a typical accelerator program.

f. Some of these banks have a start-up accelerator program that runs for 6 months.
g. A VC FinTech accelerator program launched by a financial services product company and integrator is a 12-week program encouraging early stage FinTechs working in emerging technologies like iOT, cognitive computing, enterprise blockchain and AI.
h. FinTech Innovation Lab is a 12-week program run in partnership with Accenture and the Partnership Fund for New York City as a sponsor. Multiple financial institutions are partners in the program (Source: http://FinTechinnovationlab.com/).

Coworking spaces, incubators and/or accelerators provide different aspects of facilities, mentorship and seed funding. Once a start-up is graduated and is doing sustained business as an outcome of a demo day through incubators/accelerators or by itself, it needs to find a VC who is willing to take the start-up to the next level. VCs or corporations then seek out to get a certain percentage of equity in exchange for funds and enterprise mentorships to propel the start-up to the next level. Some of the VCs that are there in the FinTech space comprise of TTV Capital, General Atlantic, Village Venture, Anthemis Group, IAF Ventures and multiple others.

Chapter 6

The Road Ahead

FinTechs started their journey in the midst of gloom and doom prophecies because of the financial meltdown. They started tapping the opportunities which were otherwise being considered as too difficult to pursue or did not have had a justifiable return on investment (ROI), or the business may not have been compliant with the regulatory requirements. Soon they started tweaking the age-old business models to make it more innovative and address the customer needs. In fact, in most of the accelerator programs the one thing that is pursued almost like a religion is the customer saying "I was waiting for this for so long and now I have it." I personally believe that this has been one of the single most important parameters that has helped FinTechs differentiate from their established peers. This approach of directly addressing the issue has its roots in providing the best customer experience. The new customer experience goes on to making the customer feel that they can do their work in a more effective manner with little effort, yet yielding greater results, thus much beyond what a digital-only experience would have provided. Initially there was a sense of skepticism in the investment community regarding the potential of FinTechs and the disruption trend they have started. Buoyed by recent success stories and many start-ups turning into unicorns (greater than a $1 billion valuation), there has been a mad rush among investors to get a piece of the pie of the next "Microsoft."

Synonymous to "there is an app for that thing," there soon started being "there is a start-up for this business." In 5 years, a host of start-ups started disrupting the market and most of them were offering a solution that would either make the business simpler or/and would be transforming the customer experience. The overlap within the start-ups started growing and it was imperative that though there is a large playing field, a start-up could only provide for a small business function within a particular segment. Additionally, since there were multiple companies offering similar functions, it resulted in considerable competition across the board.

Consequently no one start-up has been able to achieve the depth and breadth of services to seriously challenge the established financial firms. There are about 100+ payment start-ups and there are about 50+ lending start-ups in United States alone. With the market that is yet accepting these disruptions, there is bound be stagnation and competition around customer acquisitions from other start-ups.

This led to a small number of start-ups that are successful and a large number that is not able to sustain because of multiple reasons. Recently even those start-ups which were once looked upon as becoming a unicorn soon are becoming failures. Despite all of this, the investor enthusiasm around FinTechs has not only remained persistent, but is growing by the quarter. Though there have been some weak quarters or once in a while a dip in investment because of some start-up going down, but overall the sentiment is upbeat. Definitely, the FinTech world is quickly learning lessons from these failures and are doing the desired course correction.

The disruption caused by challenger banks and insurance aggregators has definitely made established firms to take notice of FinTech impact and threat from them to their business. Therefore, the financial institutions (FIs), large retailers and telecom operators are all looking to collaborate to acquire these start-ups to expand their business scope and in some cases to eliminate the competition. Consequently, successful start-ups have become an ideal acquisition target since they have the customer base, technology and functional know-how and usually a proprietary engine like a credit check engine, etc. A large number of these financial and non-FIs have started acquiring the most promising start-ups that fit their business proposition.

There is a mad rush by these large financial/non-FIs to acquire these start-ups by paying large upfront acquisition prices. Despite these institutions' readiness to shell out large sums of money, the buyouts were not easy to come by. One of the primary reasons for an established start-up not to sell out itself is that it can easily get funded from investors and will rather try to scale itself up to the next level using this funding rather than being bought by the institutions.

The established financial firms soon realized that it is a more meaningful effort to get involved with a start-up using early stage funding rather than doing a buyout at a later date. Alternatively, some of the other financial firms are exploring partnering with the start-ups rather than trying to fund them or own a piece of them. By far, partnering has been the most successful approach with a win-win for both. The partnership typically is to provide access to a bank's customer and introduce the start-ups product as a cobranded product or introduce the start-up products (business or technical) as a separate offering by the bank. An example of the same would be wealth management firms using researches and rating engines from start-ups by partnering with them, thus offering the traditional services from their existing applications and offering the disruptive services through additional channels partnering with the start-ups.

Despite all of the above, the breadth of functions that a start-up has to offer is not getting fully leveraged by the established firms. Some of the reasons are the threat of customers being poached, technology teams not collaborating and for many other such operational and business reasons. Additionally, technologies like blockchain and regulations like the second payment services directive (PSD2) are pushing these established firms to open access to their data and information. Consequently, most of these institutions realize that it is meaningful for them to collaborate together within themselves as well as with start-ups to create a common ecosystem, which subsequently becomes the launch-pad for a joint offering.

The FinTech Innovation Lab in partnership with Accenture and the Partnership Fund for New York City is a clear example of such a partnership between the established firms, start-ups and service providers. The lab has multiple FIs that are large global banks as partners along with multiple start-ups. Some of the FIs have opened up their own accelerators in partnership with different venture capitalists (VCs)/investing firms. The accelerators help these institutions collaborate with FinTechs as an early stage investor and become a part of the disruption. Some of the institutions have gone a step further in giving start-ups access to their facilities and even make them a part of the organization for 6 months. All of these are clear signs that large FIs are collaborating with FinTechs to be a part of the next wave of disruption.

Besides the FIs, there are multiple retailers and telecom companies that are looking at acquiring FinTechs as well. A telecom company based out of India which has recently launched a payment bank, has acquired a start-up, which has developed a proprietary credit scoring algorithm based on multiple conventional and nonconventional sources and digital analytics.

Until the end of 2017, investments in FinTechs were showing no signs of slowing down, though there were intermediate quarters with low investment, but from an overall perspective there has been considerable investment interest. A report from leading analysts indicate that almost half of the banks will look toward acquiring FinTechs in the next 4–5 years.

FinTechs, although being looked at with skepticism as of yet, are going to exist and will continue to disrupt in the future. Financial service businesses were underserved for a long time, even in highly banked and insured nations, while nations like India and China have a large population that do not have access to a formal financial system. This is in conjunction with technology disruptions like blockchains and application programming interfaces (APIs), will continue to reshape the industry and bring in new ways of doing business. Therefore, from an optimist view, FinTechs will do to financial industries what the iPhone did to the entire music, telephone and camera industry. If we look at it from a pessimistic or a sceptic viewpoint, there is a possibility that most of these innovations could be much ahead of their time and could meet the fate of the dot-com boom and crash or could end up like the "palm" device to be reinvented decades later as the iPad. Nevertheless, despite a possibility of a FinTech bust, the impact of the phenomenon is bright enough for people to keep venturing into this area and bring in new ways of doing business.

FinTechs as Disruptors

FinTechs have a clear differentiating edge to the traditional FIs in terms of what they offer. Some of the clear differentiators that have helped them create the desired disruption can be listed as found below.

Compelling User Experience

A large number of start-ups started by providing a differential online and mobile experience and then followed it up by providing a differential experience through all the other channels. One such example of offering the holistic customer experience would be in the case of travel-related FinTechs where the respective FinTech teams work with the customer to find the best flight options, thus assisting the customer all the way from selection of their tickets to facilitate funding for the dream vacation by offering easy options to lending. Therefore, FinTechs have been very successful in drawing attention of the prospective customers by providing a compelling experience in a very unique manner and not restricting themselves to what technology has to offer.

FinTechs have also taken support of technology disruptions like iOT and analytics to provide a very personalized customer experience to an individual or group of people together. There is an ecosystem of data analysis platforms that can help analyze data about customers. Some of these platforms even offer advice on how an investor should be investing in lending. There are a number of insurance companies that are analyzing driver behavior so they can provide an insurance appropriate to each behavior. Undoubtedly, a very exquisite, yet intuitive user experience has been the biggest disruptor from almost all of the FinTechs.

Tapping the Untapped Opportunity Space

FinTechs have disrupted the financial services market by tweaking and transforming the business and operational processes. Additionally, they have remained agile, nimble and have to worry less about regulatory compliance as compared to established. The FinTechs have remained compliance light by being focused on a single or few business processes as against a whole range of business offerings. Using technology to do what is difficult for humans have also propelled them into unchartered territories. All the above together has helped FinTechs tapping potential opportunities in areas/segments which was overlooked by the formal financial services and was left to individuals/unorganized players. Using mobile money in regions of Africa has helped the unbanked to make purchases using online and mobile channels. Credit scoring companies have used alternative algorithms that rely on unconventional data sources to determine creditworthiness, and have enabled a large number of people with low or no credit scores to borrow money. One of the FinTechs allows opening a bank account using selfies, thus onboarding a large number of millennials quickly. There are lending companies offering safeguard funds for investors in a lending start-up that safeguards investors in case of defaults by the borrowers. The entire concept of peer-to-peer (P2P) lending and P2P insurance is an opportunity in which most established firms did not venture into until FinTechs disrupted the market. FinTechs are even disrupting the way donations are done. There are FinTechs that have enabled a customer to donate while insuring themselves thus enabling people to give back for a cause while they are getting themselves insured.

These start-ups have also used technology to venture into areas which were yet unexplored. Some of the technologies like robo-advising have really helped to bring in customers who could not afford huge fees for a typical wealth advisor. Insurance premium payments have been brought down significantly and quick claim settlements have been made possible based on actual feeds received from iOT devices rather than basing them on past trends and assumptions respectively. Currency exchanges in Africa using Bitcoin and mobile money has enabled a large community of unbanked individuals and traders to conduct banking and cross-border transactions, thus becoming an important medium to drive financial inclusion in Africa.

Automation for Efficiency and Effectiveness

Traditional FIs have over time built a significant infrastructure and age-old software systems, that have evolved with business and therefore have a huge percentage of custom logic. Additionally, since a large part of these systems have been built in a patch-work manner to address the immediate business needs, even a simple action like providing a loan eligibility approval may take hours/days for them. Technically, it would mean that the system responsible for providing the eligibility approval will have to wait for the batch of requests coming from multiple sources to be processed by a centralized system. The processing would typically happen at the end of the day to optimize the server utilization. The processing time would multiply every time if something is missing from the application or if the information does not seem to be correct. Therefore, it could take days or weeks before the relevant eligibility approvals are in place. A large number of processes in most of these established firms are still done manually owing to data, software and hardware limitations.

FinTechs have differentiated themselves here by automating a large part of the processes including the capability to run analytics on a huge amount of data in minutes. This has resulted in delivering a near-instant personalized customer experience. They have automated their processes, using the latest business rules engines and business workflow managers. This gives them a capability to tweak business rules almost on a daily basis, thus churning out more offers and lucrative deals on a daily or weekly basis. A large part of application intelligence has also been automated through machine learning, enabling them to address a large number of requests in minutes, if not seconds. Besides having "the feature that I want," a quick response "almost near instant" has been the second most important element why FinTechs are a success.

Using Unconventional Channels to Market Themselves

FinTechs were the early adopters of social media and with the total users of social network estimated to be 2.5 billion by 2018, it is obvious that they have been successful in getting the attention they need from their customers. Additionally, most of the customers FinTechs have been targeting are mobile device users, and mobile as a device has made usage of social media and peer-to-peer (P2P) communication very easy. FinTechs have therefore captured the "WOW" moment of the customers and are pushing them to refer the app/application to their friend/contact. In fact, some FinTechs have incentivized the referral by giving the referrer free wealth management services up to a certain amount for every person he/she refers. Payment platforms are even enabled for gifting, using social media for purchases made on e-commerce sites and for booking travel and movie tickets on their respective booking sites.

The entire P2P payment, lending and insurance business is based on building communities and enabling transactions based on trust. Most of the P2P platforms use social media extensively to add customers directly through the user's contact/friend lists. Some of the platforms like Snapchat, Wechat and Facebook use payment as part of their social media applications. The payment application by some of the FinTechs, use social networks to allow payments to be made seamlessly through its application. The impact is so visible that even established banks are now leveraging social media to enable their business. Some of the well-known banks globally have enabled payments capability using Facebook and Twitter.

Agile and Asset Light

Traditional businesses were built on software solutions and hardware hosted within the premises. In fact, a decade back it was usually considered as one of the selling propositions for banks, boasting about their investments in hardware and software. This was also used to serve as a barrier for new entrants in the financial services space as it required a large amount of up-front costs. Start-ups, in contrast, have most of their hardware in the cloud and software is usually built from scratch with the most efficient tool sets. This helps them to be asset light and enables them to convert a large part of their upfront asset costs to pay-per-use expenses. The saving is either passed on to the customer or is built into the investments as expenses incurred per customer. In both the cases, since most of the hardware and software is on a pay-per-use basis, there is no up-front costs that start-ups have to bear. The start-up workforce usually employs10+ people and goes up to 100+ people when they are really growing. Most of the workforce usually gets equity as part of their compensation. With a high likelihood of getting good valuations for the equity they own, most of the employees will leave after the start-up is taken over by another company or goes public. All of these factors make these start-ups asset light as they have very little long-term commitments for infrastructure and manpower and they can scale up or scale down on short notice. From a consumer/customer's perspective, the pay-per-use model brings down the cost when the product is not used, and the high usage typically would mean higher utility of the corresponding application, therefore the customer does not mind paying more for the same. Consequently, therefore everybody gets a fair share of their charge for using their share of the platform. Though this is notional, more often than not customers feel they are being reasonably charged by a start-up as against an established FI. Start-ups collaborate and outsource a large part of their noncore business either through incubators, co-working spaces or just by collaborating with other start-ups. Consequently, they are asset light and can focus on delivering value to the customer and not spend their time managing operations.

Collaboration with Peers and Competitors

Large FIs traditionally operate in silos and sometimes rolling out business products similar to a product launched by another division of the same company within the same country or by the same division in another country. Essentially, even though the product across different departments would be similar, they would yet be reluctant to share the same service provider. As a result, each service provider usually has a dedicated set-up for each department, thus not being able to benefit from the advantages of shared services. Since start-ups have very focused business propositions to address, they can afford to collaborate with other FinTechs for most of their noncore functions. An example would be a large number of FinTechs in payment and lending space are collaborating with regtechs for regulatory compliance. The collaboration of a large number of FinTechs have also exposed their core-engines through APIs to be used by other FinTechs.

There are cloud-based FinTechs that have APIs for messaging, voice, video and authentication. Xignite, a company that started as a wealth management platform, soon created their own sets of APIs to access market data and they currently have 50 Web services, offer more than 1,000 APIs, serve more than 1 trillion API calls annually and count 1,000 innovative companies as their clients. They have the leading FinTech disruptors as their clients, namely Betterment, FutureAdvisor, Motif Investing, Personal Capital, Robinhood, SoFi, StockTwits, Wealthfront and Yodlee. Advisors and developers can launch their trading platforms and offer trades using trading FinTech platform APIs.

Besides collaborating with other FinTechs as mentioned above, most of the FinTechs are now also collaborating with banks and competitors to leverage the unique factors from individual set-ups.

Collaboration, therefore, has helped FinTechs expand their customer base, focus on their key offerings and exposing their proprietary functionality to other FinTechs/consuming applications, thus helping create a plug and play ecosystem for the entire financial services industry. This in turn has helped the customer get a lower price to pay for the same functionality, as now the overall cost to deliver the functionality is shared by the ecosystem instead of a single player.

All the above factors today have provided the secret sauce for a start-up and can be summarized as: "FinTechs provide customer delight by providing an impeccable customer experience and a functionality that he/she has been waiting for at an affordable price to the customer with a near-instant experience."

Recent Failures and Lessons Learned

FinTechs, like any other start-ups, have their share of failures as well. Some of the reasons why FinTechs typically fail are listed below:

1. One of the primary reasons for failure is not being able to get the next round of funding. Most of the FinTech firms are asset light and primarily dependent on investor money to continue operation and most importantly, to scale. If they do not get appropriate funding for the next set of investments to be made, then they have no alternative but to shut down the operations.

   Platc is one such example where the company wanted to build and deliver the most technically ambitious smart card on the planet. They were planning to bundle all cards including debit cards, credit cards, loyalty and multiple other functions into a single card. They were way ahead in their development and had multibillion dollars' worth of preorders, which is exactly when they ran out of funding options and they have now been acquired by Edge Mobile Payments. (Source: https://www.plastc.com/).

2. The second most often cause of FinTech failure is getting too ambitious based on the early results. FinTechs are one of the most talked about topic and with the investor frenzy around the space, there is a great possibility that the founders/promoters get too carried away with the potential offering they have. It is a big possibility that they may mistakenly extrapolate the initial trends for future results, yet base the plans completely on the same. One of the largest mobile service providers in South Africa, discontinued their service, offering mobile money in that country. They did not do as well as they did in other countries and decided to discontinue this service. Going by the reasons stated by the company, it is clearly an example of an assumption going wrong regarding the trend of being successful in one nation would work the same for other nations as well.

3. The third reason, more often than not, is that the competition is able to get a major share of the initial customer base resulting in one of the competing companies going out of business. Intense competition between two of the leading personal finance management FinTechs and the one who launched first, losing out to it's competitor is a clear example of such a scenario. Both FinTechs have had the same idea of aggregating user accounts and helping users manage their personal finances. The first FinTech shut down 3 years after being considered a leader in personal finance space. Some of the reasons

why the competitor could get a larger share of users on its platform was its seamless customer experience, from logging in to giving up-front personal finance management options, with very little user intervention. The customer experience at the first FinTech was not that friendly and soon a majority of the customers shifted to the competitor leading to the shut-down of the first FinTech.

4. There is a temptation to exaggerate results to keep investors happy. Once a start-up has achieved some level of success, there are many investors who are willing to invest and the frenzy goes on from the first round to second round. The survival of these companies is at times dependent on how they can showcase better results quarter on quarter. In the financial world, things may not move so fast on a quarter on quarter basis, though the long-term bet by investors, instead of looking for short-term benefits, may be appropriate. More often than not, the pressure is so immense that they end up creating false orders, loan books, etc. to show investors that there is a healthy growth. Consequently, this then leads to the erosion of investor confidence and ultimately closure of the company.

Investors for one of the FinTechs in the P2P lending firm did due diligence on the company filings of its loan book and uncovered a systematic fraud attempt which ended up exaggerating their loan book. The same was published in the media, and the CEO had to resign to gain back the public trust.

Another start-up which rose to being a unicorn with a value of $2.7 billion ended up claiming 1,000+ clients while most of these clients had signed a nonbinding letter of intent expressing interest in the product. A leading auditing company confirmed less than 10% of them were actual orders of the total clients claimed by the FinTech to have on board. Because of this, the FinTech in question completely collapsed and then there were multiple allegations on its team of how they have misused their funds.

This is clear example of promoters/founders cooking their books to get investor attention and next round of funding.

5. There is a wrong marketing strategy. In their enthusiasm a large number of FinTech start-ups were using all channels of marketing without understanding the impact their marketing message would have. Additionally, the FinTechs grossly underestimated the negative impact a particular medium/channel for advertising or pushing their product will have on peoples' minds. In most of the countries people do not want to publicly share their financial information and if any FinTech is using financial information to promote its product or as a feature within their product, then the it will not be accepted. One example for this is a FinTech that came up with an innovative concept, that allowed users to publicize their debit and credit card purchase information on a social media-type platform and make the act of buying a social event. The feature did not sit well with a lot of users due to concerns over

having sensitive financial information in the public domain. This in turn resulted in demise of this FinTech.

Another Chinese start-up, shut itself down 5 years after its launch, was a group-buying website that offered deals to customers at local merchants. It was similar to a large global group-buying FinTech based out of the United States, which also has a large share in this company. The United States-based FinTech insisted that this China-based FinTech use mass email marketing, despite being warned that Chinese people seldom read that type of email, resulting into the subsequent collapse of the China-based FinTech.

These are clear examples of using wrong marketing strategies with the right product that can mean the end of the product or the start-up.

Financial Institutions Collaborating with FinTechs to Create an Ecosystem

In and around 2008 when the FinTech revolution started, there was almost a sense of competition if not rivalry between the established FIs and most of the start-ups. A large group of established financial players embarked on a fast-track transformative journey by creating innovation labs and a separate group/department to focus on innovation. After experimenting with these concepts for a certain time frame, these large FIs realized that they could bring in infrastructure, resources and investment capital, but they could not transform the culture to the extent to replicate the disruptive capability of FinTech.

Some of the established financial firms realizing this, tried partnering or acquiring the start-ups. This worked for a while, but after some months or years they again hit a roadblock from a cultural and focus perspective. With passing time, the gap was widening and albeit most of these FinTechs were only having a small percentage share of the overall business, but the pace of growth was threatening for the established banks and insurance companies. One of the interesting aspects in all of these were FinTechs by now were also realizing that they would need to partner with an existing financial provider to complete the value chain in the business. All of these together were further promoted through multiple initiatives in the form of accelerators, pushed by the established banks and insurance companies. The effort of all of these organizations and FinTechs was now to create an ecosystem where both of them could benefit through collaboration. The different strategies established by FIs that are used to collaborate with FinTechs are explained below.

Partnering with FinTechs to Increase Their Offering

This is considered as one of the most viable options used by multiple FIs to make FinTech disruptions a part of their offering. Multiple FIs have created separate departments to scout for new FinTechs so they can partner up with them.

A large bank has partnered with an online lender to generate loans for the bank's customer base. Some of the examples of recent partnerships between established firms and start-ups include:

- Multiple established insurers are partnering with well-known start-ups specializing in on-demand insurance for utility items like mobile phones, etc.
- A Canadian bank has partnered with a wealth FinTech to provide flexible financing and with another lending FinTech to allow one-click online lending solutions.
- A large global bank has entered into a partnership with a FinTech firm to allow the bank's clients to digitally manage their supply chains and working capital requirements.

All of these partnerships have happened in last 3–4 years and there is an increasing trend of FIs working with FinTechs,rather than competing against them. It is a clear indicator that more and more FinTechs will be partnering with banks/insurance agencies to marry their agility with the maturity and brand of large FIs.

Using FinTech Products by White-Labeling or by Cobranding

A large number of banks, instead of spending time in forming partnership or mergers which would come with their limitations in terms of a skill gap and different priorities for each of the stake-holders, have started buying product licenses of established FinTech players and using them as part of their offering. The product thus purchased is either made available as a white-labeled product or a cobranded product.

- A very well-known small business lender white-labels its lending platform to be included as offerings by other lenders for lending to small businesses.
- A large European bank has plugged into a very well-known payment API provider to offer their customers real-time money transfers and other related services.
- A Personal Financial Management (PFM) firm and a competitor to one of the large personal finance management FinTech have partnered with a large UK bank to provide a best in class savings and debit account, thus enabling customers with a complete personal finance solution that includes planning, managing, saving and spending money.
- A large bank in the UK has partnered with a funding circle to offer its customers small business loans.
- A large payment provider and P2P lender announced a partnership to provide/enable loans to small- and medium-sized businesses (SMBs).
- A large insurance provider is building its financial advising platform by building its own code and integrating a start-up code as well.

- A SME lender start-up is now selling its customer's onboarding and other platforms as white-labeled products to multiple banks.
- All of these and many more such partnerships are a clear indicator that more and more FIs are either integrating FinTech products as part of their offering or are using them through cobranding.

Acquiring FinTech Companies

Some of the large FIs have taken a different approach to managing FinTech disruption. They have started acquiring finetchs to augment their portfolio of services. Some examples are shown below:

1. A financial advisor platform based in the United States is a wealth-planning system for financial advisors. Initially, a mutual insurer offering dental insurance products and funding vehicles for 401k plans, annuities and other financial products invested in this platform. The platform was bought by an established financial wealth management firm to provide the next broker and advisor platform to its brokers and advisors, respectively.
2. Another United States-based life insurance giant acquired a New York-based FinTech start-up that sells financial planning software and provides online financial plans and phone consultations with a certified financial planner. A year later this start-up team has helped the insurer build a redesigned online portal and mobile app that the insurer clients can use to manage their finances. These tools can help clients and advisors by putting assets, liabilities, and insurance in one place.
3. A large card processing firm acquired a payment processor. The payment provider is an innovative provider of payment processing technology, and already is one of the card processor's largest distribution partners. It processes approximately $26 billion of volume annually from around 67,000 merchants.
4. Another large card processing firm has acquired a payment system company. The payment processing firm based out of the UK processes almost all the salaries and more than two-thirds of household bills in the UK.
5. A large payment provider has acquired multiple start-ups to strengthen its position as the largest payment provider. It bought a cloud-based multichannel bill payment processor to reach out to Americans who are living paycheck-to-paycheck. They bought a commerce solution provider to offer a complete commerce solution to their merchants. They acquired another start-up so that they could leverage mobile transactions from their platform and increase its capability to do cross-border money transfers and remittances. They acquired multiple other companies to increase security, get expertise in store-branded credit cards, gift cards and loyalty offers.

6. A French bank acquired a German start-up to provide a digital interface to its banking platform. The start-up was an entirely online-based bank that prides itself on completing all of its services in under 60 seconds.

In most cases, after the FinTech acquisition the acquired company is operating as a separate entity or otherwise it is entirely merged into the parent company with no branding of the existing company. Irrespective of the mechanism of acquisition, the parent companies in almost all the cases have largely benefitted by incorporating the disruptions in their offerings by acquiring FinTechs.

Engaging FinTech Companies through Investment/Accelerator Programs

A large number of banks, technology providers and service integrators are engaged in building the ecosystem for encouraging FinTech innovations and investing early into these innovative FinTechs. As the FinTechs proceed to becoming a success, these institutions can either acquire them, partner with them or work with them to create a new entity altogether. Some of the examples below highlight the different approaches taken by multiple institutions to build the collaboration ecosystem:

- Some of the estimates indicate that three of the largest FinTech investors are large global banks and/or their financial investment arms.
- A large number of established banks are promising to help start-ups build the next generation disruptors through their accelerator programs, usually in return for equity and in hope of identifying future disruptors.
- Multiple technology service providers and product companies have launched their digital academies and innovation centers to help start-ups build innovative ideas using their platforms, respectively.
- A large core banking platform provider has launched its MarketPlace, wherein business apps are sourced from partners, FinTech providers and innovators. These innovative apps are introduced in the market by the core banking platform using its marketplace, which in itself has now become a leading digital native platform.
- A large global bank has funded an enterprise data management firm to enable the launch of their financial analytics platform.

The Future of FinTechs

In the last decade, FinTechs have had a rollercoaster ride. The rise and fall of investment frenzies in FinTechs over the last 3 years is a clear sign of the industry's doubt that these start-ups will be successful. Despite this, in 2016, VC-backed FinTech companies worldwide raised over $10 billion for about 1,000 deals. Though less than a year later, there still is no sign of investor interest fading away. Companies with greater than $1 billion valuations are referred to as Unicorns. The list below elaborates some of these unicorns and their business (disruptive):

- One of the biggest P2P lending platforms who are launching their wealth management platform as-well.
- A payment company that has built a machine learning-based fraud detection system.
- An Internet only insurer.
- Offering the largest digital and m-commerce platform in India
- Connecting students and alumni through a dedicated lending pool and an original social community.
- Offering a free credit monitoring and personal financial management service.
- A FinTech that has built its health insurance offering around the Affordable Care Act.
- Offering financial inclusion to the unbanked having mobile devices.
- Providing single click, single page-based payments.

A handful of these unicorns have been in legal trouble and/or are facing pressure due to frauds in peer group companies.

It is imperative that FinTechs are scaling up, but the journey has not been smooth. Established financial firms collaborating with FinTech firms are adding new dimensions to the entire ecosystem and there are very bright chances that this mechanism of coexistence will become more of a norm than exception. Millennials and digital natives are further fueling the FinTech disruptions by opting to interact with devices, than the traditional way of being explained in person. The future of FinTechs would largely be influenced by these millennials as they will soon be one of the largest groups of earners. They would also be inheriting a large wealth from earlier generations. Since millennials will be inheriting a large wealth at the start of their financial existence, they will be more inclined to spend than to save. Additionally, enforced by globalization, a lot of these millennials will be travelling and changing their location of work, stay, etc. This will lead most of them to rent rather than buy, thus leading to a more pay-per-use economy rather than owning assets. Lastly, owing to the standardization of needs and available facilities, a large number of millennials will prefer to share rather than own and keep it to themselves. This will further fuel a new kind of economy, the sharing economy where people will be sharing books, apartments, cars, etc. The sharing economy will further challenge the norms of the existing financial services industry, as the existing system encourages ownership to sharing. The deteriorating environmental conditions also will bring a shift in investment priorities to encourage more environmental-friendly options like renewable energy, etc. rather than profitability as the only goal. This shift in investment patterns will further disrupt the traditional wealth management industry which is primarily focused on profitability at any cost.

The New Financial World

Therefore, influenced by all the above and many other current and future trends, FinTechs could transform the financial industry in some of the belowmentioned ways.

1. FinTechs, with their superior customer experience are not only disrupting the existing financial services, but are slowly increasing their captive customers. Very soon it is possible that FinTechs will have a larger customer base than their established peers. Additionally, equipped with regulations like PSD2, most of the FinTechs will have access to customer data and information. The API-fication will further fuel the need for sharing of information between FinTechs and the established players. All these factors together might end up with FinTechs becoming the customer-facing interface, powered by data and information coming from established firms, thereby reducing the established firms to be more of back office firms responsible for ensuring transactions are seamlessly handled in the core systems. The established financial firms acting as back-office transaction engines could result into a major part of their revenue coming from only the transactions being conducted through them. Since this would be more of a back-office operation, this could soon become customer agnostic service, and the price points being charged for this could become competitive with the peers in the industry. The competition could drive the price points further down leading to a very low margin and high-risk business for established firms. This is in contrast to the premium these firms charge today for owning the customer relationship. An example would be the wallet FinTechs that have built the customer relationship and loyalty over a time period, could become the primary interface for all the payments made in the future, and the credit card-issuing banks would remain a back office transaction engine for validating and authorizing payments. This could also be the biggest threat to the revenue base of most of the established financial firms.
2. As most of the FinTech firms transition themselves from a formation phase into a stable phase, they will start generating significant revenue. Since, most of these FinTech firms are agile and incur less infrastructure and manpower spend than their established peers, they will be able to generate margins in multiples to their peers. With good margins and backed by investor money, they could start acquiring more companies and could become global players. Acquisitions could help them increasing the breadth of services, they can offer and soon would be able to overtake their established peers with respect to financial performance.

Therefore, the FinTechs who hold lesser valuation today could start commanding high valuations like other tech start-ups in other business domains like, Uber, Amazon and Google. The biggest barrier for most FinTechs today is they have differentiation but they do not have scale. FinTechs, after achieving scale would be able to overcome this barrier and then overtake their established peers. Though this is more easily prophesied than what would happen in reality, but nevertheless this could be one of the possible outcomes, if not globally but for sure in some of the countries. This transition could be further fueled if the established financial firms foray into adventurism, as was the case during the financial crisis and end up being bankrupt.

3. Technologies like API-fication and regulations like PSD2 will have far reaching impact on the financial services industry of tomorrow. A large part of the customer experience around financial service, currently being offered by established firms, could be made available by FinTechs while they connect to established firms core processing engines through APIs. Additionally, in the current state of the industry, a large part of the end-to-end supply chain is owned by large and established banks. The FinTechs are ironically operating in a collaborative model of sharing and outsourcing noncore elements of the supply chain. An example would be if a personal financial management is core for a customer, then the company would only focus on the same and would get information on the customer's account from existing banks through APIs, instead of building the same with themselves. This is one of the reasons why a large number of challenger banks have also been popular as compared to their established peers. The supply chain in its current state is primarily owned end-to-end by established firms except in very few areas like the cards payment processing, loan recovery and reinsurance.

The point to be noticed here is that the fragmentation of financial services businesses equipped with API-fication could unleash an era of business function outsourcing. This would mean that instead of banks and FinTechs increasing their breadth of services, they would focus on one particular service, and for all the other services they would consume the same from other firms established in that specific business domain. Therefore, it is very much possible that a firm would offer only mortgage and lending as its core services and would partner or collaborate with other firms for providing wealth management services. Therefore, there would be firms offering specialty services and partnering with others to provide value-added services. If the industry moves toward operating in this service-centric model, then FinTechs will have the first mover advantage as they are currently operating in the same model. The service-centric model is quite opposite to the consolidation of services that has been adopted by established firms, but either one has a fair chance of becoming the leader if this is the way industry operates in future.

4. A large number of FinTechs and established firms are exposing their core services and platform capabilities using API-fication. This has led to easy

access to information and functionality for a third party to develop a customer experience around the same, package it and white-label the same as services offered by the respective firms. Additionally, a large number of FinTechs are realizing the business and technology product they offer can be sold as licensed or pay-per-use services to their peers, while they are competing with them at the same time. This model is also quite prevalent in the automotive industry where a particular car manufacturing company uses an engine from another company for the cars being sold under their brand names. This could very well mean that FinTechs could start offering their proprietary functional capability, including their customer experience, as a widget within the product or platform of an established firm or FinTech as one of the value-added services. An example would be if a company has been able to develop a risk model for impact of global events on a customer's portfolio, then they could offer it as a widget to any company that is providing a wealth-advising platform.

As in case of other possibilities, either this could be the only way forward for FinTechs in the future or this could be one of the ways for monetizing their services without getting into the race to scale themselves. There is a very big possibility that this could be what a large number of niche FinTechs would resort to, as this would give them the capability to keep working and improvising on their platforms and at the same time demand a premium for their superior services. This would also ensure that the technology start-ups keep their focus on technology platforms and collaborate with business experts to provide a complete offering. The same is evident in the case of companies offering alternate ways of credit scoring, outsourcing their platform to be embedded as value-added services for lending banks. Another example would be the case of technology companies tracking driver behavior to embed theirs services as widgets in an application from an automobile insurance provider.

5. The existing financial world is operating in silos resulting in a distorted experience to the end consumer. An example of the same would be—a customer would typically purchase insurance policy for auto, health, life, etc. from different providers. To access and manage the policies, a customer has to log-in into multiple applications provided by respective insurance provider. Some of these boundaries are getting challenged by FinTechs, but still there are ample opportunities to collapse boundaries between industries like banking, cards, insurance, retail and telecom. FinTechs are rightly placed in breaking these boundaries, as compared to their established peers, because they are building their brand from scratch. Thus, it is much easier for a personal financial management FinTech to start offering insurance services from a large established insurer than the insurer to offer banking and card services. The large firms could also face regulation barriers. Though regulations like PSD2 are an exception, soon the governments could help encourage breaking boundaries in the future if the disruption is highly impactful.

The seamless way of navigating across multiple business domains is also quite similar to how real life works. An individual on a weekend can watch movie, visit a bank, visit an insurance company while buying groceries in a supermarket and may end his/her day reading a magazine or book within an application like Kindle from Amazon. The concept of aggregating services is also referred to as a marketplace and is currently more prevalent in the retail business. The same can then be extended to a multiple industry domain where an individual can get access to all the financial services seamlessly as in the case of a supermarket. This would also help these financial services companies to offer their services stacked in virtual aisles as in case of a retail supermarket. One of the possible futures for FinTechs could be to build such supermarkets and have services from other FinTechs alongside the offerings from established firms in the same financial services supermarket.

6. A large number of FinTechs have started taking steps to solve some of the socio-economic issues like marriage counseling, poverty eradication, financial inclusion, etc., while keeping the business profitable. In the traditional business, a firm can either be a business enterprise or a charitable organization. The only form of charity the business enterprises can be involved in is by spending their corporate social responsibility funds. There is no emphasis on handling socioeconomic issues as part of the business itself. FinTechs, through their innovative offerings, have been able to charter a new course of doing social good while remaining profitable. Unicorns like Mozido and FinTech firms like Givesurance and OpenInvest are helping socioeconomic causes while at the same time remaining profitable.

The success of this phenomenon and deteriorating environmental and socioeconomic conditions globally could lead to social revolution, leading to a socioeconomic agenda from governments globally. This would be somewhere between a pure capitalist or a pure socialist form of government. This could further enforce businesses to move away from a purely capitalist agenda and government-owned establishments to become profitable while continuing to address the social agenda. These factors together could lead to a new generation of businesses that would be profitable as well as tackle socioeconomic issues. Therefore, in this new world order, FinTechs would be well placed, since they would have an experience of managing the same in the most difficult of conditions. Among all the future possibilities, the possibility of a FinTech term being changed to socioeconomic financial technology services industry is also highly probable.

The abovementioned possibilities are some of the prophecies that can be made for the future of FinTechs based on the current trends, though there can be many other possibilities that could emerge through war, environment degradation and lead to other revolutions like the FinTech revolution. Nevertheless, disruptions would continue and FinTechs would keep us surprised every time as more energy and thoughts start getting precipitated in the financial services industry.

Technology Empowering the Tomorrow Land in Financial Service

While the future of FinTechs would largely be impacted by the directions the industry takes, the technology disruptions would also have a large influence on how the FinTechs shape up their offerings in the future. Research reports by leading analysts indicate very few start-ups are actually using the technology to cause disruptions. In fact, a large number is using the same to cause process improvements.

Some of the possible ways technology will disrupt the industry and reshape the FinTech world include:

1. Chatbot and AI is changing the customer experience dramatically—A large part of FinTechs and the financial services world is relying on getting customer attention by giving a superior customer experience. Some of the approaches in providing superior customer experience include offering personalized information, helping through friendly in-person assistance, providing timely alerts and notifications and offering geolocation specific services. The important aspect to note here is that most of the abovementioned experiences would include a manual intervention and therefore would primarily be dependent on the individual delivering the service to customer. Though there are means and measures to monitor the performance of individuals, the past trends have indicated that services deteriorate with scale.

   Chatbots and AI are the first steps in providing a machine-driven customer experience and it is being touted as the next big revolution in the business services industry. FinTechs have been at the forefront for using AI and chatbots to not only provide a superior customer experience, but to reduce spending on manpower by promoting machine-driven business servicing. A crucial aspect of an AI-driven machine response gets better with time as the bots start learning more aspects of linguistic and behavioral responses. Since FinTechs are already ahead in offering these services, they would be able to create a more robust information repository for responses. In the future, a large number of FinTechs will be able to offer a near-complete machine led customer service, thus reshaping the FinTech and financial services industry to be more machine-driven than having a human interface.

2. Personalization would transform the way we conduct financial services— Leveraging the machine-learning capability as mentioned in the previous point, FinTechs would be able to analyze the needs and wants of an individual and therefore would be capable of offering more than financial services. The analytics and machine-learning capabilities are already being put

to use by a large number of FinTechs in suggesting promotions and offers that would suite an individual and has a very high likelihood of availing the same. The advancement in these technologies would further encourage these start-ups to offer services that would typically fail in the retail, telecom and travel domains. Using these technologies, the FinTechs could start personalizing the choices available to a customer in matters of grocery shopping, clothing, tours and multiple other such elements that varies from individual to individual. Therefore, it is highly probable that FinTechs could start personalizing aspects of an individual's daily life beyond providing only financial services. This would also help them edge over their established peers driving greater acceptability and loyalty.

3. Biometrics may eliminate the need of processes like know your customer (KYC) and authentication—One of the most influencing technology disruptions that could reshape not only the FinTech industry but the entire financial world is the increased usage of biometrics for identification and authorization. Currently, biometrics is being viewed with skepticism in the financial industry and has not been fully adopted as the only means of identification and authorization. The advancement in technology on this front would help FinTechs and the financial world to eliminate the login-password-related customer experience. The elimination of keying in a login-password would dramatically open up interaction possibilities in the financial world.

The same coupled with advancement in payment and mobile device technologies could mean the elimination of wallets and transforming of the payment experience. Some of the possibilities that FinTechs could be offering in the future are payments through voice or eye movements. The entire thing could go a step further through the advancement in existing speech recognition technologies like Siri and Alexa to combine shopping, listening, texting and viewing through a single interface at the same time. Therefore, you could watch a promotion, talk to their representative, compare alternate products and listen to reviews from earlier buyers at the same time. Like 2G and 3G helped the data services to be always on and eliminated the need for dialing in every time, similarly biometrics could keep an individual always authenticated without a need to specifically authenticate every time.

4. Implementation of just-in-time for financial services—A large of part of the financial world is currently dependent on the principle of pooling the money by all the members. Any claimant will be paid back from the pool with an underlying assumption that all of the members will not claim their money back at the same time. The same principle is being challenged by P2P lenders and insurers like Prosper and Lemonade. The P2P business model has been made possible because of technology that helps people connect seamlessly. One of the essential elements in such an arrangement is trust.

The technology disruptions like blockchain and smart contract could take the trust between various firms to the next level, thus building a transparent system that works across the industry. FinTechs, like in the case of other tech innovations, will be able to use the same to bring about a new level of trust and transparency between multiple financial services entities. This coupled by advances in multiple other technology areas like biometrics, mobile devices and machine learning would bring in the capability of just-in-time for all the financial services. This would mean that anybody having a lending require-ment would be able to seamlessly choose between the best lending offer, iden-tify the best service provider and be able to see the impact of the same on his/her financial planning and finally decide to pay or not. Leveraging the advancement in technology, FinTechs will be able to apply the concept of just-in-time across all the domain areas within the financial industry such as insurance, wealth management, banking, etc. This could further be leveraged to build transparency and trust across other industries like retail and telecom, to have a seamless just-in-time supply chain across the industry, thus making the optimum use of demand and supply across the industry and the respec-tive value chains.

5. Blockchain starts managing all multiparty interactions like family finances, financial dispute resolution, etc.—All blockchain implementations are cur-rently restricted to either generating cryptocurrencies or otherwise offering solutions to cross-border transaction and currency exchanges. There are ongoing initiatives by FinTechs to build KYCs and some corporate banking transactions using blockchain that have met limited success. The advance-ment in technology, infrastructure and understanding of blockchains pow-ered by smart contracts will help FinTechs push the boundaries to make it available to all multiparty distributed ledger transactions. Some places where the distributed ledger capability of blockchain could be employed is for man-aging family finances and investments, if the same involves a large number of family members. Creating a will for a financial asset, again involves mul-tiple family members. The same could also be leveraged by FinTechs in the future to build and develop resolution systems for all financial transactions and instruments. Since most of the entities in dispute resolution systems are distributed entities and have a compelling need of trust between the entities. Therefore, it is imperative that blockchain would be one of the technologies that would dominate the ways of working in the financial services industry disrupted by FinTechs in the future.

Local Solutions for a Global Service

In addition to the shift in the way business will be conducted in future, driven by technology disruptions, the future of FinTechs will also be dependent upon the acceptance of FinTechs within multiple countries. An additional aspect that would drive the acceptance of FinTechs in these countries would be with regulatory and government support. This would also be dependent upon how FinTechs pursue collaboration and their relationships with the local governments. One example of how these things could impact the future prospects of a start-up is banning a leading taxi service aggregator of its services in London, owing to issues with complying to the regulations. In addition to the regulatory requirement, FinTechs would be able to strike success globally if they are able to understand the need of locals within a specific area and are able to tweak their platform to address the same. FinTechs have a high possibility of adapting to the local needs owing to their agile culture and set-up. Some of the business and technology areas that could be adopted by FinTechs in some of the prominent countries and can make them a leader there are:

1. India—The opportunity for FinTechs in India leans toward financial inclusion. With a large part of the country unbanked and being the second most populace country in the world, there is huge potential for driving financial inclusion. The same has been simplified further by the introduction of a biometrics-based KYC by the government of India. The financial inclusion would further open up opportunities in all the financial services including lending, payments, banking and wealth management. Currently, a large portion of this is managed by local moneylenders and between communities. A survey by one of the government agencies in India pointed out that about half of farm households are financially excluded from both formal/informal sources and only about one-third have access to formal sources of credit.

2. China—With the highest level of Internet and mobile penetration coupled with a low penetration of formal banking, China is an ideal ground for FinTechs to transform the underlying financial industry landscape. Additionally, due to the opening up of their economy in the last few decades, the high-income middle-class population is growing exponentially. The high-earning middle-class population is in desperate need of their wealth being managed. Additionally, the universal social credit system, that will be rolled out by 2020, will further open up an entirely new era for the transformation of financial services. The system will further open up a host of opportunities for FinTechs to provide solutions for the financial services industry. As of this writing, two out of the top five unicorns are from China which is a clear indication that some of the potential is getting translated into success stories. Still there is a lot of ground to be covered to make financial services accessible to unbanked individuals and small and medium enterprises.

   In the last few years, a large number of FinTechs in China have been shut down resulting in losses for the customers and investors. In the lending space alone, almost half of the P2P lenders have been shut down. The government has realized the need to take regulatory measures in all the different services being offered by FinTechs. Though at a nascent stage, it is very likely that regulations related to data privacy and minimum capital requirements for P2P lenders will help eliminate the non-serious players from the industry and a future full of exponential growth for FinTechs.

China, through the World Trade Organization (WTO) provisions, have been forced to open up its economies to foreign players and consequently, global card players have been allowed to file licenses as independent card processors. Since the existing Chinese companies have been operating as monopolistic service providers, there is a large possibility that their customer experience may not be up to the mark, which could therefore open up probable opportunities in this space.

3. Africa—As in case of India and China, financial inclusion is one of the most thriving yet partially tapped opportunities within Africa. Cross-border transactions is another area that is getting redefined in Africa through cryptocurrencies and blockchain. Since a large part of the African economy is dependent on cross-border trade and remittances, it is imperative that FinTechs would be more successful foraying into these trades. Blockchain could also help prevent security issues plaguing most of the African online industry. Additionally, consistent regulatory standards across all the countries would help FinTechs generate critical mass in the future, thus building a case for large-scale transformation.

   The financial status of individuals across different countries in Africa varies. Therefore, a FinTech planning to provide a single solution across the entire continent may experience success in a few countries and failures in most of the others. In contrast, building a solution specific to a country may not generate enough revenue and profitability as compared to the investment required, thus not offering a lucrative opportunity for investors to invest into the start-up. Therefore, FinTechs in Africa would be able to survive and achieve scale by creating a solution that can be easily tweaked to local requirements and would have enough government and regulatory support in the respective countries. These solutions also need to be backed up by enough security provisions to ensure trust and confidence of their customers and investors are maintained.

4. The United States, the UK, and Europe—About 80%–90% of the existing FinTechs are from the United States and Europe. The entire FinTech space is crowded in both of these continents. Yet, there are huge untapped opportunities that can be fulfilled by FinTechs in the future. A large portion of FinTechs in these continents could, in the future, move toward consolidation across the financial industry value chain or could be influenced by their adaptability to the sharing economy. This would primarily depend upon the direction the financial services industry moves toward. Additionally, the FinTechs that are able to implement personalization using AI would be the ones that would redefine the future. One of the interesting trends in these continents have been the emergence of online retail giants and their influence on closing down brick and mortar businesses. The trend is expected to continue in financial services as well, with more market shares picking up for online insurers, challenger banks and robo-advising.

Again, as in the case of Africa, FinTech companies in Europe would also benefit by the advancement of blockchain technologies, since a large part of financial transactions in these countries involve cross-border transactions with multiple currencies. The regulatory mandate of PSD2 implementation across these countries would also mean an entire new economy centered around API-fication, resulting in a huge potential for FinTechs.

Summarily, FinTechs who have the capability to adapt to local rules and regulatory frameworks will be more successful globally.

All of the above clearly reflect that the FinTech story has just begun and it is far from even reaching the stage of full growth. There will be more twists and turns as more technology disruptions evolve and the traditional way of doing financial business is challenged every day. Poetically, the following could be said about the future of FinTechs: "The future is bright, the road is tough, but the hope of a better future is far more encouraging, thus eliminating any chance of failure."

Index

For Product Safety Concerns and Information please contact our EU
representative GPSR@taylorandfrancis.com Taylor & Francis Verlag GmbH,
Kaufingerstraße 24, 80331 München, Germany

Printed and bound by CPI Group (UK) Ltd, Croydon, CR0 4YY
08/05/2025
01864359-0001